Miss Bax

OF THE

Embassy

COUNCILLOR'S OFFICE, LONDON EMBASSY, 1912
Mr. Irwin Laughlin and Miss Bax at work

EMILY BAX

Miss Bax
OF THE
Embassy

WITH ILLUSTRATIONS

HOUGHTON MIFFLIN COMPANY · BOSTON
1 9   The Riverside Press Cambridge   3 9

The Riverside Press
CAMBRIDGE · MASSACHUSETTS
PRINTED IN THE U.S.A.

TO

MR. JOHN RIDGELY CARTER

THE FIRST AMERICAN I EVER KNEW

Preface

I AM NOT the heroine of this book, only the most insignificant pawn in a great game — but even so the ego *will* scream occasionally!

My setting is the pre-war American Embassy at London, and my story deals with the office end of a piece of work that is always half diplomatic and half social.

The Anglo-American diplomacy of 1902 to 1914 was concerned with the clearing away of several of the vestiges of the ancient quarrel of 1776, the growing pains of American Imperialism, and the stamping into more definite outline of a new and friendly course of co-operation and understanding between the two countries. History is a slow growth; great events do not happen every day, but are the culmination of quiet years during which there is apparently nothing going on.

Such as they are, however, I offer these records of peace and war in all sincerity and humility, hoping they may at least be a reminder to many of the happy days of long ago. We were all much younger then and believed in orderly progress towards that better world which, in these more recent, disillusioned, and almost despairing years, seems to be little more than a mirage.

EMILY BAX

NEW YORK, *December*, 1938

Contents

(*ix*)

Illustrations

Personnel of the American Embassy at London
1902–1914

Ambassador, JOSEPH H. CHOATE, 1899–1905
Councillor of Embassy, HENRY WHITE, 1883–1905
(Chargé d'Affaires on several occasions)

	Second Secretary	Third Secretary	Secretaries to the Ambassador
1902	John Ridgely Carter 1894–1905	Craig W. Wadsworth	William Woodward
1903			William Phillips
1904			

Ambassador, WHITELAW REID, 1905–1912
Councillors of Embassy: JOHN RIDGELY CARTER, 1905–1908
WILLIAM PHILLIPS, 1908–1912
IRWIN LAUGHLIN, 1912–1919
(Each Chargé d'Affaires on several occasions)

1905	Craig W. Wadsworth	Lewis Einstein	DeLancey K. Jay
1906		U. Grant-Smith	
1907			Sheldon Whitehouse
1908			Ogden Reid
1909	Hugh S. Gibson	Arthur Orr	Elliot Bacon
1910	Leland Harrison	S. L. Crosby	Lydig Hoyt
1911	F. Morris Dearing		C. L. Cooke
1912	William P. Cresson	Hallett Johnson	Stedman Hanks

Irwin Laughlin, Chargé d'Affaires ad interim, December 1912 to May 1913

Ambassador, WALTER HINES PAGE, 1913–1918
Councillor of Embassy, IRWIN LAUGHLIN, 1912–1919
(Several times Chargé d'Affaires)

1913	Edward Bell	Elbridge Gerry Greene	Harold Fowler
1914			Clifford Carver

NAVAL AND MILITARY ATTACHÉS

	Naval Attaché	Military Attaché
1902–03	Commander RICHARDSON CLOVER	Major EDWARD B. CASSATT
1904–06	Captain CHARLES H. STOCKTON	Major JOHN H. BEACOM
1906	Lieutenant-Commander JOHN H. GIBBONS	Major JOHN H. BEACOM
1907–08	Lieutenant-Commander JOHN H. GIBBONS	Captain SYDNEY A. CLOMAN
1909–10	Commander EDWARD SIMPSON	Major STEPHEN L'H. SLOCUM
1912–14	Commander POWERS SYMINGTON	Major GEORGE O. SQUIER

CHANCERY STAFF

Messrs. CHARLES, FRANK, and EDWARD HODSON, clerks, messengers, etc. (altogether about fifty years)
WILLIAM L. FAIRBANKS, clerk, 1912–1914
EMILY BAX, Clerk and Secretary to the Councillor of Embassy, 1902–1914
MARGERY FORD, stenographer to Ambassador PAGE, 1913–1918
(As soon as the World War began both Diplomatic and clerical staffs were greatly augmented)

How I, an English girl, came to the American Embassy.
1902

It was Miss Garretson of the United States — not I — who had the honour of being the first woman to be employed at the American Embassy at London. That was in those far-off days of 1902 — in the world that knew little of movies, nothing of radio, and had not yet gone through the Gethsemane of the World War. I was the second, but at least I can boast that I was the first *Englishwoman* to be employed there, and I dare say it is also safe to assume that I was the first Englishwoman ever employed in any Embassy of the United States. There are none left now, for those who helped out during the World War have gone, and American citizens have taken their places. But from 1902 to 1913 I reigned alone. No other woman shared with me those pleasant years, and no other woman could have received her initiation into the mysteries of Anglo-American diplomacy under more informed and distinguished auspices.

I never knew this predecessor of mine, Miss Garretson. After but a few months she was taken ill and had to return home, and the Embassy, not again caring to assume the responsibility for an American woman alone in London (how amusing *that* sounds!), chose me to succeed her partly because my family was close at hand. But although I never met Miss Garretson I have always felt that she laid a good secretarial foundation for me, because, naturally, if the Embassy had not found her useful, she would have had no successor. She had, in the short time, managed to 'make a place for herself,' and indeed she had impressed herself upon the Embassy so completely that it was many months before I found my own feet, my training and background having been very different.

I offer my credentials, then, for those who must always begin neatly at the beginning. Born of most respectable British parents in a suburb of London called Tooting, I took my first step on the educational ladder by winning a scholarship which took me to the Grey Coat Hospital Foundation School at Westminster, a renowned institution with a long and interesting history. It had graduated from being a mere leper hospital in Queen Elizabeth's day because of a scarcity of lepers, into a girls' orphanage in Queen Anne's day, the transition having been financed by the levy of a tax of ninepence each upon every worthy citizen of Westminster to build an endowment for the education of female orphans. This endowment was further augmented by the sale of the hair of the orphans to make wigs for the gentlemen of the Court, and, presumably to secure the maximum crop, the dainty darlings were fed on a diet that included several pints of ale a day!

By the time I arrived, nearly two hundred years later, stepping shyly down from the great gate into the courtyard that led to the front door, the official orphans had gone and the Grey Coat become a girls' day school. It still retained — for ceremonial use — the old uniform of grey dress, white apron, white mobcap with strings tied demurely under the chin, and its special interest in orphans, of whom I was one — or half-orphan as the Americans have it — for my father had died, leaving my mother with five children, of whom I was the eldest.

The Grey Coat was the sort of school where young ladies *were* young ladies and not hoydens, where no jewellery was permitted, no make-up or artificial curls, where no student might step out over the threshold without *both* gloves on, and from the gate of which there issued every Ash Wednesday and Ascension Day a long ribbon of girls, two and two, winding their way to Westminster Abbey for the afternoon service. This parade was ostensibly for spiritual rejuvenation, but I darkly suspected that it had a second motive — to maintain our relationship with the Abbey and thereby perchance some day secure a share of the Westminster boys' playing fields in Vincent Square near-by, which, so far as I know, has not yet been accomplished!

The Grey Coat was the most charming of schools, with uneven floors, shallow wooden staircases with broad balustrades, and the stained-glass window at the top of the front staircase containing the school crest depicting a boy watering a young tree, with the inscription underneath, 'God giveth the increase.' I shall always love and venerate it, for its spirit has flavoured my life and given me a nostalgia for simple and dignified things. The spreading before us of a continual feast of new ideas, to be adopted or rejected as we chose, the inspiring teachers, and the big garden at the back where on spring afternoons the girls of the Upper School hoed and planted each her own little bit of earth, getting it ready for Prize Day in June, have particularly warm niches in my memory. The shrill bark of the shaggy eager white dog who assisted everybody so valiantly with the digging still rings in my ears, and I can remember now the depressing sight of those same little gardens at the end of the summer holidays after the chickens had been running loose over them for two months. How incongruous it seems now to remember that we could stand in the quaint old garden, with its trees, its long straight walks filled with stately hollyhocks and lilies, and hear the far-off cheep of the school chickens, while on the other side of the high wall the London traffic went roaring by.

When it came time for me to consider my next step, the headmistress, Miss Elsie Day, a splendid woman, was very sympathetic with my desire to try something different from teaching or nursing, the only two professions that seemed to be open for women. She had heard of a lady who had recently established an office where a few girls might learn to play what she called the 'little black pianos,' and who also — she lowered her voice reverently — had an office actually in the House of Lords! With such reservations as she must have felt in handing over one of her lambs to be devoured in this strange world of masculine activity, she explained the matter to me, and after a serious talk of the 'Be-good-sweet-maid' type, mixed with some more hard-headed bits of practical advice, she waved me off to see the lady in question.

Miss A——, a smart, thin, acidulous, hard-bitten blonde, received me with extreme caution, and did her best, by the skilful manipulation of her *pince-nez*, to break down any resistance on my part that might hamper her in making a good bargain. Yes, she said, her establishment in the House had actually, at that very moment, a vacancy for a quiet, well-behaved young lady. She went on to tell me of the great responsibility that would devolve upon me if — if — she decided to give me this unique opportunity! She warned me that the office there was tentative; that there had been a good deal of opposition to having a 'passel of wimmen' in the Parliament buildings, and that the office was only on sufferance. Her young ladies, therefore, must always consider themselves to be, and act like, visitors, with no rights whatever, otherwise some day the enterprise might be voted a 'mistake' and the office closed. Such a weight upon my thin shoulders made me speechless, and as though that was what she had been waiting for, Miss A—— gave a wintry smile and agreed to squeeze me in! It was arranged that I should be 'apprenticed' for one year at a premium of Five Pounds (which I borrowed from my grandfather and faithfully repaid with my first earnings), during which time I would do whatever was required of me, and have a chance to learn — Miss A—— waved the hand which held the *pince-nez* elegantly off into the remote distance — *Everything!*

With what trepidation, mingled with pride, I set forth that first day! Accompanied by an older girl who knew the ropes, I marched along the asphalted walks towards the somewhat ornate Gothic-Tudor Parliament buildings with who knows what of expectations and hopes! I was to become a shorthand-typist! And in the House of Lords! Was ever mortal so fortunate! My heart was beating fast and I wanted to sing, while, as though to lend emphasis to my joy, the bells of Saint Margaret's Church were clanging a merry peal for some other woman entering on a new career too — albeit a different one, that of matrimony. She didn't know that I shared her peal, but I did, for I felt that the day was just as momentous for me as for her.

It didn't take long to find out what Miss A——'s elegant wave meant. It meant that I was the office girl, to run errands, buy stamps, and make the tea every afternoon. There was an old typewriter on which I might practise, and indeed I could learn anything so long as it didn't inconvenience the office. So, hidden behind a tall screen, on which 'V.R.' was conspicuously burned to show that it was the property of the British Government and had once belonged to the late Queen Victoria, I spent every spare moment industriously pounding away. I also taught myself shorthand — perhaps the loneliest, dreariest job I ever tackled — and though Sir Isaac Pitman might have difficulty in recognizing his offspring I am still able to read without difficulty notes that I made then.

Outside our windows on the second floor all sorts of interesting things passed by to distract my attention. There were weddings almost every day at Saint Margaret's, and occasionally a procession of lawyers in wigs and gowns would cross the street below going from the House of Lords to the Abbey for some ceremony. Even members of the Royal Family came rattling down to the House of Lords occasionally to listen to a debate, and foreign gentlemen called Ambassadors were on hand every afternoon. The way the policemen planted their feet down heavily and saluted as the carriages drew up below was most impressive.

Our nearest neighbour was Mr. Henry Labouchere, the famous editor of *Truth*, who lived opposite. He used to take his fat little dog for an airing every morning, and his chief fame in my eyes was not his eminence as an editor, but the shocking rumour that he had discarded as misfits over two hundred sets of false teeth, and that while he talked to callers the misfit of the moment grinned from the blotting pad beside him.

As soon as I had learned some typing, I began to take my part in the general work of the office, and when my shorthand improved to about fifty words a minute, to take dictation from eminent gentlemen (who must have been very easy to please) and whose names are writ large in English history, among them Mr. Reginald McKenna, Mr. Arthur Balfour, Mr. Edward Colston, Mr. James Hozier (a Scottish Member who wrote to the tax authorities complaining that he hadn't been charged enough), and the Member for Grimsby, the great fishing centre, who looked and smelled like a fish. My work had little to do with affairs of state. The letters I wrote were usually brief missives enclosing cheques to cricket and football clubs wishing them a good season, or regretting that business in the House made it impossible for honourable Members to open bazaars several hundred miles away, but in lieu of that might they venture to enclose a small cheque? In addition to working with the Members, we sent out calls to Committee meetings, and a number of journalists came up regularly to dictate their stories, my favourite being the somewhat grumpy Mr. Crowell of the *London Scotsman*, who always kept his hat on with the same explanation every day: 'I haven't as much hair on the top of my head as you have.' Occasionally a Member would give me a card for the Ladies' Gallery of the House of Commons — the sessions of the House of Lords were always very dull — and from behind the screen put there — so I had been told — so that the charming feminine vista above should not make the legislators below tongue-tied — would listen to dry-as-dust debates, feeling that this screen was also a Mistake!

The day before Parliament rose for the autumn Recess was the end of my apprenticeship. I had worked until almost eleven o'clock that evening finishing up the last details, and, as I wearily walked down the stairs on my way out, the Division Bell, to find out if a quorum still remained in the House, had just finished ringing, followed in a few minutes by the Bell announcing that the House had risen. Saint Stephen's Hall was filled with Members and clerks hurrying out, in their silk hats and frock coats, carrying umbrellas and bags, and, listening to the shrill distant whistling for cabs, I thought idly how different the scene must have been a hundred years before, when Members gathered in groups to go home together through the dark streets as a protection against the footpads of the city. Now all they had to do was to call a hansom and drive off safely where they would.

Back we went to the Victoria Street office where I had first talked with Miss A—— to remain crowded there until the House met again. She would be glad to have me stay on, she said, and would even *pay* me something, so that, in itself, was success! But I was ready for something else, so not long afterward, when a request came from the American Embassy farther down the street to send someone over to do a few hours' secretarial work, I was the one chosen to go. And I never returned!

2

The Chancery of the American Embassy and the men I found there.
1902

I$_T$ IS about three weeks later that, in the little back room on
the ground floor of the Chancery of the American Embassy at
the Court of Saint James's, I am awaiting the arrival of Mr.
John Ridgely Carter, Second Secretary of the Embassy, whose
office I share.

I have hung up my coat and hat on the hook on the end of
the bookcase farthest from the door (Mr. Carter uses the one
at the other end), thrust my galoshes out of sight, taken the
tin cover off the lumbering typewriter, and, standing on the
low fender in front of the fire, survey as much of my non-
descript countenance as can be seen reflected in the face of the
clock over the mantelpiece — the only mirror there is. It is
discouragingly much as usual, with nothing more to mar it
than a speck of London's special soot. Stepping down again,
I put on a fresh supply of coal, wind up the clock and put it
right by Big Ben which has just kindly struck for my benefit.

Now I turn my most devoted maternal attention to Mr.
Carter's desk, in the usual twitter of the shy young girl towards the lares and penates of a handsome, Godlike representative of the opposite sex who is not only her employer but a
foreigner, an American! I carefully dust the desk in accordance with the secretarial lore of those days, read over most
painstakingly several Instructions and a couple of cables which
have arrived from the Department of State at Washington

since the night before, and are now lying, properly indexed and stamped, on the right-hand side of the immaculate blotter. Mr. Carter's personal letters, as naturally the most important — especially as there are some from America among them — grace the centre, and on the other side is a miscellaneous pile of communications addressed impersonally to the Embassy.

I take out the old nibs and replace them with some of the horrid J pens which Mr. Carter most unaccountably prefers, make sure that the pencils are sharp, and that the reference books are all there (for unauthorized persons often walk off with them as soon as my back is turned) — the Statesman's Year-Book, Hazell's Annual, Whitaker's Almanack, Burke's Peerage, the Blue Book, various Social Registers, the Register of the Department of State, the latest issue of the List of the Corps Diplomatiques in London, furnished monthly by the Foreign Office (a cross against the names of the married), and finally the 'Instructions to Diplomatic Officers of the United States.' These sit comfortably and compactly side by side on a sliding rack at the back of the desk, while in front a silver paper-cutter, glistening like a dagger in the thin ray of sunlight peeping over the edge of the roof opposite, casts a sinister note over the otherwise cheery though businesslike setting. A silver candlestick, with matches, snuffers, and a stick of red sealing wax, completes the picture. I grind up the calendar to the proper day, put Mr. Carter's swivel chair so that it covers the shabby spot on the carpet, and, standing back, survey the whole. Experimentally I raise the window a trifle, and as there is no draught to blow the papers, open it wider. . . .

Now I turn to my own desk nearer the door, dust it much less tenderly, hurriedly see that pens, pencils, and typewriter are in order and that the stationery is complete and tidy. A large picture of Mr. Carter, painted by Sargent, staring down at me from the wall above the desk catches my eye. I smile back daringly, as I would never think of smiling at the original. The eyes stare blankly into mine. They fascinate me. I sit down and give myself a shake. That is not the way to behave in an office. . . . I hope it won't be too busy a day. Mr. Carter should be in any minute now. I fold my hands and wait. . . .

. . . It doesn't seem possible that I can actually be the same girl who, such a short time ago, came to the Embassy so full of mingled alarm, interest, and excitement, to do a few hours' typewriting and other office work. That first morning, as I marched, actually with chattering teeth, into the front entrance of the apartment building which housed the Chancery of those days — noticing, as I had so many times before on my way to school and to the House of Lords, the little black board with its incredible 'American Embassy, *Hours 11 to 3*,' at which the passing clerks and typists stared with such amazed envy — how could I have foreseen that the mere act of stepping across that threshold was to change my whole life? It was just as well I didn't know, for had any such suspicion crossed my mind I might have hesitated. But I should have gone forward in the end, for I have the restless love of adventure and change of my roystering, roving, maternal Devonshire seafaring ancestors, who could never resist a beckoning finger, whether it pointed to Heaven or Hell. Now the finger had beckoned me — not very far, it is true. But wasn't that an open door I saw in the distance?

After a few days Mr. Carter suggested that I remain permanently at the Embassy, and I was thinking it over when it was suddenly decided for me by one of those seemingly trivial incidents that often determine the great decisions of life. Walking down Victoria Street towards the station and home after the day's work was finished, a movement close by caught my attention, and glancing up I saw Mr. Carter driving by in a hansom. He was waving his hat and smiling at me in the most cordial way, and it was such an unexpectedly jolly little greeting as to be irresistible, and as I nodded stiffly back I knew that I could not bear to think that any other girl might use that typewriter and take dictation from that delightful man. I would be the one!

And so, without any of the preliminaries of travel, I came under the jurisdiction of the United States, and as a minor member of the Embassy staff found myself pledged to new loyalties without the necessity of shedding any of the old. For it seemed that on that most English of streets, with Westminster Abbey at one end and Victoria Station at the other, there was a bit of America over which England had no jurisdiction, and this was to prove my gateway to a fulfilment very different from any I could ever have dreamed of.

My mother, paternal grandfather, and aunts had been most interested in this step of mine into the glamorous unknown, for Americans, though 'foreigners,' were peculiarly attractive to everyone in England. It was felt that, although they ought to be more like us, they were annoyingly and persistently different. None of the family would have had the slightest interest if I had announced that I was to be employed at the French or German or any other of the foreign Embassies, and indeed, in that case, would undoubtedly have preferred me to remain safely in the House of Lords. But the *American Embassy!!* That was entirely different and intriguing. And as, apart from the history I had learned at school, most of what I had gathered about America came from the Elsie books and what was told me by our next-door neighbours, who had lived 'over there' for some years, I can safely claim to have been attracted into the orbit of the United States unhampered by any preconceived notions.

Those neighbours who had lived somewhere in America were the son of an English bishop and his wife and three children, banished, we suspected, when the young man had married his sister's governess. But after some years they had returned to England — to the wrath of the children — and from what they told us we gathered that America was a rough sort of place where no regular meals were ever taken. Whenever one was hungry, one went to the larder, cut off what they called a 'thumb piece' of anything that happened to be there — mostly a pie of some kind — and ate it there and then without the bother of setting the table, knives or forks, or other silly fuss of that sort. Other scraps of knowledge that interested us were the great numbers of huge trees in every direction, some of which the bishop's son had chopped down with his own little hatchet, and this now hung in their hall as a memento of more adventurous days. I remember once, after he had been drinking too heavily and was exceedingly quarrelsome, that he threatened to keep his hand in by 'cutting down' one of the other neighbours, a fiery little Scotchman with a most aggressive beard and indiscreet tongue who had referred to him as a 'drunken sot.' With dreadful joy I watched him march, axe over shoulder, to the kitchen door of the fiery little man's house and enquire whether he was at home. But whoever answered his knock, seeing the axe, shrieked and slammed the door in his face....

Frank Hodson, assistant Messenger of the Embassy — his father Charles Hodson was the Messenger — an Englishman with a jolly face, dark hair with a curl in it, and a way with the ladies, admitted me with some ceremony that first morning of my formal incumbency, saying how glad he was that I was now 'one of us.' Hardly allowing me time to take off my hat and coat, he volunteered to give me my first lesson in Embassy personages, and Embassy etiquette. Up to then Mr. Carter was the only Secretary I had actually met, though an older man, Mr. Henry White, had stood in the doorway a day or two before and, while speaking with Mr. Carter, nodded speculatively at me....

The head of everybody, began Frank, lifting his head towards the ceiling and rolling the words off his tongue as though he were invoking the name of some deity, was His

Excellency the Honourable Joseph H. Choate, a very great man, who, with his secretary, was just now away in Egypt, but would be coming back after Christmas. Mr. Choate represented the President of the United States to the King of England and was treated exactly as the President himself would be treated if he ever came to England on a visit. . . . Eh? No, he won't come. And don't interrupt! Mr. Choate was accordingly almost as exalted as a member of the Royal Family — more exalted than the Members of the House of Commons or even of the House of Lords. He knew the King and Queen intimately — *intimately* — Frank nodded his head solemnly. He sometimes went to Windsor Castle to stay with the King and Queen, and was also a frequent visitor to Buckingham Palace — and even old Queen Victoria — God bless her — had liked him very much, though he certainly didn't deserve it, for — Frank paused a moment — he had begun by making a most terrible error — the sort of thing that is *never done* in England! Naturally I wanted to hear about it, so Frank, with seeming reluctance, informed me that, when Mr. Choate's appointment as Ambassador to Great Britain was announced, he met an Irish friend on the streets of New York and stopped to tell him the great news. The Irishman listened, and then retorted, 'Well, all I can say is, God save the Queen.' Mr. Choate had quite enjoyed that, and repeated it with gusto at one of the first official banquets given in London in his honour. But, to his surprise and embarrassment, the story met with freezing silence, and he learned that frivolous mentions of Her Majesty were not considered humorous.

Next to Mr. Choate — Frank ticked off his second finger — came the Mr. Henry White that I had seen, the Councillor of Embassy, now in charge of the Embassy while the Ambassador was away. It seemed that Mr. White was very important, too, though of course not *quite* so important as the Ambassador. He also knew the King and Queen intimately — *intimately* — and had been at Windsor Castle.

Then came young Mr. Carter. 'We love him and he does most of the work. That's why you and the typewriter are in his room,' said Frank. I nodded. Seemingly he also knew the King and Queen intimately — *intimately* — and had been at Windsor Castle.

There was also, it appeared, still another young man, Mr. Craig Wadsworth, the Third Secretary, now on a vacation in the United States. He would be back soon. This time there was no mention of Windsor Castle.

Last of all, Mr. William Woodward, the Ambassador's secretary and almost a diplomat, who looked after Mr. Choate. And upstairs — Frank pointed up — there were two other gentlemen, the Naval and Military Attachés, only *attached* to the Embassy. With them it appeared I should have little to do, though I might have to work for everybody else, including the Ambassador. 'And that's all the Americans there are at the Embassy,' he concluded, folding his arms with a gesture of finality.

'But' — he went on after a dramatic pause — 'there is also the English staff, Father and me, and, believe me, we do our share of the work. And now there is you, and you won't be idle either.' I could not help laughing, he looked so fat and jolly, and after a minute he laughed too.

Frank then solemnly showed me round — for up to then I had been treated as an outsider — taking care to impress me at every turn with the extreme importance of everybody and everything. As he talked, I began to get worried, for it seemed impossible, after all, that anyone so insignificant and ignorant as I was could ever hope to be of use in such a place. Frank enjoyed scaring me at first, until, seeing I was taking it seriously to heart, he relented and, giving my elbow a slight squeeze, told me that they were all 'perfect gentlemen,' that he was sure I could do all the work they would want easily — 'standing on my head' — he added to show his contempt for the simplicity of *anything* they would give me to do

— and be very happy. Especially as he would be on hand to help me, and — he swelled his too-ample chest — protect me if necessary. I did not enquire from what!

The whole place was somewhat gloomy — almost like a shabby church — and did not seem at all an appropriate setting for so much 'importance,' being merely a large flat in a residential building next door to a furniture store. It smelt dingy, too, as much of London does when the fires begin to air out chimneys that have accumulated soot all the summer. The big entrance hall, with the square table in the centre, dotted with neat piles of correspondence for everyone, had only one narrow window in the corner, against which was backed a voluminous and voluptuous lady made of plaster with a girdle of stars round her head. The thick carpet that covered the floor, the impressive bookcases filled with extra-sized volumes, which turned out not to be books, but boxes made to look like them, and the large chairs, all hinted at a well-established and permanent nation, with no flighty non-sense about them, the heavy carpets for portentous footsteps, the tall bookcases for tall men, and the ample chairs for well-upholstered citizens not easily to be dislodged — an entirely masculine setting in which any woman, at first, at any rate, would feel an intruder.

Frank led me into the large front room next to the door, the reception room where visitors were wont to keep their anxious vigil until translated either out into Victoria Street again or into the inner shrines of the Secretaries or the Ambassador; where applications for passports were taken, and a good deal of miscellaneous business transacted. As we glanced round, it seemed to me deliberately planned to inspire pessimism in the breasts of flippant callers who otherwise might have lied about their ages on their passport applications or their reasons for travelling abroad (I remember one man who said he came to England to get a bottle of stout!) or dared to ask for an interview with the Ambassador on some merely frivolous pretext. Along the table down the middle were blotters and pens placed with uncompromising regularity, while on the mantelpiece a doleful clock reminded the careless that 'tempus fugit.'

One side of the room was filled with the series of volumes of the *Foreign Relations of the United States*, which contained extracts from the diplomatic correspondence with all countries, prepared at Washington every year for general use. Seeing my interest in these — I had already made up my mind to read them — Frank said that an American Congressman had once pointed to them and enquired: 'Who are the foreign relations of the United States? Our British cousins?'

Next to the reception room, still on the front of the building and through an arch, was the Ambassador's room, into which Frank ushered me with a flourish. A large, lofty room, it had the shades pulled up to the very top to catch the meagre autumn sunshine. Wire screens at the bottom reaching up two or three feet enabled those inside to see out into a murky Victoria Street and observe the horse busses and growlers lumbering by, the hansoms mincing musically up and down, and the citizenry going about its business, and those outside to catch a cloudy wraith of the Ambassador sitting at his desk — and diplomacy actually being made. The greyish-whitish walls were almost hidden behind framed photographs of many men, whiskered gentry in high collars and stocks, some in wigs, some in hats, some bald, some smiling, some intense, some quite obviously conscious of the photographer's clamp at the back of their heads. All these seemed to be staring with alert suspicion at me, an Englishwoman, descendant of the Boston Tea Party oppressors, now come to be associated with them in a very different way.

Frank pointed to the picture above the mantelpiece. 'The Ambassador before the present one always has his picture in the centre. That is Mr. John Hay. He left here in 1899 to become Secretary of State and Mr. Choate came to be Ambassador in his place. He still has a good deal to do with the

Embassy, for he is the head of the whole Foreign Service and next to the President. You know' — Frank lowered his voice to suggest great secrecy — 'he often sends cables to Mr. Choate that need immediate action, and if Mr. Choate is out of London we telegraph them on. But we don't want the English people to know who they are from, so what do you think we do?' Thrilled, I bent to hear. 'Well, instead of saying "Hay says" we change it to "Dried grass says" — you know dried grass is hay, isn't it? Clever, isn't it, and they would never suspect, would they?' Frank giggled while I stared at the thin, eager face of Mr. Hay. I looked round again. I didn't wonder these men had rebelled when old George III treated them so badly — I was a bit vague as to details — but I couldn't help feeling sorry that there had been a revolution at all. Surely some other way could have been found. But then, if there had been no revolution there would now be no Embassy! We tiptoed out.

Back of this memorial hall room, so full of history, was Mr. Carter's little office, a gay contrast, with its red rug laid down over straw matting which Mr. Carter had had put down to remind him of the smell of his childhood home in Baltimore. Here were more bookcases, while opposite to the door a bust of George Washington stood perilously on top of a tippy highboy. A row of leather-covered chairs at the back of Mr. Carter's desk were known as the 'anxious bench,' while outside a staircase led up to the second floor where Mr. Wadsworth and the Naval and Military Attachés had their offices. All these gentlemen, on their way up and down stairs, were wont to peep through the wide crack of the door to see if Mr. Carter was in, and if he was they came in too. He would greet them cordially, exchange the latest stories and answer questions, but he never urged them to stay, for he was always busy.

Mr. White had his room down at the other extreme end of the long passage farthest from Victoria Street. It was much larger and more isolated than Mr. Carter's, and therefore quieter. Several photographs of former Councillors were on the walls, and there was the same sort of heavy carpet that graced the Ambassador's room. On the whole, it was a desolate place, for the fire was never lighted until Mr. White arrived, and there was seldom any sun.

. . . The front door opened in the distance. I heard Frank hurrying to meet Mr. Carter, while I sat at my desk listening to his approaching footsteps and his 'Good morning, Frank.' In he came, a tall, dark, most impressive-looking man (whom his friends called either 'Handsome Jack' or 'Lord Baltimore'), rather slightly built with merry brown eyes. He doffed his hat and smiled at me — his manners were most courtly and natural. Frank, shorter, stouter, came panting after, helped him off with his coat and affectionately hung up each article as it was handed to him.

'Put the gloves in the pocket. I lost a pair somewhere yesterday. I didn't leave them here, did I?'

'No, sir. Shall I make some enquiries?' — Frank was so pathetically anxious to be of help.

'Oh, don't bother. They'll turn up. They always do.'

Stepping over to the fire Mr. Carter leaned down to warm his chilly fingers. Then, noticing the open window, he hurried over and shudderingly closed it. 'Fresh air whatever the weather outside — Oh, you English!' and seated himself at his desk. 'Pouch in from Washington, I see,' he said, looking across at me. I nodded. I watched him as he went through the various documents. Finally he put down the last paper, took out a perfect handkerchief from his breast pocket, brushed some cigarette ash from his coat, and put it back again, just so!

'Now we can begin,' he said, and after a few directions as to the paper to be used — heavy double blue sheets of foolscap mostly, which permitted no erasures and left a ghostly im-

(*18*)

JOHN RIDGELY CARTER
1903

print of each letter above it — he began to dictate direct to the typewriter. No one could have been more careful than I was. Every word was of great moment, every misplaced comma a calamity, and names of places, strange to me, a nervous tension even when spelled by him letter by letter. But he was always the most patient and thoughtful of men, never hurrying, never impatient, explaining everything that was new, telling me anecdotes to illustrate the reason for doing things one way instead of another, and laughing at my questions and my ignorance.

By one o'clock most of the dictation was finished, although there remained a good deal of copying to be done. Several visitors had been interviewed, there had been many telephone calls, and a few visitors. Mr. Carter got up to go, Frank mysteriously appearing at the exact moment to help him on with his coat and remind him of the lost gloves.

'You must be ready for your lunch, too,' he said turning to me, hat in hand. 'I'll be back at three o'clock.'

I listened to his footsteps fade away, heard Frank throw open the front door, the two blasts for a hansom, and even the 'Gee-up' of the driver. Then Frank came leisurely back, slamming the front door noisily behind him. I was putting on my hat.

'Now you may go to lunch,' he said paternally, 'and you needn't hurry because he won't be here until three.'

'So he said' — how dared Frank give me orders — 'but I must hurry, for I've a lot to do.'

'You don't sa-a-a-y,' said Frank, grinning.

3

*The Venezuelan blockade. The American aftermath of the
South-African War. Visit of General Nelson A. Miles. I en-
counter my first ' hot potato.' Unclaimed estates in England.
The founding of the Rhodes Scholarships.*

1902

IT DID not take long for me to become thoroughly at home,
able to relax and to feel that, as a member of the staff, I was
entitled to be told everything! Both Mr. Hodson and Frank,
to whose office all mail and cables were delivered, were most
generous each morning in giving me what they assured me
was *almost* a strict account of everything that had occurred
since the previous evening, for the night seemed to be the
usual hours when cables came in from Washington, owing to
the five hours' difference in time between Washington and
London.

Frank and his father often spent the whole night decipher-
ing a message, and sometimes performed other mysterious
errands outside, these, I suspected, being the secrets that were
kept from me. But whatever the activities of the night, they
were both on hand in the morning fresh and good-natured.
They smiled as I came bustling in, all agog and excited, to
get the cables so as to have copies ready by the time my su-
periors arrived, and the *précis* finished which was used in the
files, instead of the actual copy, to guard the secrecy of the
code.

Mr. Hodson lived in the basement, with his family, from
which seductive odours came creeping all day long. Mr.

Hodson thoroughly believed in keeping up what he was pleased to call his 'constitution' though this was already well established — especially in front. Such good, robust, and nourishing smells of onions, stews, and kippers were they that many Americans, on being invited to lunch with the Ambassador, took a long sniff, swallowed, and accepted, only to find that it was not of those viands they were to partake.

The day after I joined the staff, Frank cornered me behind the front door and gave me a smacking kiss. Although I had expected to have to administer a lesson sooner or later — the glint in his eye was not to be mistaken — it came as a disagreeable surprise, and the hearty slap in the face with which I automatically countered made such an impression upon him that every time a new Secretary arrived to begin his duties, Frank told him about it — and always in my presence! Puffing out his cheek he would nurse it with a trembling hand and rocking to and fro would say, 'Look out for her. She's dangerous! Oh, the *slap* she gave me!' But that salutary lesson established a workable 'status quo' for good and I was always very fond of Frank.

Mr. White, almost a stranger until Mr. Carter, to my dismay, left for a brief visit to the United States, now became the Secretary with whom I worked. In a few days, I discovered that there was no need for me to be any more scared of him than I was of Mr. Carter. He spoke like an Englishman, which was not surprising when I learned that he had come to the Embassy in 1884, when Mr. James Russell Lowell was Minister, and, with the exception of a few years in between when for some political reason he had been relieved of his post, had been stationed at London ever since.

In the course of years Mr. White — according to Mr. Hodson — had grown to know more about the English side of Anglo-American relations than any of the various Ambassadors under whom he served, and was quite different from them in that he had come to London intending to make diplomacy his life-work — something new in American experience, where diplomacy was looked upon as a sort of tea-and-cakes affair that could be attended to by any fairly intelligent and socially minded gentleman without previous experience. Mr. White had now reached the highest position to which a man not a political appointee could aspire, and continued to stay on at the Embassy possibly because the Department of State didn't quite know what to do with him.

Not only was Mr. White tall and striking, but he had a most aristocratic manner. His dark eyes looked out from under bushy eyebrows, he had a most benign — almost bovine — expression, and walked with a slight limp. He was one of the politest men I had ever met, and when I heard him say of another man that he was 'polite to the point of insult,' I thought that might have applied equally well to Mr. White himself. It was difficult for me to understand his way of working at first, and as he always contrived, in spite of my agonized efforts at perfection, to make an alteration in ink on every letter, I decided I should never be able to satisfy him. But when I diffidently suggested that he make his changes in pencil so that they could be corrected on the typewriter, he seemed surprised, and explained that he always altered something to prove to the reader that he had not only signed but read the letter.

My introduction to him had been somewhat unusual. I was coming in from lunch one day just as he was on his way out. Right on the threshold of the front door he stopped — he was six feet two to my five feet one — and stared down quizzically at me.

'Er — what did you have for lunch?' he enquired.

I hesitated, astonished — Americans were certainly queer. 'I had meat pie, junket, and tea,' I replied.

'That's good,' he answered enthusiastically. 'Your predecessor didn't eat proper food and got ill and we had to send her back to the United States. I am glad you are not so foolish.'

Mr. White was always so exactly the picture of all that a great man was supposed to be, both in looks and dress and manners; he was always so busy with appointments with the most august of personages, and running in and out, announcing that he had just lunched with such and such Royalty, or that some influential man had confided some deep secret to him, that he amused me tremendously. Apparently he knew everybody of note and wanted to make sure the Embassy knew it, too. He also said and did the right thing so invariably that he seemed to have jelled into a perfect automaton, a splendid model for any young diplomat to copy — provided he knew when to stop! He was called 'Three-in-a-bed-Harry' by the spiteful, who said that his ultimate happiness would be to be able to boast of having slept three in a bed between Lord Lansdowne and Mr. Balfour. He must have read somewhere what the perfect diplomat should be and do, and copied it exactly. I liked him because he let me do anything I chose, and encouraged me with praise. But sometimes I felt a bit sorry for him.

There were several diplomatic questions going forward that autumn — among them steps for the preservation of the diminishing herds of fur seals by international agreement, the boundary of Alaska, and the abrogation of the Clayton-Bulwer Treaty between Great Britain and the United States so as to make possible the building of the Panama Canal.

But of them all the most immediate was a blockade of Venezuelan ports by combined German, Italian, and British warships to force Venezuela to pay her debts. The blockade was most irritating to the United States — always self-conscious about the Monroe Doctrine — especially as they had an inkling that Germany was using Great Britain and this debt-collecting expedition to help secure the foothold on the American coast which she so much wanted and which the United

(23)

States did not intend her to have. Mr. White's point of attack was to persuade England to withdraw her ships and agree to arbitrate, believing that if the British ships led the way Germany would be forced to follow. Mr. White went to the Foreign Office almost every day, and there was much discussion as to whether a blockade could ever really be a 'peaceful' one as this was claimed to be.

As soon as the British public became aware that the blockade displeased the United States, they insisted that it be ended, for they did not care to have their navy used to settle the difficulties of a few financiers, neither did they intend to help Germany to do anything that would make trouble with the United States.

How proud Mr. White was when the British ships were withdrawn! And what a lot of long letters and despatches he wrote about every little point! He knew men of every variety of political opinion in England and passed on their views to the authorities at Washington almost verbatim. Although the Ambassador, when he was in charge, did the actual negotiating with the Foreign Office, Mr. White seemingly danced round on the outskirts, filling in the odds and ends, not duplicating, but rather ornamenting, Mr. Choate's work. Mr. White's letters were most entertaining. He had been Secretary when Mr. Hay was Ambassador at London, so it was only natural that when Mr. Hay or anyone else in Washington wanted information about England they should ask Mr. White. Through the correspondence I came to see many eminent members of the British Government through the eyes of Americans. And most enlightening it was! Up to then these gentlemen had been mostly unknown to me, unless I happened to read their speeches in the newspapers or listened to discussions of their policies at home. Now I was being introduced to a different view of these eminent compatriots, watching them being impaled on the international pin; most disillusioning, but highly entertaining.

Of the miscellaneous correspondence that autumn a good deal was concerned with various claims arising out of the recently ended South-African War. There were requests for compensation for injuries received; complaints of American prisoners, and a continuous stream of enquiries for news of absent sons. Mothers sent money to pay for the release and passage home of sons who had joined the army under age. Wherever there was fighting, a steady stream of restless young men came hurrying to take part. Parents wanted them home — a mistake in most instances — and the Americans were never grateful to the Embassy for its intercession with the authorities, in their behalf, though their parents may have been. I remember one irate young man snatched from the jaws of death in the early months of the World War, who, in sarcastically thanking the Embassy for the trouble they had taken to get his release, suggested that next time they would do well to mind their own damned business!

In addition to such acts of mercy, business groups were always complaining about being 'discriminated against,' and we were called upon by the Department of State to champion so many causes that one Ambassador is alleged to have said that all he ever did was to harry the Government to which he was accredited in behalf of unknown Americans with absurd claims. A mass of information of one sort or another was also being constantly requested for departments of the American Government and many individuals. One department asked how the people of the islands used as naval stations of Great Britain were governed; another sent an impressive list of questions to be answered about British and Colonial coinage; the Smithsonian Institution asked for a copy of the plans of the additions being made to the Victoria and Albert Museum at South Kensington and to the Royal College of Science. These were wanted immediately — everything was wanted immediately. We sent on the request to Mr. — now Sir — Aston Webb, the architect, who sent the plans of the Victoria and Albert Museum, but said that, as he couldn't do the others in the short time allotted, he would not do them at all. Then the Smithsonian Institution said meekly that they would be glad to have them whenever Mr. Webb could conveniently do them.

As a change from strictly diplomatic routine, a problem of an entirely different nature presented itself. General Nelson Miles, the first 'hot potato' I had encountered, notified us of his imminent arrival on his way home from a Continental trip. By 'hot potato' I mean a man who believes himself to be extremely important in the United States — whether he is or not — and who, when he is abroad, expects to be treated by the diplomats as though he were. Mr. Hodson told me that diplomats were always thoroughly scared of this type of man, for they never knew what he might say of them when he got home and what harm even the most unintentional slight might do to their future. The usual procedure was to greet him fulsomely — Mr. Hodson was specially successful in this brand of 'diplomacy' — pretend that he *is* the most important person in the world, whom everybody in England is panting to meet — and hope for the best. General Miles was met at the station by Mr. Hodson with the usual pomp, and almost at once expressed a wish to see the King — or maybe Mr. White, thinking it good strategy, put it into his head. Mr. White thereupon wrote to Lord Knollys, the King's Secretary, asking whether it would be possible for the General, as the 'Lieutenant-General commanding the Army of the United States,' to have an audience with His Majesty. The King was agreeable, and the meeting took place at Windsor Castle, Mr. White going down in the train and introducing him. Needless to say the General was much gratified. But some busybody apparently afterwards told the King that Mrs. Miles was disappointed that she had not been included, and Lord Knollys, much perturbed, sent an apologetic note to the Embassy expressing the King's regret that there had been such an oversight, that Mr. White had not mentioned that the General's wife was with him, etc., etc. The General explained that he had only desired the audience in his official capacity and had not thought of including Mrs. Miles — and apparently it had not occurred to Mr. White either. So everybody was cross — extremely cross — especially Mrs. Miles, who now felt that she should have been included!

Hard on the departure of General and Mrs. Miles, Senator Kean of New Jersey sent us a list of questions about an estate in England said to be lying unclaimed in the Bank of England. In forwarding the questions the State Department instructed us to secure replies 'without incurring any expense' — another habit of theirs which met with little approval. This was my introduction to the large amount of money and unclaimed estates supposed to be in the Bank of England awaiting claimants who presumably went to the United States and never bothered to collect. This 'estate' business was — and probably still is — one of the greatest nuisances with which the Embassy had to contend.

Of them all the 'Sir Francis Drake Estate' was the worst. If Sir Francis Drake ever *did* leave any large estate from his piratical adventures, and had no relations to claim it all these years, it would long since have become the property of the British Government under the Statute of Limitations. But thousands of people wrote hopefully from the United States every year about the Drake estate, and many lawyers must have made a good living out of prosecuting claims. So notorious was it that the State Department had published a warning which they sent out broadcast, and the Embassy also had thousands of circulars on the front of which THERE ARE NO GREAT UNCLAIMED ESTATES IN ENGLAND was printed in large type.

But memories are short, and if the letters ceased coming from New England because the hopeful clients there had been disillusioned, they soon began again from the Middle West or the South, where someone else had started a new hare. A circular was sent in every case, on which was added, in case they wished to pursue the matter further, the names of two or three trustworthy American lawyers in London. They probably found them as much a nuisance as the Embassy did.

Mr. J. Arthur Barratt, one of these lawyers, told me amusing sequels from time to time: of the lady who said there was no doubt of her claim, as her family were direct descendants of the Virgin Queen Elizabeth; of the Irish woman who claimed some English estate, had nothing to prove it, but shouted as she left his office, 'The British Government is living on my money now.'

There was also the American lawyer who arrived in England with money and authority to collect an estate based on an error in a statement made more than a hundred years before, and who was very angry when informed of the English law which requires that 'reasonable diligence' must be shown. Mr. Barratt's view was that, if the mistake had not been noticed for more than a hundred years, it would be difficult to prove 'reasonable diligence.' He admitted that the English authorities were occasionally forced to take action against lawyers coming from the United States to prosecute claims which they knew in advance had no validity, and sometimes clapped them into jail. It was rather saddening, for most of the letters came from obviously uneducated people, written hopefully on poor paper from places in distant States, and one couldn't but regret that this bit of romance to which they clung was nothing more than an illusion.

During the previous summer the Embassy had had its fingers in the setting-up of the Rhodes Trust, the first scholarships to be established for the express purpose of promoting Anglo-American leadership through education. The money — to found scholarships at Oxford University, Mr. Rhodes's *alma mater*, for young Colonials, Americans, and a few Germans — was provided by the will of Cecil Rhodes, an Englishman who had made a fortune in South Africa. It was such a huge sum that, before deciding on the details of administration, the Trustees asked the Embassy to secure the views of authorities in the United States, especially as to the best way Mr. Rhodes's purposes could be achieved and on what basis the choice of American scholars should be made. As the opinions asked for were from individuals scattered through many States, Mr. Choate was not sure whether it was the function of the Federal Government to get them, but in sending on the request he expressed the hope that, 'as it is a matter of first-rate importance to the whole country, I think you may find a way....'

The only question the State Department asked in agreeing to get the opinions was the date of the will — omitted from the printed copy, and necessary because the scholarships were limited to 'the *present* States and Territories.' Many replies dribbled in to the Embassy all the winter and were forwarded to the Secretary. I remember one from the Governor of some State, who not only gave his opinion, for which he hadn't been asked, but, apparently under the impression that he had some right of choice, selected a student long before the machinery had been set up. And there was one eager young man from Alaska who wrote the Embassy to please inform him of *everything immediately*, though he added pathetically that the mails were so slow that he couldn't possibly hear in time to apply the first year.

I was especially interested in the Rhodes Scholarships because my mother's brother, who lived in South Africa, had known Mr. Rhodes. This uncle had come to visit us a year or two before, and his stories of digging diamonds at Kimberley, of the Jameson Raid, and other events in South Africa made me want to go there. At the first breath of the coming Boer War, after sitting on his verandah several nights with a loaded gun to protect his family, he told us he had sent them south to Cape Colony and remained in Johannesburg to await events. But one day, as he was eating his dinner, something startled him, and getting up from the table he closed his door behind him and went to join the British army. Two years afterwards he returned, to find a young forest grown up round his house, and on forcing his way through he found the dirty dishes still on the table just as he had left them, and the only sign that the Boers had been in — probably to look for fire-arms — was the top of the piano open! The Boers were gentlemen, he said.

Two disappointments marked that fall. One was that no one stayed late enough to need tea, and the other, that the board outside, with its 'American Embassy, *hours 11 to 3,*' on which I had secretly built high hopes, meant exactly nothing so far as I was concerned. But I soon forgot these disillusionments in the fascinations of the new work and in dealing with so many different and surprising subjects. America had jumped out of the history book and become a real place, and Americans real people.

I meet my first Ambassador, Mr. Joseph H. Choate.
1903

THE subconscious and idealized picture I had of an Ambassador was of a most glamorous individual, a Personage in splendid attire with much gold lace and a feather in his hat (either an Admiral or Yankee Doodle), escorted by a large retinue! I must have seen such a picture somewhere, or it was connected, perhaps, in some way with the history I had learned, for I had also a vague impression that Ambassadors were rather sinister. The Embassy had been such a peaceful, pleasant place up to now that I did not look forward to the changes that the approaching great man might bring. Would there be, perchance, horses charging away from the front door on which messengers would be riding furiously on mysterious errands, varlets standing round, crimson carpet spread before the front door as His Excellency sailed through with something of the glory of an Eastern Potentate?

Of *course* it wouldn't be like that, for hadn't I listened to so much about American 'simplicity' already that I was heartily sick of the word, and, as the Embassy contingent fund was always empty, wondered whether simplicity was merely a sentimental cloak for meanness? The continual talk about the undesirability of show in a simple country like America, and how the United States had risen above all such things, bored me, because the Americans I had met did not belong in that simple picture at all. I couldn't help feeling, however, a

(*31*)

sense of disappointment that when the Ambassador did appear he would bring with him no romance, no mystery, no retainers waiting hat over heart for his command — no Cinderella coach! Why did the American Government actually pride itself on being drab?

'No romance!' jeered Mr. Hodson when I expressed some such ideas to him. 'You don't know romance when you see it. Think of the two countries and their history, America once a colony of England built up in large part by Englishmen, then the quarrel between them, the Revolutionary War, the signing of the Declaration of Independence and all the bitterness that followed, and now the long process of healing, in which every Ambassador sent from the United States is doing his share, going on right before our eyes. We in England are doing our part, too, to forget that old quarrel and foster the friendship that lies deeper than political differences, and treat each Ambassador in his turn as a very special guest. We don't think of him as a diplomat only, who may turn out to be an enemy any day and go away with our secrets under his hat. We don't even think it necessary that he should be an accomplished diplomat. We prefer the American Ambassador to be an accomplished speaker, willing to speak on any and every occasion.

'The arrival of a new American Ambassador is always an event, and if, during the time of his stay in England, he does not become one of the most popular of personages, it is likely to be entirely his own fault. Courted on every hand, he has a most pleasant time, even though he is expected to take an interest in purely British affairs that would never be demanded of any other Ambassador. He may begin by conducting himself as an outsider, but we persist in considering him one of ourselves, with the added glamour that comes from his being a distinguished visitor from that most romantic of countries, America, where, as some of us understand it, life is one long thrill and the houses almost touch the sky. So, of course, American Ambassadors being only human, and exceedingly flattered by the universal appreciation with which their every word is treated, may seem sometimes to become so Anglophile that it is hardly to be wondered at, perhaps, that the American Government — watching distrustfully from afar — sometimes deems it unwise to keep a man in London more than a very few years, fearing the effect of this most insidious form of flattery upon his plain Americanism....'

At last, towards the end of January, when London is at its sloppiest, gloomiest, deadest, and chilliest, the Ambassador came. Frank had met him at the station, so on returning from lunch that afternoon I was awestruck to be informed that, as Mr. Choate would be going to the Foreign Office for his first official reception with Lord Lansdowne at three o'clock, he might drop in afterwards to send a report of his conversation to Washington — and might want me!

'Has he heard about me?'

'Of course not, silly,' said Frank, 'but he will be expecting *someone.*'

It was not until after four o'clock that I heard the front door slam back on its hinges and a new voice speaking to Frank. Then I watched a strange back receding into the front room, with Frank following after, and in a few minutes he came trotting excitedly out again, and announced with a sort of hiss —

'His Excellency wants you. Bring your notebook and don't be frightened. He doesn't bite.'

Notebook in hand and trying to look debonair, I marched in, Frank calling from the rear, 'Miss Bax, Your Excellency.'

Before me a rather heavy man with untidy, sparse, mouse-colored hair, still wearing his overcoat, as the room was cold, sat hunched up in a chair that seemed a little bit on the small side. He had an almost querulous expression on his face. *This* the Ambassador! He was a terrible disappointment. There was nothing in the least picturesque about him — nothing. After a moment he glanced up from the paper he was studying, and I found myself, 'standing with reluctant feet' — as it were — enveloped in an instantaneous summing-up of myself, my potentialities, my shiny nose, my heavy shoes, my pathetic immaturity. Paralyzed, I stared back, feeling like a rabbit in front of a bright light. Then he smiled — a warm, revealing, and most enchantingly roguish smile — and relieved, captivated against my will, I smiled hesitatingly back.

'Sit down,' he said, pointing with a pudgy hand to the chair by his side. 'I am glad to see you. Can you write stenography?'

I hesitated.

'Shorthand?' explained Mr. Choate.

'A little,' I replied, 'but I can write very fast on the typewriter from dictation.'

'Can you, indeed?' — as surprised as though I had confidentially informed him I could work miracles — 'Well, that's splendid.'

Without more ado we adjourned to Mr. Carter's room and he began to dictate the report of his conference with Lord Lansdowne, and a cable to Washington about some point on which he needed further information. He must have been satisfied, for after that he dictated to me three or four times a week on all sorts of subjects, official Notes and Despatches as well as a great many personal letters. All of his letters were urbane, substantial and 'meaty,' not the thin, talky missives of the cautious, which official diplomacy must so often hide behind, but rather brief notes which managed to contain everything necessary. Many of them were written to Mr. John Hay and President Roosevelt, and to fellow lawyers and friends in such places as Salem, Marblehead, Boston, and Beverly — to me ever after names of romance hinting at a lovelier America than I could ever have suspected to exist.

Mr. Carter — after his first surprise on his return at finding Mr. Choate dictating in his room — seemed rather to enjoy it, though it probably hindered his own work more or less. Mr. Choate liked to have an audience. Sometimes he would ask me to read a letter aloud, and then ask, 'Well, Judge Carter, is that all right?' (he called all the secretaries Judges), and Mr. Carter, who had been dutifully listening, would make the appropriate comment. And then, just to plague me, he would say, 'And I hope it pleases you, too?' He would sometimes fix his eyes on me in a stare — not looking *at* but through me — until I would begin to feel the muscles at the back of my neck contract and my head being forced back, mesmerized just like a rabbit, and would glance at Mr. Carter for reassurance. His smile would untie the knot.

One day, in writing to Mr. Elihu Root, who was about to come to England as one of the Commissioners in the Alaska Boundary Tribunal, he shot at me suddenly:

'I suppose you don't know how to spell Elihu?'

Taken off my guard and wishing to please, although I knew perfectly well, I murmured, 'No.'

'You *don't!*' he whispered in pretended astonishment and sorrow. 'But it's in the Bible.'

I grinned sheepishly.

I had heard from the beginning what a most distinguished and clever man Mr. Choate was, but I soon found out for myself many other ways in which he was very clever, too. He could go out of the room in the middle of a sentence, interview a caller, and come back and go on dictating exactly where he had left off — without asking me to read back! But his long sentences worried me. He would go on and on until I grew more and more fidgety, for I had been most carefully taught that long sentences were to be avoided, and had no idea that the great may take liberties even with grammar that would never be permitted to the meek and lowly. Finally, one day, when he had dictated more than enough to fill a whole sheet of foolscap without a single full stop, and there didn't seem to be any prospect of one, I interrupted firmly:

'Don't you think you should begin another sentence?'

He stopped and stared with astonishment and annoyance, for it was probably the first time in his whole career that anyone had dared to question his use of English, and even Mr. Carter seemed startled. Then he said solemnly:

'You don't approve of long sentences?'

'No.'

'I'm sorry. I didn't realize that this *was* so long. Perhaps, when we have finished, you might go through and put in whatever punctuation you think it ought to have, will you?'

He went on again, me quite unconscious of the secretarial enormity I had committed, and afterwards I changed the despatch, and in my own opinion improved it considerably, and Mr. Choate signed it. I have always had a particularly tender feeling for him on account of that incident when he was big enough to be so kind and understanding and human. No lesser man would have acted in that protective, kindly way.

Mr. Carter should have been back from his vacation immediately after Mr. Choate's return, but I had been warned by Mr. Hodson that when he went to the United States it was always difficult for him to drag himself away. His intentions were of the best, but something important always turned up to delay him. Two or three cables had come announcing his sailing, but he didn't come, and Mr. Choate began to be quite cross. At last, however, he arrived. Mr. Choate had come in early that morning, so when I heard a lighter step crossing the hall, I suspected it was the truant. It didn't take a minute to warn him that Mr. Choate had come and there was a rod in pickle for him. With the merest word of greeting he caught up a document and hurried into the Ambassador's room, smiling, confident. But Mr. Choate, sitting at his desk absorbed, apparently did not hear him. Mr. Carter stood at the side of the desk waiting, 'listening to the clock ticking' as he told me afterwards. Finally Mr. Choate looked up, gave a theatrical start, stared as at something new and strange, and, shading his eyes with his hand, enquired,

'Can this be Mr. Carter? *How you've grown!*'

Mr. Woodward, the serious-minded secretary to the Ambassador, turned over to me — his first attention — a notebook containing a complicated system of accounts of the Egyptian trip, with various currencies involved. He had paid part of the expenses and Mr. Choate part, and would I please find out how much he owed Mr. Choate? I wrestled with this mess for a long time, and, arithmetic not being my strongest point, I dare say that the resulting figure was, to put it generously, approximate. But Mr. Woodward was entirely satisfied, thanked me cordially, waved aside my doubts, and didn't even check it! I was astonished that anyone could take money so lightly, and such large sums, too. How wealthy they must all be!

The attitude of the Secretaries towards Mr. Choate was charming. There was a deference and a regard that was most interesting to watch, and their affection and devotion were obvious and unquestioned. Through my crack in the door I would see Mr. Choate arrive in the mornings, silk hat, flower in his coat, gloves and walking-stick, with Mr. Woodward following slightly behind, a regular courtier, lacking only the Sir Walter Raleigh cloak to put down in case mud had to be crossed. A few minutes would elapse, and, leaving Mr. Choate to open his personal mail, Mr. Woodward would come slipping into Mr. Carter's room, and soon the two of them would be talking jovially about their doings of the previous evening. It wouldn't be long before Mr. Choate, hearing the laughter, would come in, too, all ready to have a part in whatever fun was going on. What jolly times they had! I had known few men, and none in the least like them. Sometimes I used to creep out, feeling that perhaps I ought to, though I should have much preferred to stay, for men talked about such interesting things. Sometimes I did stay, for they didn't seem to mind. Mr. Choate would listen while Mr. Carter retailed all sorts of gossip, and sometimes added his quota.

And when all the stories came to an end, and Mr. Choate reluctantly got up to go, he would turn round as he reached the door, shake his head mournfully and say, 'Judge Carter, I am positively ashamed of you. You are a sad gossip!' and back we would go to more serious matters.

All these new impressions poured over me from every side, and I should like to have asked many questions. But I was always careful to be discreet, cautioned that that was the proper attitude of any woman who wished to succeed in business — and wasn't diplomatic business the most important of all? But after a time it didn't seem necessary to be quite so careful, for the Embassy seemed to be amused at my questions rather than censorious. There was a warm human quality about them all; they were refreshingly alive and interested in everything, and extremely alert where any matter remotely allied to their work was concerned; their slang was marvellous, and I absorbed it as fast as I could from obliging young gentlemen (some of them Secretaries from other Capitals visiting in London) who were only too pleased to teach me — sometimes they taught me things that I had to unlearn hurriedly. I remember my wrath at seeing myself described in a letter of one of them as that 'yellow-soap damsel in your office.'

Americans apparently didn't mind showing their feelings in a way that disturbed my English reserve. The Secretaries didn't act at all as I had expected foreigners to act, and none of them were in the least like Elsie Dinsmore's father. I was never hurt by anything they said, nor indeed knew whether they had any reservations in their professed liking for England. We didn't talk about that. I chatted with Mr. Carter about my own family sometimes, and he talked of his so much that I soon felt I knew them well — his wife, a charming petite lady with beautiful blonde hair who came in occasionally, his little daughter Mildred, his pride and joy, and his son Bernard — Bunny — a year or two younger, who used to come and meet his father in the afternoons during his holidays.

I shall never forget the first time I lunched with Mr. and Mrs. Carter. Three times my stiff and large and slippery napkin slid off my sloping knees, and three times the butler picked it up and carefully put it back. If it had gone down once more, I should have had screaming hysterics!

Instead of correcting, they encouraged and praised me. I was made to feel myself a real part of the staff and little — apparently — was concealed from me. No one cautioned me about repeating outside anything I heard or wrote inside, nor gave me any particular instructions. Probably they guessed that I would say nothing, more flattered to appear to be concealing information than to impart it. I loved to be mysterious, though I never reached that apex of diplomatic reticence which hesitates to admit that it is a fine day when the sun is shining and there isn't a cloud in the sky. The real truth was very different. The Embassy knew that I was far too ignorant to be able to judge between what was important and what was not; that they could safely discuss anything in front of me without my understanding more than its most obvious implications, and that all sorts of confidential material might go safely through my fingers without penetrating deeper.

I see myself as I was then — and a most discouraging picture it is — clad in a light blue flannel shirt with stiff linen collar, broad black petersham belt around my alleged waist, dark skirt, very long and gored, with a braid on the bottom that I was always catching my heel in, sturdy shoes and woollen stockings, my hair parted on the side and slicked back into a hard knot at the back of my neck, without a hint of a curl. A rather florid complexion and a nose the lustre of which had never been dimmed by the profane touch of a powder puff, complete an awful *ensemble* of the snappy business woman of the early nineteen hundreds. I must have been a source of innocent merriment to everyone as I sat primly on a fat ' Atlas of the world,' to raise me to the required height, trying to look the part of a full-fledged secretary.

Outside the doors of 123 Victoria Street, while the English half of my world was being thoroughly disrupted — or should I say modified — by this American challenge to all my certainties, things continued to go along just the same. Queen Victoria had been dead two years, and her eldest son Edward VII had succeeded her. Her death had brought the end of the cramping ultra-respectability which she had exemplified, and, as though a spring had been released, the reign of Edward VII had begun on an entirely different note, with an almost gleeful expectation on the part of everybody of having a good time. Wealth was increasing, labour was becoming vocal, and women, casting aside scornfully the ideal of large families, bonnets and bombazine, for which Queen Victoria and the ever-lamented Prince Consort had stood so valiantly, were beginning to seek broader fields of experience. With this spirit of release and pleasure King Edward VII was in full sympathy. He, too, was freed at last from his dominating mother, and intended, in the few short years remaining to him, to lead his country in better and more gracious ways of living, for he was no puritan, but a sophisticated, experienced man of the world who loved life and people and the more glamorous aspects of kingship. A firm believer in peace, he used his charming personality always to that end, and was particularly friendly and cordial to the diplomats at his Court.

Into this compact, comfortable British world of mine, more or less in the hands of Queen Victoria's children, intermarried as they were with the Royalties of many other countries and between them ruling practically the entire globe — so I believed — I now had to find a place for far-distant America. The Americans had a President instead of a King at the head of affairs (with no place for a British princess) and had gone on building up their country with little interest in other nations. That job now well in hand, they had begun, under the leadership of the ambitious Mr. Theodore Roosevelt, to encourage aspirations towards world trade, world friendship, and co-operation.

Naturally enough, while America's thoughts were mainly directed to home affairs, her diplomats had been rather outside of the political and international happenings of the rest of the world. Their function in England had actually been little more than to maintain friendly relations and a waiting brief for their country, as one by one the disagreements arising out of the War of Independence were settled by diplomatic methods. So American diplomats were received everywhere with friendliness, no one suspected them of chicanery, there was no need to watch them. Every nation sought their friendship and the friendship of their country. Especially was this true of England, who saw in them people of her own race, with the same traditions and ideals.

On the American side of the Atlantic, however, Anglo-American relations were not quite so peaceable, for the Irish there were apparently as active as they were on the English side, where their own interests were concerned. So much was this so that an anti-British bias sometimes crept into the State Department's correspondence — or so it seemed to me. Even admitting that England's record in Ireland left something to be desired, I could not see why it was any business of the United States Government, nor why every Anglo-American question must necessarily be inspected through Irish glasses. The Irish who had emigrated to the United States to settle had become American citizens and some of them powerful politically. Yet they remained Irish, too, and continued to harass the British Government from across the Atlantic. Among the leaders in the United States was Mr. Henry Cabot Lodge, the Republican Senator from Massachusetts, a State which contained a great number of Irish-Americans. Mr. Lodge was not an Irishman, but his attitude got him the Irish vote, which he certainly deserved, for he was always pretending to see that bogey man, the hand of England, in any sinister happening anywhere in the United States. The right to fish off the coasts of Newfoundland by both Canadians and Americans was one bone of contention during those years — until it was arbitrated in 1910 — in which Mr. Lodge's championship of his Massachusetts fishermen was often carried farther than seemed ethically justifiable.

To offset this Irish bias the American diplomats at London did not hesitate to modify truculent instructions. They also went over in advance with a fine-tooth comb any official speech the Ambassador was about to make in England, to be sure that no political capital could be made out of it by the Irish in the United States, and whether anything was included that, by the wildest stretch of the imagination, might be interpreted by them as 'truckling to the British,' an accusation continually hurled at Mr. Choate, to his somewhat wry delight. Indeed, the diplomats at London did their best to hold the scales of diplomatic dealings level while the small minority of Irish in the United States led that country by the nose in their determination to use them to wring Home Rule for Ireland from the British Government by sheer nuisance tactics.

On the other hand, the Irish in Ireland, though always pressing their monotonous demand for Home Rule, were personally very friendly with the English people. Hundreds of thousands of them lived contentedly in England and the British Civil Service was filled with them, for underneath all the political differences there was — and still is — a profound respect on both sides. But Home Rule had become a political plank of the Democratic Party in the United States, raised anew in every election. It is probable that without the encouragement and financial assistance of Irish-Americans the differences between Ireland and England could have been adjusted many years before they were.

It was Mr. Dooley, the famous Irish-American humorous character created by Mr. Finley P. Dunne, who expressed so delightfully in his articles the mixture of friendliness and impudent familiarity which typified the Irish-American attitude to England. Said Mr. Dooley, speaking of Mr. Choate:

> Why we shud sind an ambassador to th' Court iv Saint James I don't know, though it may be an ol' custom kept up f'r to plaze th' people iv Omaha. He's a good man, th' Ambassadure, who is inthrajoocing th' American joke in England. Hogan says th' diff'rence between an American joke an' an English joke is th' place to laugh. In an American joke ye laugh just afther th' point if at all, but in an English joke ye laugh eyether before th' point or afther th' decease of th' joker. The Ambassadure hopes to inthrajooce a cross iv th' two, that ye don't laugh at all, that will be suited to the English market. His expeeriment so far has been encouraging.

There was certainly nothing disagreeable about that. It amused everybody. But, as the Embassy found out from time to time, there was another side, and a fear that if the United States insisted on putting itself in the line of fire when England and Ireland were shooting at each other, someone might get hit — and no American diplomat in England could be careless with that possibility before him.

Social events of the 1903 season. Early Courts of King Edward VII. The American diplomatic dress. Americans at the Courts. The Embassy's troubles in connection with presentations. Visit of the King to France and the resulting Entente Cordiale. The visit of Admiral Cotton and the American Squadron.

1903

Mr. CRAIG WADSWORTH, junior member of the staff, the last to return from his vacation in readiness for the 1903 season, was very different from what I had expected — as everybody always is! A short, thickset young man with dark glasses, he was so shy that his relations with me at first were confined mostly to nods and stammers. He was clean-shaven, and this caused a shout of merriment that first morning when he came in to Mr. Carter to report his return. 'Well, Craig, so here you are. But what have you done with your moustache?' While Mr. Carter indulged himself in this piece of acting — for we had heard all about it already — Mr. Wadsworth stood scowling and made no reply. He had, it appeared, lost a bet made with a fellow passenger in mid-Atlantic that, if his horse Portlight II did not win a race that was running in England that day, he would shave off half of it — and the horse didn't win!

Although a good bit of work was waiting for him, it wasn't long before he and Mr. Woodward began trotting off together to many race-courses, and it may have been then that Mr. Woodward became inoculated with the love of the turf that has since made him one of America's race-horse owners, and a winner of some of the most famous races. I should like to have gone with them, for I had heard about racing all my life, and the thousands of vehicles, from coaches to donkey barrows, that drove down to Epsom every year for the Derby and Oaks used to pass our very door. My grandfather was in the habit of going to Ascot — his principal bean-o of the year — sending on two extra horses ahead to an inn halfway along the road to await his arrival, and then, with a fellow enthusiast of his, starting off the following morning in a light trap with a hamper of food and drink under the seat. 'The Races' were a great British institution. But Mr. Wadsworth went Mr. Woodward one better. He had a race-horse of his own.

Mr. Wadsworth's particular duties as Third Secretary were to handle correspondence with and about Consuls (particularly the securing of their Exequaturs and Certificates of Appointment), to write many miscellaneous letters, to interview callers, and in his spare time to keep the archives up to date by hand-writing into the current bulky volume the official Notes, Despatches, and cables that came in and out of the Embassy, by which method he would, presumably, in time come to know how to phrase them himself.

He was a bit bandy from much riding — couldn't stop a pig in a passage as Frank picturesquely put it — and rumour had it that he had fallen from a horse in his youth and still felt the effects in his back. He was also — so said Frank — a *very* brave man who had fought a duel — in France — in defence of the name of some fair lady. But who she was, and the details of this most thrilling story, Frank would not divulge — and therefore didn't know! I liked Mr. Wadsworth very much when I got to know him, and what he thought of me may be guessed by the gifts he gave me from time to time, handsome editions of the *Meditations of Marcus Aurelius*, the *Poems* of Tennyson, etc.

My first interest in him was aroused by his habit, in the middle of the morning, of partaking of a brew which Frank used to bring up from the basement and present in a glass on a silver tray with an air of one offering the head of John the Baptist. I was told it was a mixture of milk and lemon juice, warmed to some exact degree of heat and reputed to be good for something. I never discovered what that was, and didn't enquire in case it might be something I shouldn't want to hear, and, given encouragement, Frank would have been only too delighted to tell me. I heard other interesting bits of news about Mr. Wadsworth from Frank *via* the valet, for butlers and valets and chauffeurs, awaiting orders, haunted the Hodson office, and Frank was always ready to pass on as much as I would listen to. I learned from this lively back-stairs centre that Mr. Wadsworth had a different suit of clothes for every day of the month, complete with all the etceteras, the rotation in the wearing of which was fixed and determined permanently, that there were dozens of miscellaneous suits and hats for special occasions; and that in general he had enough clothes to outfit an entire regiment. 'And,' added Frank, getting the last ounce from the monstrous tale, 'he is always buying new ones.'

The following month the beginning of the 1903 season was formally ushered in by the receipt of a Note on very handsome stationery (a double gilt-edged sheet with the Royal monogram on both the Note and the envelope), announcing that His Majesty the King would hold the first Levee of the season at Saint James's Palace on the twenty-third of February at twelve o'clock noon. To this first Levee of the year the entire Embassy was expected to go, and, as Mr. Wadsworth had been appointed to London since the previous summer, he would be officially presented. The Ambassador had likewise decided to present, in the Diplomatic Circle (reserved for diplomats and the *most* distinguished guests) the President of the forthcoming St. Louis Exposition, Mr. David R. Francis, and his associate Mr. John Barrett, who had recently arrived in London to support the official invitation given by the American Government to the British Government to send delegates to, and take part in, the Exposition.

Court announcements requiring equally felicitous replies, Mr. Carter wrote them in his beautifully clear handwriting on the Embassy's most impressive stationery. (It wasn't very long before they began to be typewritten!)

To the Master of the Ceremonies went the first two Notes, giving the names of those who would attend and those who would be presented:

> The American Ambassador presents his compliments to His Majesty's Master of the Ceremonies and begs to inform him that the names of the Gentlemen of this Embassy who will have the honour of attending the Levee on the 23rd, are as follows: Captain Richardson Clover, Naval Attaché; Major Edward B. Cassatt, Military Attaché; and Mr. John Ridgely Carter, Second Secretary. Mr. Henry White, Councillor of Embassy, is unavoidably prevented from attending, owing to his absence in the United States.

> The American Ambassador presents his compliments to His Majesty's Master of the Ceremonies and begs to acquaint him that, accompanied by the Gentlemen of the Embassy, he will have the honour of attending the Levee which is to be held on the 23rd instant. Mr. Choate will also have the honour of presenting to His Majesty on that occasion, in the Diplomatic Circle, Mr. Craig W. Wadsworth, Third Secretary of the Embassy; the Honourable David R. Francis, President of the St. Louis Exposition of 1904; and the Honourable John Barrett, late United States Minister to Siam and a Commissioner of the St. Louis Exposition.

That took care of the diplomatic end, but as the Consul-General at London and a mere civilian were also to be presented, this time in the General Circle, a notification had to be sent to the Lord Chamberlain:

> The American Ambassador presents his compliments to the Lord Chamberlain and begs to acquaint His Lordship that he will have

the honour of presenting, in the General Circle, at the Levee which is to be held by His Majesty the King on the 23rd instant, Mr. H. Clay Evans, the American Consul-General at London, and Mr. George H. B. Hill of the United States.

Carriage tickets, ensuring that the carriages of those attending the Levee were properly taken care of, being always extremely scarce, an extra one had to be asked for — this time from the Lord Steward:

> The American Ambassador presents his compliments to the Lord Steward and would be obliged if His Lordship would be so good as to cause him to be furnished with two additional carriage tickets for the Levee of the 23rd instant, one for his own carriage and the other for that of the Military Attaché. Three tickets have already been addressed to the Chargé d'Affaires.

A slight reminder, this last, that the Ambassador had returned and was in charge of the Embassy — a point which had most unaccountably been overlooked.

The morning of the twenty-third accordingly found the Embassy deserted, for every Secretary and Attaché, and all the rest of the gentlemen to be presented, had gone to the Levee, after the usual last-minute flurry about details that were not quite clear to the distracted Mr. Wadsworth, in this his first official appearance in his new rôle. He was disappointed that he was not to wear knee breeches, though the Commissioners would wear them. He had thought that they were part of his apparel, too, but it seemed that, for diplomats, these beautiful nether appendages were reserved for evening functions.

He remembered that when he was in Washington, just after his appointment, how eagerly he had gazed, in the books of the past, at pictures of gentlemen in gorgeous uniforms, with oak-leaf designs down the front of their coats, and had been amazed and delighted to find that these bright birds were Americans and this decorated attire the American official diplomatic dress. Why, then, was it not worn now? It seemed, on enquiry, that President Jefferson had not cared for it.

Mr. Wadsworth felt very nervous as he followed his chiefs into the Levee, and as he made his bow to the King, experienced some flutterings that certainly had no proper place in his American heart. He refused to be impressed, for why should a king be any different from anyone else? But, notwithstanding his intellectual rejection of a difference, the defiant pumping of his heart showed that old ancestral ties were not quite dead. On the way out the Ambassador introduced him to several colleagues, and the act of his presentation made him a fully accredited member of the Corps Diplomatiques.

After Mr. Wadsworth had been to Court several times, he didn't take it so hard. Once, indeed, he arrived at Saint James's Palace for a Levee in his knee breeches. Discovering his error in time, he rushed home to change and arrived back just in time to meet the others coming away and the King gone.

In March the King and Queen held a Court at which several American ladies were presented. The evening Courts, introduced the year before by King Edward to take the place of the afternoon Drawing-Rooms of Queen Victoria, were to be continued, for they had been most popular. The varied uniforms of the Court officials, of army and navy officers, civil servants and Indian Princes, and the brilliant uniforms of the European and Asiatic diplomats made a splendid background.

All through the reign this magnificence was maintained. The glories that had been packed away for many years were brought out and aired. More than nine hundred invitations had been issued the previous year for the first Courts of the King's reign, and even then but a small proportion of the ladies could be accommodated. So this first Court of 1903 had much of the pomp and ceremony of the previous year.

In those days, and indeed so long as he remained at the Embassy, Mr. Carter handled most of the social correspondence and made the Court arrangements. Of course I, too, soon learned much about Embassy etiquette, the necessity for the right costume at all times, and the proper way to write appropriate and pompous Notes. I wrote many notes to gentlemen about to be presented giving them the necessary particulars — the black silk stockings (with a pair of white ones underneath to give the proper sheen), the shoes with jet (not steel) buckles, the full Court dress with knee breeches, the cocked hat and sword. And I also told them that this Court dress, with the exception of the stockings and shoes, could be hired. But whether they bought or hired it I noticed that most of them managed to have their photographs taken!

As a matter of fact, the American uniform worn by diplomats in England had been agreed upon by the two Governments after a good deal of trouble. At first the United States had conformed to the usages of European diplomacy, and the dress for American diplomats in 1819 was very handsome. But this was modified in 1828, and again in 1853 was considered too fine. So far as England was concerned, the last word was spoken the following year when this dress was agreed to with Mr. Dallas, then the American Minister: 'At Levees a suit of black evening clothes with white neckcloth, sword and cocked hat and at Drawing-Rooms or other full-dress occasions breeches and buckles.'

Squabbles about American Court dress raged at most of the Courts of Europe, where 'simplicity' was everywhere resented, until, by a resolution approved March 27, 1867, Congress prohibited persons in the diplomatic service of the United States from 'wearing any uniform or official costume not previously authorized by Congress.' But Congress could not compel other countries to receive diplomats who did not comply with the universal dress regulations. Indeed, as late as 1899, the Russian Government having refused to admit an American Ambassador not in the prescribed dress, the Department of State's views were threshed out in a long Instruction to Mr. Charlemagne Tower, then Ambassador at St. Petersburg, by the indefatigable Mr. A. A. Adee, the State Department expert, who in the end left the question 'to your own good judgment.' But the American Ambassador at London remains the most conspicuous person at the Court, 'a crow among the birds of paradise.'

The Court dress regulations for ladies changed little, and had mostly to do with the length of train, the right way to put on the three Prince of Wales feathers above the head (worn so that they can be clearly seen on approaching the Presence), the length of the veil, and the gloves. For the débutante the dress was expected to be white, usually soft white, like tulle or chiffon. Other ladies could wear any colour they liked — white or mauve or blue or green being the best because these did not clash with the red uniforms of the Court officials. American girls usually needed a lesson in the curtsey, as they were apt to be a little too extreme in their obeisance for the daughters of a democracy. All this and much else was made plain to each in turn by Mr. Carter, and he gave them all sorts of other hints for their general comfort. 'Don't,' he would say to a lady planning to carry a bouquet. 'There's no place to put it down, and you'll need your hands.'

In Mr. Choate's time we had many rehearsals in Mr. Carter's little office. But when Mr. Reid came, two years later, to be Ambassador, these were transferred to Dorchester House (his private residence) where the facilities were more in keeping with the size of the ballroom at Buckingham Palace. Mr. Carter had information about hairdressers, costumiers, and styles at his finger-tips and was quite accustomed to advising about them. No wonder that 'Mr. Dooley' said that First Secretaries (and Second Secretaries too) are autocrats. They have to be! Any man appointed to be Secretary of Embassy at London will do well to take a course in dress materials. For if he can tell ladies that a certain colour or style looks particularly well under the lights of Buckingham Palace, he is well on his way to popularity.

I used to follow the excited ladies in my mind as in their

carriages they joined the line in the Mall waiting to be admitted to Buckingham Palace, about nine o'clock. With hundreds of others I would sometimes stroll along the Mall on the night of a Court hoping to see someone I knew. A few of the passers-by were not very polite as they stared into the carriages with their noses actually pressed against the glass and made remarks that were all too audible to the exhibits within. 'Oh, look at that old guy,' one would say, pointing to an elderly lady sitting with her eyes closed, her expression that of an aristocrat being taunted by the mob on her way to the guillotine. 'Give my love to the King, deary,' would bring a shade down hastily or the poor little victim would pretend to be deaf. The waiting in line was the worst part, and was so tedious that habitués took along knitting or a pack of cards, and some had a bite or a nip to revive their fainting spirits. As nine o'clock approached, however, the line would begin to move up until in due time the Palace was reached. The doings inside did not interest me. I knew them by heart, so, as soon as the carriages began to move, I went home.

Various stories I remember of small happenings, one that the gliding by of so many trains was apt to make the onlookers giddy, and therefore the King and Queen kept their heads turned away until each lady was actually curtseying before them. But one little page, standing beside Queen Alexandra, who had not been warned, was suddenly and violently sick and had to be carried out. Refreshments were served in the room beyond the Throne Room and photographers' shops remained open all night. Many private supper parties followed, so the morning after a Court most of the Secretaries would come in late, sleepy, but full of amusing incidents. They were always delighted when the American ladies looked well.

The actual presentation was the culmination of weeks of trouble for the Embassy, for there are certain people who believe themselves to be above regulations, and apparently feel that their personality needs an individualized setting. But if they are persistent their persistence is as nothing to the icy immobility of the Lord Chamberlain, schooled by years of experience. Tears and prayers, blandishments and threats are of no avail. Obey the regulations to the letter or stay away! The Corps Diplomatiques understand this perfectly well and are not so foolish as to butt their heads against a stone wall, but less sophisticated and spoiled ladies sometimes ride for a fall.

There was the noted poetess Ella Wheeler Wilcox, who arrived in London for her presentation with her dress already made, white, with a frieze of water-lilies round the hem. That was all right. But when she announced that her head-dress was to be a band of the same water-lilies, Mr. Carter — or perhaps it was Mr. William Phillips who succeeded him — explained that the regulations called for three feathers and veil, and that no change was possible. But she airily waved him aside. That was all stuff and nonsense. She herself would see the Lord Chamberlain and everything would be all right. So she talked to the Lord Chamberlain, not once but many times, and after days of honeyed appeals and lamentations, it was borne in upon her that she must either dress like everybody else or stay at home. Presented in veil and feathers she was a chastened woman!

Many other amusing incidents about Americans at the Courts were told from time to time. I remember that when the two Misses Shonts, daughters of the late Theodore Shonts, were presented, they looked so magnificent that King Edward nudged Queen Alexandra violently to call her attention to them. Poor Queen Alexandra was so deaf that this was the only way to get her 'ear.'

Another time there was consternation at the Embassy when the daughter of Mrs. Lawrence Townsend, wife of the American Minister to Belgium, was presented. King Edward liked Mrs. Townsend very much, so when she came forward

(53)

to present her daughter he was all smiles. But whether Miss Townsend didn't want to go to the Court or had quarrelled with her mother about something else, she raised her hands high above her head in a 'pigeon wing' as she curtseyed, to the utter bewilderment of everybody including the King and Queen. They left London the following morning, for the season was ruined for Miss Townsend.

As soon as the spring Courts were over, the King went to Paris to make a visit, although many people felt he would not be well received. But within forty-eight hours his gracious manners, coupled with the conspicuous homage he rendered to the French flag, captivated the French people, who crowded the streets when he left, shouting, 'Vive notre Roi.' By this visit was the ground laid for the Entente Cordiale with France which proved its value at the beginning of the World War, and a few months later a return visit to London by President Loubet of France further cemented it.

The summer of 1903 was memorable also for the visit to Portsmouth of an American squadron on its way back to the United States after paying a visit to Kiel. The King was particularly anxious to secure a visit, too. He had no intention of letting Germany get ahead of him in compliments to the United States, and as President Loubet was coming, it would be a suitable opportunity to show honour to the American Squadron as well.

On the night of the Court Ball given in honour of President Loubet, Lord Selborne, first Lord of the Admiralty, gave a dinner for the American officers, and some of them went on to the Ball. The final instructions sent to the Embassy were:

The King wishes the thirty officers of the United States Navy who are coming to the Ball tonight to assemble in the white drawing-room at 10.20 P.M. in order that they may be presented to Their Majesties. The Lord Chamberlain also invites the Ambassador and Mr. White to attend with them.

The officers were presented to the King by Mr. Choate and were received by the Queen. The floor of Buckingham Palace was so crowded that there was room for very little dancing. The American officers wore their special full-dress uniforms with swallow-tailed coats and plenty of gold lace. The next day they attended a Review at Aldershot in which the Military Attaché took part, the War Office having kindly suggested providing him with a 'charger,' and in the evening a dinner was given for them at Buckingham Palace at which Mr. Choate sat on the King's right hand and Admiral Cotton on his left, with the Prince of Wales opposite. Among others present were Mr. Balfour, Mr. Joseph Chamberlain, Lord Lansdowne, and Sir Michael Herbert, British Ambassador to the United States. The King toasted the President and Mr. Choate toasted the King and the guests stayed until long after midnight.

Mr. James McNeill Whistler, the great American painter, died in London in July, a great loss to the American Colony and to art in general, and Lord Salisbury the following month. Mr. White made a mistake in his quarterly accounts and was told by the Treasury Department that 'if you have nothing further to offer I will thank you to credit the United States in your next account of salary with the amount of ninety-nine cents'; Messrs. Root and Turner arrived as American Commissioners to adjudicate the Alaska Boundary (Mr. Lodge, the third Commissioner had already arrived), and Mr. Carter, who had been appointed Secretary, spent much time at the Foreign Office helping with the arrangements. Major John H. Beacom was designated Military Attaché to succeed Captain Cassatt; and presumably to fortify them for the forthcoming Tribunal. Mr. Choate and Mr. White asked for the free entry of cases of whiskey and champagne.

$$\boxed{6}$$

The Alaska Boundary Tribunal. The death of Sir Michael Herbert. The relations between the Embassy and the Foreign Office. Lord Lansdowne. An Oriental Minister makes a call at the Chancery.

1903

T HAT autumn of 1903 was my introduction to the mysteries of an International Tribunal. All through the summer we had been making preparations for it, until there couldn't have been a document of the time of the Revolution and after that had remotely to do with the North American Continent adjacent to Alaska that had not been taken out of its file, dusted, copied, and used. Such far-reaching preparations were almost frightening, and the thing that haunted me most was the responsibility that dwelt in the briefest note. Suppose one of the notes that I typed had a mistake in it that hundreds of years from now might make the decision of an International Tribunal different!

The settlement of the exact boundary between the United States and Canada in Alaska, which had been a source of irritation ever since the Revolution, had grown more difficult since the discovery of gold in Alaska had made that country a more desirable possession. Each side felt the need for a settlement, but naturally wanted the boundary changed to its own advantage, so, though the matter was always cropping up, it remained unsettled. Mr. Hay finally made up his mind to tackle it, and in 1901, after several deadlocks, presented to Lord Pauncefote, British Ambassador at Washington, the American view of where the boundary should come. This did not meet with Canadian approval, so they suggested the fairest thing to do was to arbitrate. But the United States refused to arbitrate, and the matter was again shelved until after the death of Lord Pauncefote. Sir Michael Herbert succeeded him, a young, enthusiastic diplomat who had the confidence of the Foreign Office. Again the question was re-opened and in due time a treaty was made and ratified by the Senate.

Under this treaty the case was to be arbitrated at London by a joint commission of six impartial jurists — three from the United States and three from Canada — one of the three on the Canadian side to be Lord Alverstone, the Lord Chief Justice of England. The American delegates were Messrs. Root, Lodge, and Turner, and the Canadians Jetté and Aylesworth. Mr. Hay wrote informally to Mr. Choate asking him to be one of the American Counsel, but he declined, saying he was sure that if the Foreign Office had had any idea that he would sit as a lawyer in the Tribunal they would not have treated him with so much candour — and indeed might consider his appointment as taking an unfair advantage. He also felt that the whole diplomatic world would condemn him, for it was well understood everywhere that the place of an Ambassador was on the side lines — impartial. He promised, however, to offer the same aid and advice to whatever counsel should be retained as the Foreign Office would give to the British law officers. That was the most he could do, though, eminent lawyer as he was, he would in any other circumstances have been honoured to have a part in such an international gathering — the only one, I believe, held in London during his term of office.

Fortunately Mr. Hay withdrew his suggestion. The Embassy felt it was curious that Mr. Hay, familiar with the ethics and etiquette of diplomacy, should have put Mr. Choate in such an embarrassing position. But probably Mr. Hay was only carrying out instructions from 'higher up.'

The American Commissioners, counsel, and staff reached London in August, and there were many preliminary consultations and last-minute discussions at the Embassy. Mr. Carter was at the Foreign Office a good deal. A series of apartments there was set aside, and everything done for the comfort and convenience of the party, and four American reporters were given permission to attend the meetings. Men connected with the Tribunal were in and out of the Embassy all day long, and the cabmen must have made a killing, as even their horses standing outside set out instantly in the direction of the Foreign Office whenever anyone from '123' got in. Mr. Carter warned me that I was not to do anything for any of these gentlemen. My work was for the Embassy only. So, much as I should like to have had my fingers deeper in the pie, I was firmly kept out — for my own good I was told!

Some weeks before the Commission arrived, the Embassy had received from the usual expatriate living in London the customary warning of what would happen if the United States were foolish enough to take part in any international meeting in that Capital which was supposed to weave over Americans a magic spell so powerful that they could not defend themselves — London! Our correspondent, who may have had his tongue in his cheek, asked us to forward the letter to the Commission, and it was sent along to the State Department, without acknowledgment or comment of any sort. It said:

I am greatly surprised to see by the New York *World* that you intend to hold your meetings here in London. It shows you lack a clear knowledge of the condition of things here. There is positively strong *Magnetic Influence* here in London that the English use to debilitate the American, and which at the same time holds the Englishman so strong that the American actually wilts before him.... Mr. Choate is also a victim....

'Dear me,' said Mr. Choate when Mr. Carter handed it to him. 'I must look into this. Have I wilted? Have I been debilitated?' Mr. Carter laughed. There was no need for words. One thing we were sure of and that was that the writer did not know Mr. Choate. The Ambassador sometimes looked rather grim when stupid and ignorant criticisms poured in upon him, but this particular one amused him. 'Send it along and warn them,' he said, handing it back to Mr. Carter.

The Tribunal held its first session at the Foreign Office on September 3 for the ceremonial exchange of credentials, and the meetings continued uninterruptedly until the thirtieth of September when everybody was shocked to hear of the death in England of Sir Michael Herbert, the Ambassador who had done so much to make the Tribunal possible.

The session adjourned, and many of the delegates attended the funeral a day or two later in Wiltshire. Then on went the meetings again, with many social interludes to lighten the burden of work and to show the delegates a picture of indoor English hospitality, for the weather was awful. As an introduction a banquet was given by the Lord Mayor at the Mansion House, at which the famous turtle soup was the first course; followed a few days later by a dinner in honour of Lord Alverstone given by the Goldsmiths Company — of which he was a member — to which the whole Tribunal was invited. Lord Roberts also, as head of the Pilgrims, presided at a reception and dinner for them, and they met the King in special audience. All the three American Commissioners were amiable. Of them all it was Mr. Lodge who interested me most, for I had heard so much of his dislike for England. Yet when I met him he was so friendly that I was rather nonplussed. Mr. Root struck me as rather austere and Mr. Turner made no impression on me whatever.

Mr. Choate and Mr. Carter alternated in being at the Foreign Office, and of course Mr. White was in and out with Mr. Lodge and other important people, leaving Mr. Wadsworth to do the routine work of the Embassy. Mr. Carter continued to attend to most of his usual duties, although the members of the Tribunal were constantly bothering him about the smallest details, especially their dress and manners for special occasions. Mr. Choate found time to dictate many reports and letters to me. I remember an amusing story which he preceded by saying, with one of his impish glances, 'You won't understand this.' The story was of a Southerner who was asked by an Englishman if anything could have prevented the American Civil War. 'Oh, yes,' replied the Southerner. 'If Plymouth Rock had landed on the Pilgrim Fathers instead of the Pilgrims Fathers landing on Plymouth Rock, there would have been no war.'

The Canadian case was not especially strong — Mr. Choate told me all they really wanted was a port on that coast — and the realization that Canada could not have prevented the United States from making any boundary it chose by force must have been clear to them. It was soon evident also that the two Canadians were, like the three Americans, absolutely committed to their side, so the decision actually rested upon Lord Alverstone, and on October 29, by voting for the American side, he determined the boundary. There was bitter disappointment and criticism of Lord Alverstone in Canada, but that gentleman was said to have told them bluntly that if they had wanted to guarantee a victory they should not have put their case in the hands of a British judge.

Mr. Choate, in a speech at the Pilgrims a few weeks afterwards, paid a high tribute to Sir Michael Herbert and suggested that his name be given to one of the peaks on the Alaska frontier that lifted 'its sublime and soaring summit to the Arctic skies.' It was in that same speech that Mr. Choate, doing some facetious advertising for the St. Louis Exhibition, invited the Lord Mayor to visit it and reproduce the entire Lord Mayor's Show in the very heart of America. This caused some merriment, but the proposal to name a peak Mount Herbert was cordially approved by both the Governments. A nice spoonful of jam I thought it.

The bills for printing, postage, and thousands of incidentals paid and the delegates safely started on their way home, things thankfully settled down again into the routine of the commonplace day. 'Thank goodness they're gone,' said Mr. Carter, yawning. 'And don't mention Alaska Boundary to me again. The Foreign Office will never be the same after what the charging mobs have done to the carpets.'

The relations between the Embassy and the Foreign Office were always most cordial. The Foreign Office, sacred to the making of what is known as 'British policy' — a complicated and serious matter — is a place which an Englishman instinctively tiptoes past. All the men in the Diplomatic Service of Great Britain are trained by years of service for the work they are doing, for no mere temporary hit-and-miss handling of international questions is permitted to interfere with what Edward Carpenter calls the 'long surge of history.' Such is the effect produced that even as one steps over the mat at the door there is a sense of momentous thought being expended on far-off affairs, and of events moving slowly and inevitably towards — well — something!

Lord Lansdowne, the Secretary of State for Foreign Affairs, a member of the Conservative Party which remained in power until 1905, was an interesting personality. While Liberals in general thought he should have been court-martialled for his mismanagement of things in South Africa during the Boer War, Conservatives believed that the world-wide impression of the Machiavellian policy of England was due to the fact that, being partly French himself, Lord Lansdowne could understand the Continental as well as the English mind. He was an extremely wealthy man, starting life with fourteen titles, an enormous rent-roll and social position of the best, and later he married a great heiress and had a seat in the House of Lords.

He seemed to know so much that Mr. Choate referred to him once in a speech as 'Lord Lansdowne from whom no secrets are hid,' and on another occasion reminded him that, as there was nothing but fresh air and salt water between his estate in Ireland and Mr. Choate's home in the United States, friendship between them should be easy. But with all his urbanity Lord Lansdowne maintained the inflexible tradition of the Foreign Office never to be on too intimate terms with any foreign diplomat — a rule of discretion which must have been uncommonly useful many times.

I never remember any high British official coming to the Chancery for official purposes. On the occasions when they called on the Ambassador they presumably chose his residence, even though the Chancery was the official Embassy because it was the only place the rent of which was paid for by the United States Government, and where the code and archives were kept. Neither did other Ambassadors and Ministers of foreign countries come to the Chancery as a rule. But I remember one afternoon when a new Oriental Minister to London made his first call at the Chancery during a period when Mr. Carter was Chargé d'Affaires. I was in the Ambassador's room with Mr. Carter when His Excellency, clad in gorgeous raiment, was announced by a twittering Frank, and, though I was working at the side desk, found myself taking an unwilling part in the ceremonies. For on entering the room His Oriental Excellency bowed deeply first to the Chargé d'Affaires and then to me. We both bowed low in return, then he bowed again and we bowed, and as it looked as though we were in for a long session, I hurriedly effaced myself when his back was turned, and was no more seen. But his memory lingered on, for his clothes had apparently been packed in camphor!

7

*The American Colony at London, and its relations with the
Embassy and with the Court. Valuable historical researches in
England by American scholars. The English social year.*

1903

IT HAD been a matter of surprise to me — almost resentment
at first — to find how many Americans there were living in
England. If anyone had asked me I should have said that
England was almost entirely British — with a few foreigners
I might have added as an afterthought — a few American
Duchesses — and of course lots of visitors in the summer.

Seemingly, however, there were thousands of foreigners living in England, and far more Americans than any others. They
had their own clubs, helped their own indigent countrymen,
loudly proclaimed their American citizenship at least once a
year, and the rest of the time went their way in neighbourly
friendliness with their British hosts. They made few demands
on the Embassy, and were of all classes. The small group of
Americans who owned houses in England and came over every
summer, like the Carnegies, Morgans, Bradley-Martins,
Jameses, Phippses, Drexels, Mrs. John Mackay, and many
others, added much to London society and were warmly welcomed and feted.

There were also many other representative American women
living in London then: Mrs. Craigie, who, under the name of
John Oliver Hobbs, wrote most of her books about England;
Mrs. George Cornwallis West (formerly Lady Randolph
Churchill), Mrs. Arthur Paget, Consuelo, Duchess of Man-

chester (whose recipe for a successful party was to have it include a Duke, a Beauty, and a Ham), Mrs. Adair (the aunt of Mr. Wadsworth), Lady Cheylesmore, the Marchioness of Dufferin, Lady Curzon, Mrs. Joseph Chamberlain, and many others.

There was also the Astor family. Mr. Astor was the butt of the American papers because he had dared to become a British subject, and inferentially spend his money in England. As a matter of fact he probably wanted to have some public office, to participate in the Government of England and serve in Parliament, for in England men of wealth and standing are automatically expected to assume some responsibility for the community, whereas public office in the United States, so I had been told, is largely in the hands of professional politicians.

Most of the American men belonged to the American Society, founded in 1899 to be a convenient meeting-place for the business men who were extending trade and adding the spice of American aggression and cocksureness to British stodginess and conservatism. I never went to any of the Independence Day Banquets — the great event of the Society's year — because they admitted no women to the floor, and to sit in the gallery munching sandwiches and drinking coffee with such American wives as enjoy looking down on the bald heads, and only smelling the delectable odours of turkey, did not seem to me worth the trouble. It was undoubtedly at one of these banquets that Mr. Choate, glancing up at the hunger-pinched faces, tried to comfort them — if it *was* any comfort — by remarking that he now knew what the Psalmist had in mind when he said that God made man a little lower than the angels.

The Benevolent Fund of the American Society was added later, to aid Americans in distress. It was amazing how many there were who demanded help, either to return home — the usual plea — or for some other reason not quite so commendable. If one could believe what they told us, there had been Americans in every earthquake and major catastrophe of recent years, and all of them had with great heroism made their way to London, and now only wanted to get *Home*, from which, never again, please God, would they ever stray. So common was this plea of an American, who wanted above all things to 'Get Home to God's Own Country,' that when, at one of the banquets Mr. Choate quizzically enquired, 'Have any of you gentlemen ever seen a stranded American?' his question was received with derisive laughter, provoked by the picture of the average well-fed American who applied for help.

No assistance whatever was given by the American Government to its citizens abroad with the exception of needy *American* seamen shipped on *American* ships — a combination so rare that those eligible were hardly more than two or three a year. For those the Consulate-General, at no expense to the Government, arranged return passage on any convenient ship, usually as part of the crew. All other casualties were left to private charity. Mr. Walter Hempstock, who looked after the routine administration of the Benevolent Fund, told me that he never had the slightest difficulty in getting any money required, and in an emergency Americans in London would send cheques by messengers or authorize large expenditures without any hesitation.

Many and varied were the stories told by gentlemen and ladies of the 'itching foot,' who had sailed away from home looking for adventure, for change, or for the Holy Grail, and found themselves friendless in London without funds. To their indignant surprise work was hard to find. American ways were different, and though some of them found a place and a few achieved fame and fortune, the shiftless, the casual, and the men who were restricted in their abilities found their prospects worse than at home. The saddest of these were the 'cattle stiffs,' young men who had been crimped in American ports and at the end of the trip put ashore penniless in England, to get home as best they could.

Confidence men took their toll, and I remember one eminent

American gentleman who, explaining that he had been cleaned out, asked the Embassy to send a cable in his behalf. The money came at once, but the very next day he was back for another one to be sent as the same confidence man had tricked him again. All money from America for relief was sent to the Embassy, to establish good faith, and forwarded by them to the Society.

There were also a great many *bona-fide* students who spent more than they intended, and among the flotsam and jetsam of the international floating population who exist no one knows how, there were naturally a few Americans. Many were given loans and shipped home. And how grateful some of them were and how quickly they repaid the loan! But some of them neither repaid nor were grateful. Many refused to go home. They had been long abroad and felt more at home in London. They might as well starve in England as in the United States. But they did not starve. Americans were far too generous for that.

But there were many pitiful cases. Several middle-aged women, musicians or third-rate painters, looking shabby and half-starved, used to haunt the Embassy trying to sell tickets for their sad little shows, or just to have a chat with other Americans. The Society would gladly have paid their passages home to be rid of them, but their 'art,' they said, made it essential for them to remain. They told me privately they didn't want to go because their relatives didn't want them. No one wanted them. The English would not help them either. If they had been able to do the commonplace things of life, house work or office work, the Embassy or Consulate or some of the American firms might have employed them. But they were all artists, starving, striving, and a few of them had become 'abnormal' with discouragement, frustration, and disappointment.

The American Women's Club gave the women their meeting-place. In those days most of the American women living in England were rather diffident — a quality which the men had escaped entirely. They found London a chilly and unsociable place. Not that anyone was unfriendly, but simply that the English people didn't bother about them. They treated them exactly as they did each other, with utter indifference, and felt no more obligation to entertain them than they did their English neighbours. It wasn't until the World War that the splendid help given by the American women in England overcame those barriers and the English women got over their shyness.

In addition to these strictly American societies, Anglo-American relations were taken care of by the Pilgrims, started a few years before largely through the energy of Mr. (now Sir) Harry E. Brittain, an Englishman with organizing ability, a friendly feeling for people, and the urge to promote increased good relations between his country and the United States. There had been a succession of strictly American societies through the years — London was said to be strewn with their corpses — but this was different in that it was to include both British and Americans, and there was to be a branch in New York. Membership, the qualification being public service — the Army and Navy, science, literature, art, diplomacy, extensive travel, etc. — extends throughout the English-speaking world. It is not so much a club as a means of entertaining visiting public men, so that the 'Pilgrim' from England will receive as hearty a welcome in New York as his American confrère does in London.

The inaugural banquet of the Pilgrims was held at the Carlton Hotel in 1902, just before the Coronation of King Edward VII. It was presided over by Lord Roberts, the first Honorary President, and Senator Chauncey Depew made an excellent speech to a most distinguished audience. The Pilgrims held their banquets at no set times, and were careful never to encroach upon the three dates sacred to the American Society — Washington's Birthday, the Fourth of July, and

Thanksgiving Day. Naturally many of the members of the American Society were also members of the Pilgrims.

Notable Pilgrim dinners, held on many occasions, have always been and still are some of the most colourful held in London. While the American Society banquets reminded Americans of home, its habits, its food, and its claim to their love and loyalty, the Pilgrim Dinners were strictly occasions for exhibiting and promoting Anglo-American solidarity.

There was also, of course, the Consulate-General in the City of London, in charge of American commercial interests, with whom our relations were official and more or less friendly: and the Despatch Agency, called 'Uncle Sam's Post Office,' which took care of official mail for the whole of Europe and the ships at sea, and personally handled the official pouches to and from the State Department. These were put on board at Southampton by the Despatch Agent or his assistant, and on the arrival of the ship at New York taken off by an official there and sent to Washington. Mr. C. J. Petherick, an Englishman, did most of the work of the Agency while I was at the Embassy, as the official Despatch Agent was usually an American resident of London engaged in some other business, whose appointment was merely a political honour. Mr. Petherick was assisted by Mr. Frank Gurney, another Englishman, who succeeded Mr. Petherick on the latter's death. Since the World War, however, an American citizen has been appointed Despatch Agent, who gives all his time to it.

Many little human incidents enliven the monotonous arrival and departure of pouches and the distribution of mail. I remember the postman bringing in a postcard one morning addressed in a childish hand to — Bryan, London, England. The British Post Office didn't know what to do with it! The Embassy turned it over to the Despatch Agency, and Mr. Gurney recollected a young officer on one of the ships of the South Atlantic Station, somewhere off Brazil, whose name was Bryan, so, as the card bore an American stamp, he sent it off on the chance. It looked, he said, as though a tiny child had popped the card into the letter-box for her daddy far away, all unconscious of the big world and the slight chance of its ever reaching him. But it did, thanks to Mr. Gurney!

Of the thousands of other Americans who have done or were then doing valuable work in England in many fields there is no room to speak, though the contribution made to historical study by the late Mr. Benjamin Franklin Stevens — who was also, for some years, a most popular Despatch Agent, an old man, when I knew him — deserves to be recalled, for it was perhaps as great as any made by an individual American in that line. Mr. Stevens, a Vermonter, came to London to carry on business as an Anglo-American literary agent and bookseller, and was soon searching, cataloguing, and transcribing papers in the Public Record Office on the history of one of the States. As he came to realize the masses of unclassified papers there were, not only of one State but of all the thirteen original American Colonies, he decided to make an Index of at least some of the material, especially papers relating to the Revolutionary War.

The diplomatic papers and correspondence of the Negotiations for Peace in 1781–83 by which the United States took their place among the nations, seeming to him an appropriate starting-point, his first Index was limited to that. But the brief period of the peace negotiations soon widened to include the military events of the preceding years and his plan was changed so that his Index should begin in 1773, the year of the Boston Tea Party, and include every paper in both the national and private collections from then on to 1783. His aim was not to write a history, but to provide material for future historians. He did not confine himself to British archives alone. Those of Paris, Madrid, and The Hague were gone through also, and an elaborate system was built up to ensure as much accuracy as possible.

The great work well under way, and Mr. Stevens not a

wealthy man, he applied to Congress for aid, thinking that the Government of his country would be eager to sustain this patriotic effort. In support of his application petitions were sent to Washington, drawn up and signed by the presidents and faculties of the leading colleges, by the committees of historical societies, by leading American statesmen, and such eminent individuals as James Russell Lowell, Francis Parkman, Edward Everett Hale, John Bigelow, and hundreds of others, and also received the strong recommendation of the State Department. But, although it passed the Senate by a unanimous vote and was most favourably reported to the House, the jealousy of one man — a 'learned' but 'unnamed' historian! — was able to destroy the interest of the House in this valuable piece of research. This man, to whom the proposal was referred for his opinion, reported against it. As Mr. Stevens records:

> The chairman of the Sub-Committee [of the House of Representatives] briefly repeated the historian's arguments to the effect that the history of the United States had been carefully written; that it was a pity to give the rising generation references to the chapter and verse of original authorities, as the simple fact of such references implied a possible absence of accuracy in the quotations or conclusions; and that the Government need not incur expense by adopting the plan. The matter never came to a vote in the House, as it was suppressed in Committee.

How great Mr. Stevens's disappointment was he never said, but as no other help was forthcoming he went on year after year providing the funds for it. He didn't live to finish it. It was completed by his wife, and when published made twenty-five volumes, on which he had worked for thirty years. It is known as the 'Facsimile of Manuscripts.'

Along with this great Facsimile, Mr. Stevens published several other valuable historical volumes dealing with Anglo-American relations, and made some interesting discoveries which he passed on to the State Department from time to time.

On one occasion he pointed out that the examination of the State Papers showed how, through the operation of its secret service, the British Government secured its majorities to force the war policy against America, and another time he sent them an account of an electric apparatus once owned by Benjamin Franklin which he had unearthed somewhere in London.

Later in life Mr. Stevens took an Englishman, Mr. Henry J. Brown, who had been with him for many years, into partnership. The headquarters of Stevens & Brown at 4 Trafalgar Square (until the building was pulled down recently) was sacred to Anglo-American activities, and particularly, when it was the headquarters of the Despatch Agency, was crowded day after day with the Americans whose unofficial club it was.

Mr. Stevens was also one of the most enthusiastic members of the Whitefriars, one of the oldest literary coteries of London, which used to meet at Doctor Johnson's house, and of which the American Ambassador is always an honorary member. Mr. John L. Griffiths, one of the most popular of the Consuls-General in my time, was one of the pillars of this club and a frequent speaker. At one time Mr. Griffiths was invited to give a lecture on Benjamin Franklin. He said he would, but when he got to the meeting he announced that as he had left his manuscript at home he would speak on George Washington instead.

Mr. Griffiths' reluctance to speak on Benjamin Franklin reminds me of a dilemma which Ambassador Page handled with his usual ease during the time of America's neutrality in 1915. He had been invited to make an address on George Washington, a subject rather difficult because of 'entangling alliances' with which Mr. Page disagreed, for he was then all for increasing Anglo-American entanglements. He avoided political pitfalls, however, by speaking of the education of George Washington, a subject which was quite safe and about which he could be as vague as he chose!

Of the thousands of visitors who came every year to visit

England, the vast majority were Americans. Some came to look up family records and re-establish personal relationships with their British kin. To these it was a sort of eager home-coming, a return based on deep emotional stirrings. Americans seemed to know more and to care more for the historic places than the English themselves. They had been brought up to reverence Shakespeare, Milton, Westminster Abbey, and the Tower of London, and they were so sincere and frank in their admiration that they rather embarrassed their hosts, who may keep such things hidden in their hearts, but are rather slow at talking about them — except, of course, the poets and writers, who have no proper reticence anyhow! American visitors introduced England to the English. They loved and revered everything, and one enthusiastic lady was quoted as having said to a group of Englishwomen — who, incidentally, would like to have torn her limb from limb — that she thought it might be a good idea to tow the funny little island across the Atlantic and anchor it off Long Island so that it would be more accessible! England was a sort of 'pet' of these American visitors, and they used to pretend it was so small that they were afraid of falling off the edge.

All these visitors were exceedingly welcome in England and much liked. But there was another entirely different small group of women who had come to London to try to secure the social recognition that was denied them at home, and these were the bane of the Embassy. Many of them were wives or widows of men who had made large fortunes in Alaska and in the West in curious ways. Being uncultured and ignorant of everything except the value of money and an in-flated idea of its ability to buy anything, and kept out of social circles in America, they looked abroad for an entrée. A few such women had in former years managed to catch the eye of the Prince of Wales, and a most discriminating eye it was! But now that he was King, it was not so easy for *them*, al-though the more representative Americans were able to enjoy his friendship in a way that had not been possible in the previous reign, for Queen Victoria made no secret of the fact that she did not like American women.

King Edward VII, however, was much amused by their clothes, their dash, their gaiety, and their independence. Some of them were married to Englishmen and a part of English society, and others were the wives of prosperous American business men. The majority of American women living in London were most charming in every way. But the others — an extremely small number fortunately — were of the brand to banish sleep from the eyes of the most weary diplomat who had any official responsibility for them in a foreign land.

While to the uninitiated it may seem to make very little difference who goes to Court, apart from the satisfying of personal vanity — which so many Americans appear to think is the only reason — actually a presentation is the public introduction of an American citizen, vouched for by the Representative of the President, to a foreign Sovereign. Presentations are not by any means always for social purposes. There are much broader implications than that. Occasionally a presentation is a prelude to the husband of the lady acquiring business advantage in England, the parade of his wife's beauty and jewels being also a parade of the husband's credit in the same way as the presentation is the sign of his social acceptance. Sometimes it is to introduce a family who intend to become permanent additions to the American Colony in London and who desire to take their place in the conventional manner; and often the presentation of a débutante introduces to Their Majesties publicly the daughter of an old friend. All presentations of Americans must be made through the Embassy and at the discretion of the Ambassador, and no one has a *right* to be presented. It is only a courtesy extended by the King and Queen to distinguished foreigners, and that the privilege has been stretched to much greater proportions in the case of Americans is due to the feeling of kinship that the English people have for Americans and because they enjoy having them in London and want to do their utmost to make their visit pleasant.

With this large and increasing constituency, part of the Embassy's energy was directed to promoting a unique and individualized brand of social Anglo-American diplomacy entirely apart from the international business exchanges. The Anglo-American diplomacy carried on at London perhaps could be more accurately described as two separate and distinct pieces of work. The two Governments might be diplomatically at odds, but, whatever these differences, there was always a tremendous amount of social friendship between the two peoples. The English might and often did distrust and even dislike the American Government, but they had cordial liking for Americans as individuals and were sometimes sorry for them when their Government did not seem to represent the same friendly views that they expressed so warmly.

To take care of this 'social diplomacy' the Embassy every year (or it did until Ambassador Kennedy recently changed things) opens its books on January 1 to receive applications for all Court privileges for that year. Such ladies and gentlemen as wish to be presented make formal application, and if they are not known to the Embassy furnish letters of introduction from Americans with whom the Embassy is well acquainted, or from officials of high standing given for that specific purpose. The number of places for unofficial Americans is strictly limited, and the competition is very keen, so the annual attempt to feed five thousand applicants with a few small loaves and fishes is an unenviable one.

On January 1 the list of Americans who wish to attend the Ascot races in the Royal Enclosure opens also. This is a privilege which many Americans specially desire, whether they own horses which are running or are merely spectators, for in the Royal Enclosure during that week one may rub shoulders with most of the great and not-so-great of many countries. The Royal Family — unless there is Court mourning — attends. Any American, like anybody else, is at liberty to go to the course by paying his railway fare and entrance to the stands, but since the accession of Edward VII any foreigners wishing to have a place in the Royal Enclosure have been obliged to secure vouchers through the Embassy. So here again the miracle of the feeding of the five thousand is annually repeated.

There are invitations also to be coaxed for Court balls, banquets, garden parties at Buckingham Palace and Windsor Castle, gala performances at the opera, and other special entertainments, invitations for all of which are secured for Americans through the Embassy; so those who have been presented and who know and enjoy London make their applications early.

From January to July, then, even if the diplomatic horizon is clear, the lives of the Ambassador and Councillor of Embassy are one long nightmare. The junior members of the staff may disport themselves at the balls and garden parties with beautiful ladies, meet all sorts of amusing people and have a glorious time. But with the Ambassador and Councillor it is very different. Their pleasure is almost overridden by that 'care which, on the horseman's back perching, unseatest.' For should an unpresentable American be presented, something done which should not be done or something not done which should be done, the responsibility is on the Embassy.

All through January, while the Embassy is busy informing applicants that their names have been entered, the social population of London is absent either seeking sunshine on the Riviera or freezing in its country houses. The two early Courts and Levees usually held in February bring them back for a short time, Parliament begins its sessions, and the American ladies who have been chosen for the early Courts arrive and make their bow. Some entertaining is done, but with the coming of Ash Wednesday everything stops, and the English people — supposedly keeping their Lenten fast (Parliament can apparently work and fast, too) — either go South again or return to the country.

Easter brings everybody back, and soon the great houses of Mayfair, Park Lane, Carlton House Terrace, and Piccadilly open. Flowers are seen blooming in boxes, curtains appear at windows, and carriages stand at the doors. Steamers begin to arrive crowded with Australians and New Zealanders, South Africans, Indians, Canadians, Continental Europeans, and Americans, until the streets are filled with a medley of people of every nationality, the whole world apparently crowding into London. All foreign Ambassadors on leave return, the flag goes up at Buckingham Palace, and Their Majesties arrive, cheered all the way through beflagged streets from station to palace. The weather usually cheers up, too, although it is often May or early June before winter finally retreats and makes way for spring, with birds and flowers and genial warmth and long evenings encouraging the new and tender green of the parks and ornamenting the tidy beds with a riot of blossom. Rotten Row is filled with equestrians in the mornings and pedestrians in the afternoons, to say nothing of hundreds of nursemaids with perambulators and rosy-cheeked children. London is alive, gay, beautiful, easy-going, with everybody having a part in the pleasure.

The late Courts and Levees take place in May and June, foreign Royal visitors come and go welcomed with roars of applause from masses of excited Britons standing on the pavements and clinging to the lamp-posts, bands playing their own national anthems and special addresses of welcome from ridiculous looking officials all dressed up. The Royal guests are entertained with Court balls, garden parties, special pilgrimages to spots sacred to them, and in their turn give receptions at their own Embassy to the Diplomatic Corps and to the people of their own country, and finally are sent on their homeward way through more cheering crowds and their Royal host to see them off. New plays are to be seen, new musicians to be heard, tea on the Terrace of the House of Commons is popular, the best oratory is heard in both Houses of Parliament, and there are great balls and receptions in the historic houses of the political parties.

The Court leaves London at the end of June for Windsor, for the King and Queen usually go to the Ascot races once or twice. On Gold Cup Day they drive in procession from the end of Windsor Park down the hill — two miles long — to the course. Crowded on both sides of the course with thousands of their subjects, they drive along smiling and bowing, their open carriage drawn by cream ponies with postillions in bright red coats and white breeches. Following them, come the rest of the Royal Family and the Lords and Ladies in Waiting. As the procession draws near to the Royal Box and Enclosure, the noises of the paddock subside, the guns boom, bookmakers cease their raucous barks, and everybody stands at the rail. The Royal Enclosure looks like a sea of lovely nodding flowers as the ladies droop their heads in unison and curtsey to the ground, and the men, hatless, bow low to their Sovereigns. No one can look at such a spontaneous and dignified demonstration without being much moved. A few moments, and then the King and Queen appear in the handsomely decorated Royal Box and the racing starts. Between the races they come down into the Enclosure and mix with their guests. No wonder Americans like to be included, for Ascot is one of the most beautiful of race-courses, with the long green lane leading up to Windsor Park and Castle, down which the gay procession advances, looking like a handsome velvet band of carpet startlingly green and young and luscious.

Ascot over, the Embassy may now close its books, fold its hands, and either one by one a-holidaying go, or return to the more prosaic exchanges of diplomatic give-and-take. Its con-

tact with the Court for the rest of the year will be more inter-
mittent. There may perchance be invitations to the Ambassador or Councillor to visit Windsor Castle. Appropriate
felicitations will be officially exchanged between the King
and the President on their respective birthdays, important
people will come from Washington armed with letters of introduction and wish to meet the King, and will be presented, if
the King is agreeable, by the Ambassador. Large numbers of
gifts, suitable and unsuitable, will be received for presentation to the King, and either returned — the usual course — or
sent on through the Foreign Office. Many Americans will
write letters to the King, and should a Royal wedding occur
there will be no end to the gifts which generous Americans
will want to bestow.

Truly the width and depth and general inclusiveness of
social Anglo-American diplomacy before the World War was
unfathomable. It was always far-reaching and unexpected,
though thoroughly disarming and friendly.

8

*The Russo-Japanese War. The secret marriage of Mr. Marshall
Field. J. S. Sargent and his portraits of Mr. Choate. Mr.
Henry James. American oratory. Mr. William Jennings Bryan
speaks at a dinner of the American Society. Rivalry of Senator Chauncey M. Depew and Mr. Choate as after-dinner
speakers.*

1904

THE war between Russia and Japan which began early in
1904 made little difference to the Embassy except for some exchanges with the Foreign Office in regard to the neutrality of
China and questions of contraband, and continued on its
dreary way until, owing to defeats in the field and dissatisfaction at home, Russia was crushed. The following June President Roosevelt arbitrated between them, and with the signing
in the United States of the Treaty of Portsmouth in September
the war ended.

The Embassy received most of its official information about
this treaty and the President's success as an arbitrator through
the newspapers, for it was not until some time after that the
Department of State began sending out what they called 'Information Series' material. Up to then it had not been their
regular custom to furnish anything of general interest. But
many diplomats were beginning to clamour for something
more, not at all content with odds and ends doled out only
when it was necessary. They felt they ought to be reporting
more of the incidents and impressions which lay a little outside of the precise instructions sent to them, in the way that

Mr. White did so successfully. Specially noteworthy speeches and statements had always been forwarded, as of interest, but, as all that ever came in reply was a mere acknowledgment without further comment, the Embassies did not feel encouraged to go to great lengths.

There seemed to be little attempt to include the American diplomats in the world policy that was developing. They learned something of it when they went to Washington on leave, but when in the field they often felt all too isolated. In the many Anglo-American negotiations which were being handled through the British Embassy at Washington, the London Embassy was usually better informed, but the State Department seemingly had no means of keeping us up to date with negotiations proceeding in Russia, Persia, or any other country unless these negotiations also included the British Government.

It didn't matter so much in London, where the Embassy personnel was experienced and cultured, and their relations with their fellow diplomats were intimate enough to ensure their being kept up to date by them on matters of general interest. But on the whole American diplomacy suffered from this rather narrow view, and occasionally America's diplomats had been known to slip up in keeping the State Department informed of treaties actually in the making.

The senior diplomats wrote some of their opinions to Washington, but these went in personal letters, for, owing to the lack of secrecy, a diplomat was always fearful of putting too much in writing. The smallness of the staff at the State Department apparently made it impossible to do more than deal with each situation with the utmost economy of secretarial assistance, and then only with the two or three Embassies concerned. The newspapers invariably knew more than the Embassy on matters of immediate interest, so Mr. Carter had long ago developed a defence mechanism, which he hoped was convincing, of looking wise and saying nothing. Perhaps

Mr. White was better informed. He may have received replies to some of his personal letters, but ordinarily the official cables and instructions were abrupt.

The Embassy, in brief, did good work with little machinery, human or otherwise, and very little money. Through the friendly help of the American newspaper correspondents at London, they were able, however, to keep themselves alive to what was going on especially as the correspondents rang up whenever they had any news that they thought the Embassy ought to have, or would confirm. This group held a reception almost every afternoon in the Hodson office, where old Mr. Hodson, in lieu of news, would tell them anecdotes, and recite the poems of James Russell Lowell and John Hay. There was Mr. Warren T. Mason of the Scripps Agency, a witty, black-haired young man with thick lenses to his glasses, who was reputed to be a first-rate story-teller; Mr. George Denny of the Associated Press with a most trustworthy face and quiet manner, who had been bear-leader to some of the sons of the King of Siam in a trip round the world and had some cuff-links of Oriental design to prove it; Mr. Frederick Moore, also of the Associated Press, known to his friends as the 'Virginian' because he looked like the famous cowboy of that grand story, and could lounge against a doorpost gracefully; Mr. Kaufmann Spears, a most soulful, poetic gentleman; Mr. Lambert of the New York *Sun* who knew more gossip than anyone else; Mr. I. N. Ford of the New York *Tribune*, Mr. Frank Dilnot and Mr. A. A. Milne, the last two Britishers, and several others.

Mr. Marshall Field was married that spring — or it may have been the spring of the following year — at Saint Margaret's, Westminster, and, so secret was the wedding that even I was cautioned to say nothing about it. But, as all I knew of Mr. Field was that he kept a big shop in Chicago, his matrimonial affairs did not interest me. Not long afterwards he died, and it became necessary, in settling up the estate, to prove that this London marriage had taken place, so the attorneys asked the Embassy to arrange for the clergyman who had performed the ceremony to go to Chicago to testify. Mr. Hodson telephoned to him — I think he was one of the assistant curates — and asked him to call at the Embassy, and when he arrived the following morning he was brought in to Mr. Carter's office with much ceremony. He was a nervous little man, so Mr. Carter chatted pleasantly for a few minutes to make him feel at ease, and then asked him to go to Chicago, explaining what was wanted.

I never saw such utter astonishment and apprehension in anyone's face before. His eyes fairly stuck out of his head. 'Go to America!' he gasped, as though it was a trip to the moon which was being suggested. 'Go to America! But I couldn't get such a long holiday as that. Oh, no, it's perfectly impossible.' Mr. Carter waited a minute and then ventured:

'You would be doing the Field family a service, and, after all, Chicago isn't very far nowadays. I am sure you would find it a most interesting trip and we will make the arrangements and pay all the expenses.' But it looked as though he could never bring himself to consider it seriously until Mr. Carter said: 'And why not take your wife with you? She would like a sea voyage, I'm sure, and it would be entirely proper for her expenses to come out of the estate too.'

I sat at my desk, but managed to watch him, his consternation, and then his dawning realization, and finally a smile. 'I don't really know *what* to say. Of course it would be wonderful, and I'm sure my wife would be most happy — and — I *dare say*, after all, I *could* manage to be away.' He smiled almost roguishly.

'Well, then, that's settled,' said Mr. Carter, rising briskly to his feet. 'Now I will turn you over to Mr. Hodson and he will see that everything is done to make you comfortable. And — pleasant trip.'

It was some weeks later that he was ushered in again. Mr. Hodson whispered:

'The clergyman to see you, sir. You know — the man who went to Chicago.' Mr. Carter looked up.

'Oh, he's back. Did he enjoy himself?'

'Not 'arf,' said Mr. Hodson, laughing.

And when he came in how different he was. He had on new clothes, his looks had improved, he walked with a new assurance. Marching over to Mr. Carter, he shook hands cordially.

'I really don't know how to thank you for everything,' he said, and there was a quiver in his voice. 'It has been a wonderful experience. We could never have made a trip like that under any other circumstances, and both my wife and I thank you. In Chicago everybody was very, very kind.'

Seeing how friendly and pleasant most American men were who came in to see Mr. Carter, I used to listen to their conversations, and if one happened to be left alone with me I studied him surreptitiously. Most of these gentlemen were Senators, Ambassadors, Congressmen, or other influential men who were quite ready to be talkative, especially when they found out I was English. They told me the most amazing things that they pretended were happening in America, and I remember an exhaustive account given me one day by Senator Spooner, while he waited to see Mr. Choate, of a particularly brutal murder of a girl in a taxicab in Brooklyn, upon which he asked my opinion. I had no opinion that I was willing to pass on to this most entertaining gentleman, much to his disappointment, though he was full of absurd suggestions as to the whys and wherefores. Finally he asked what I should have done if some man had tried to murder me in a cab, and when I demurely replied, 'Get out,' he rocked with laughter.

Many other well-dressed elderly gentlemen in light suits and buttonholes, panama hats and square-toed shoes with humps on them, used Mr. Carter's room for an anteroom, and while waiting for the Ambassador tried to draw me out on many personal subjects. Some asked about my family, my religious opinions, and what I thought of the United States, and when I said I had never seen the United States, they enthusiastically invited me to come at any time. It must have been hard going for them to maintain any conversation at all, for I did nothing to encourage them. Sometimes, on Mr. Carter's return, I would notice an exchange of glances. But when I reported the invitation, he told me it didn't mean a thing!

Among the famous men who came to the Embassy seldom, but who when he did was treated like a king, was the painter John S. Sargent, who was not only a great painter, but a heavy man with phenomenal powers of work — boasted, indeed, that he could go on without stopping for twenty-four hours — but who was so shy as to be a constant target for jokers and an embarrassment to his friends.

Mr. Sargent presided on one occasion at a dinner given to Rodin at the newly organized branch of the Royal Academy on condition that no speech was expected of him. He was, therefore, enjoying himself, all unconscious that a group of his students had decided otherwise. These began to call for a speech so vociferously that he was finally forced reluctantly to his feet. But, as usual, every word deserted him. He hemmed and hawed, but not one intelligent sentence was forthcoming while he stood miserably looking to the ceiling for help. The sight was particularly ridiculous because of his size, and because it seemed impossible that such a splendid specimen of humanity should actually be unable to find a word. In the end, without saying anything he had to sit down, to the applause and cheerful cat-calls and jeers of his students, who, though they treated him so cavalierly, loved him and had great reverence for him.

A year before that Mr. Sargent had undertaken to paint two official portraits of Mr. Choate, one, I believe, for the Bar Association of New York, and one for some legal fraternity in

JOSEPH H. CHOATE: A PORTRAIT SKETCH BY JOHN S. SARGENT

England. Mrs. Choate went with the Ambassador to Mr. Sargent's studio, full of the importance of the portraits and eloquent as to what she thought would be the best pose. Mr. Sargent, polite, friendly, said he was counting on Mrs. Choate's suggestions, but instead of dismissing this as a mere pleasantry, Mrs. Choate took it seriously, and Mr. Sargent found out he had made a great mistake. It seemed that Mrs. Choate in her youth had painted flowers — perhaps on china — and as an experienced artist had much advice to offer. The consequence was that Mr. Sargent, temperamental and used to working without any suggestions or advice whatsoever, was entirely 'put off,' and the finished portraits, though they have their points of excellence, lack a certain spontaneous zest for life which his friends found the most infectious thing about Mr. Choate. A secret plan was hatched soon after that Mr. Sargent would make a sketch of Mr. Choate for his friends, which would be the Mr. Choate they knew. It was not until a few months before Mr. Choate left London that the opportunity came, and one morning Mr. Carter slipped off with Mr. Choate to Mr. Sargent's studio. The occasion was extremely hilarious, mirth on every face, and with this background Mr. Sargent, in three hours, finished the sketch of Mr. Choate which is included here, a perfect likeness.

Mr. Sargent was a great favourite with everybody — with the possible exception of the State Department — for, in spite of pleas on the part of American artists that he remember that he was a citizen of the United States and act accordingly, he chose to take it very calmly. American artists disliked intensely to see Mr. Sargent's pictures placed in foreign exhibits as part of the British, instead of the American School. I remember one occasion of an exhibition at one of the capitals of South America, when again Americans found to their wrath that several of Mr. Sargent's pictures were hung with those of the British School. The Embassy was asked by the State Department to persuade Mr. Sargent to have them moved into the American section. But all that could be got from him was a statement that as a member of the British Academy, he was subject to the rules of the Academy, and they could put his pictures where they would. Everybody knew he was an American, he said, and what did it matter? The only concession to American opinion that he made was the suggestion that as there were many other pictures of his in the United States they could be gathered together and hung in the American section. He didn't take citizenship as a serious matter at all — no one did in those days — although when nationalism raised its head and it became necessary for Americans to register at the Consulate-General every year to preserve their citizenship, he carefully registered.

I remember the occasion when a very beautiful young American woman in London wished him to paint her portrait, and many of her friends supported her in telling Mr. Sargent what a lovely picture she would make. But he did not like what he had heard of the lady, and to the bombardment of requests he said: 'I don't care whether she would make a lovely picture or not. I won't paint her. I am not going to have anyone use me to advertise herself!' And he never did! He and Henry James were good friends, and there were several others of that group of cultured Americans who made London their second home, with whom the Embassy was on terms of cordial friendship. Henry James, who lived comfortably not far from London and mixed with Americans and English irrespective of their nationality, actually, at the age of seventy-one, became a British subject after the beginning of the World War, Percy Lubbock in the 'Letters of Henry James,' published after his death, giving as his reason: 'The challenge of the war with Germany roused him [James] to a height of passion he had never touched before in the outer world; and if the strain of it exhausted his strength, as well it might, it gave him one last year of the fullest and deepest experience he had ever known. It wore out his body which was too tired and spent to live longer; but he carried away the power of its spirit in its prime,' a demonstration of sympathy which touched Englishmen deeply.

Mr. Woodward resigned and Mr. William Phillips came to be Secretary to the Ambassador in his place. Mr. Phillips was a tall, slender, blond young man with a most winning manner, and with such a fresh almost girlish complexion that, as he came from Boston, it was not surprising that he should soon be nicknamed — behind his back — 'The Puritan Maiden.' He took his place immediately in the Embassy social circle, for he had much poise and dignity and the others liked him enormously, though they occasionally pretended that he had to be lived up to, for he was most industrious and punctilious about matters which had long since become routine to the others. Mr. Phillips came in every morning with Mr. Choate, often quite winded, having walked across the Green Park with him from Carlton House Terrace, for Mr. Choate was a fast walker.

When Mrs. Choate was away, or the Ambassador wanted to return to the Chancery immediately, he and Mr. Phillips would have their lunch in the dairy next door. Mr. Choate declared he liked eating there because it was clean, the food good and plain, and there were plenty of pretty girls to look at. The two would sit opposite each other at a tiny table, jostled by waitresses and customers and seemingly quite content and interested. While Mr. Choate watched the girls eating their lunches and took note of the sticky pastries they seemed to prefer, and dodged the hundreds of cups of strong tea that went sweeping past his head, Mr. Phillips watched over Mr. Choate, for he, like everybody else, soon came absolutely under the spell of his whimsical and most engaging personality.

I used to think sometimes that Mr. Choate deliberately lunched at this place to annoy Mr. White, because whenever

Mr. Choate had eaten there he would make an opportunity of telling the impatient Mr. White about it. 'You know, Harry,' he would say confidentially, 'it doesn't matter *how* much I eat. I have never yet managed to spend a shilling.' But Mr. White was 'not amused,' so naturally Mr. Choate could always find something more to tell him, and would do it so innocently that poor Mr. White, with little sense of humour, could never be sure whether or not he was being 'spoofed.' I don't believe wild horses could ever have dragged *him* into such a place.

After lunch Mr. Choate would fall asleep at his desk, and put his foot on the bell underneath, which would ring and ring until someone had to be bold enough either to wake him up or move his foot while he slept, a ticklish business. One day when Frank, on his knees, was very gently sliding his foot off the bell, Mr. Choate woke and, as Frank struggled speechless to his feet, enquired, 'And what is this, might I ask? Worship or murder?' Mr. Phillips didn't like to have Mr. Choate sleep, for he did not think it good for an old man to dream his life away, so they usually woke him by making a noise, and he would then go on with his work, with a joke about the earnest souls who wouldn't let him have his forty winks in peace as the other animals did.

Talkative visitors didn't have much chance to spread themselves with Mr. Choate. He would listen patiently for a certain time, and then, perhaps actually in the middle of one of their most impressive sentences, he would rise to his feet, and, holding out his hand, say cordially, 'So delighted to have seen you,' and before the startled caller could collect his wits he was on his way out. That was a trick Ambassador Reid never learned. He did not seem able to get rid of callers until they had poured out everything they had come to say, but Mr. Choate could — and did.

A tremendous amount of oratory enlivened our days, for every American who came to London seemed to have something to say, and the Embassy felt responsible for these utterances. There was Mr. William Jennings Bryan, who came that year, and, notorious as he was for his pro-Irish sympathies, for the fact that he was always attacking Mr. Hay as one of the 'slaves' of England, and was ready at any moment to put an anti-British plank in the Democratic platform to gain votes, he was considered an extremely 'hot potato,' and, because he was an excellent public speaker, one of the most poisonous variety. When Major Beacom, the Military Attaché, whose guest he was, brought him in to be introduced to me, I thought him a most charming man, and his paternal, church-elder face looked so innocent and trustworthy that I decided he must have been maligned.

But he was to speak before the American Society, and, although he had received many hints to submit his speech to the Embassy beforehand, he seemingly didn't know what they were talking about, and as no Ambassador could afford to be too dictatorial in supervising his unofficial fellow citizens, they had to let it go at that. The Ambassador had always to keep in mind that in the constant changes of government the most unlikely person might one day become President or Secretary of State and his 'boss,' and that it behooved him to take no chances with his career by minimizing the importance of anyone, however improbable he might seem at the moment.

Mr. Choate, however, did not go to the dinner unprotected. In introducing Mr. Bryan he disclaimed publicly all responsibility for him. Said he:

> It is my happy privilege as Ambassador to welcome the distinguished men and the distinguished women of my country who come over here, without regard to party, or creed, or section, or race, or colour. All men and all women of all classes and sections are my constituents as long as I am here. And so, in that spirit, I have been most happy to welcome this celebrated citizen on his too brief visit to London. I have done what I could to make his visit pleasant — and profitable. I have taken him to the Bank of England where he could make a special study

of finance and currency, and if you could have heard him cross-examining the Governor you may believe that he improved his opportunity. And then, too, he is making a tour of enquiry, an enquiry that would be worthy of the British Government itself. He sat at the feet of Asquith and Chamberlain and Goschen and Rosebery, and if, having heard all of these gentlemen in the space of about forty-eight hours, his ideas on the fiscal question are not a little mixed, you will appreciate what qualities the man has. . . .

After all the apprehension, however, Mr. Bryan made a most appealing speech.

Senator Depew was another American orator who came often to London, and, as he and Mr. Choate were rivals for the title of the greatest wit, there was always good 'listening' when the two men were on the same platform. Mr. Depew loved to poke fun at the Embassy, and on one occasion told a delighted audience an experience he claimed to have had at the Legation years before, when Mr. Lowell was Minister and Mr. James Hoppin Secretary. According to Mr. Depew he called on Mr. Hoppin, whom he knew very well, and that, without even glancing at his card or at him, Mr. Hoppin began immediately on the regular rigmarole he had evolved to answer all Americans who came to ask for favors:

> I can't understand why Americans who come over here are so anxious to get into the House of Commons. It is infinitely better for them to go to the House of Representatives or the Senate of the United States. I can't understand why they want to see the Minister of the United States. They don't seem to appreciate that every minute of his time night and day is employed in preserving the peace between the two countries and the peace of the world. I can't understand how any American could want to be presented to the Queen. The Queen doesn't want to see him or her. The Queen won't recollect who he or she is. It will cost anywhere from $500 to $1000 to go there, and it only takes a minute. . . .
>
> But, my dear friend, I want to tell you that I have found something exactly suited to a man of your quiet tastes; I have with

difficulty succeeded in procuring a few tickets under tremendous pressure, and I will give you two of them — for the Cattle Show at Reading!

When the laughter had died down, Mr. Depew added that he was sure his audience would be glad to know that when he reached home he was immediately elected a member of the New York Farmers' Club.

Some years afterwards, in 1910, I believe, at a dinner given by the Pilgrims in New York to Mr. Henry White, Mr. Depew showed that he had a broad knowledge of other diplomatic hardships at London. Said he:

> There are, I believe, about four invitations possible for a reception at Buckingham Palace and about eight to the House of Commons, and there are at least 30,000 Americans a year asking these favours. The Ambassador, wanting to retain his place, refers them to his Secretary, and Mr. White met these hundreds and thousands of Americans with an expression which meant he would do the best for them — and the best he could was that none of them got anything. That led to several additions to the expletives in the American language in regard to the manner in which we were represented abroad.

But of all the speakers Mr. Choate, to my mind, was far the best. Many stories were told which illustrate his character better than his impressive orations on state occasions could ever do. When he grew stout, as he did in his later years, he explained it was so that he could meet the English halfway. In his speeches he was always contrasting the Lion with the Eagle, and once got into trouble at home by saying that when the British Lion is about to roar even the American Eagle should hold its peace. He never tired of teasing the English people, who thoroughly enjoyed it, for they respond to that sort of approach much better than they do to professional politeness.

'How do we know that George Washington could throw a dollar across the Potomac?' he would ask, and there being no response he would go on, 'Because he chucked a Sovereign across the Atlantic.' And when on one occasion he stood up to address a large assemblage at the Fourth-of-July banquet of the American Society and saw before him, besides the Americans, a great array of Englishmen, he leaned forward and hissed incredulously, 'Can *this* be the Fourth of July? Is *this* the spirit of 1776?'

Important as these occasions were, Mr. Choate was perhaps at his best when he made extempore speeches at working men's clubs, sailors' institutes, and other gathering places of the lesser man. He was so honest and sincere and direct, and one had the feeling that he saw into the real human being and had an intense sympathy for him. This, lit up with flashing gleams of his wit, made him loved as one might love a fine opponent, not as one loves a remote saint in a stained-glass window. It was not only the British Government and the aristocracy and the learned who knew and enjoyed him. He was Ambassador to the ordinary people, too, and the masses, whom he could twist round his finger, adored him.

I heard him make a speech only once and that was when he gave away the prizes at Battersea Polytechnic, an evening and day school near London which offered courses in every known subject. Most of the students were of the struggling, ambitious lower middle class, pathetically trying to scale the ladder of success against almost insuperable odds. I had learned to cook there, so, as a great honour, they gave me a card. The 'Polly' was everything to the students, who firmly believed that what they got there would fit them for any position.

Mr. Phillips drove down to Battersea with Mr. Choate, and on the way they looked over the catalogue, probably all the preparation that Mr. Choate made. I sat near the front, and the vast hall was filled to capacity, with the American flag well in evidence. There were doubtless other speeches, though I have no memory of them, but at last Mr. Choate stepped forward, smiled, and after the usual applause, began in his vibrant, stimulating way — his grey hair waving and his fingers caressing his watch chain — to talk with that sympathetic understanding so characteristic of him. He knew what they were trying to do. He looked at their earnest faces, and saw in them the epitome of the struggle for self-determination, for a fuller life, and with his broad experience and his knowledge he talked, playing with them as he must have played with many audiences and in many courts of law. He was one of them, one with them. He was no stranger.

He talked on education. He could have compared national systems and been specific, but his theme was much broader. He had to make a place for this particular group, to include them as members and partners in the broad educational scheme, and then to point out some of the resultant responsibilities of the educated man, and he did it superbly. And, after a short interpolation about some of the actual courses offered, he brought everyone to his feet by saying slowly, impressively: 'Why, I don't call this a Polytechnic. I call it the *Battersea University*.' There was a perfect furor, many people jumping up and down in their excitement, and the boy next to me gave a quick sob.

At the end we all stood solemnly while the organ played the 'Star-Spangled Banner,' and then people began to move from the platform and to leave the seats. But Mr. Choate and Mr. Phillips stood placidly just where they were, and flurried enquiries elicited the fact that they were waiting for the National Anthem. So the organist was found and brought back and the audience returned and the whole place rang with 'God Save the King.' But even when Mr. Choate finally tore himself away from the hand-shaking and the enthusiasm, the audience would not give him up. Dozens ran along beside the car for a long distance waving their hats and cheering, and there was a sweetness and comradeship in the feeling that he had created that did more for Anglo-American relations than the noblest sentiment in the most august of language on the most official of occasions. This was another sheer triumph of personality. I never knew another Ambassador who had such a perfect understanding of the English folkways — probably because his ancestors were English — though many other Ambassadors have been very popular speakers, too.

9

The Presidential election of 1904 and its effect on the Embassy. Mr. Choate resigns and Mr. Whitelaw Reid is appointed Ambassador. Mr. Henry White is made Ambassador to Italy and Mr. Carter becomes Councillor. Farewells and plans for the future.

1905

It must have been during the summer of 1904 that I first heard about the Presidential election that was to come in November and its possible effect on the Embassy. It seemed that every Ambassador sent abroad by the United States was expected to resign every time a new President came into office — and that was very often, once every four years. Since President McKinley's assassination Mr. Theodore Roosevelt, Vice-President, had been finishing out the term, but now he was offering himself as President. If he were elected, he would probably want to put his own friends into office, and make one of them Ambassador to London, for Mr. Choate had been appointed by Mr. McKinley. And if he were not elected, and a Democratic President came into office, well — anything was possible! We were frightened of Democrats — I thought of them as our family thought of Liberals — climbers of uncertain background who were trying to scale their way into the inner circles! The election, therefore, had a most serious side for the Embassy. The Secretaries hoped to be inconspicuous enough to be overlooked in the general shake-up, but there was absolutely no chance for the Ambassador. Mr. Carter told me that the coming March was sure to make a great deal of difference, whoever was elected, but in any case Mr. Choate had already decided to resign.

Mr. White and Mr. Carter were also rather uncomfortable because of many rumours afloat of impending new regulations which would render diplomats liable to be moved about much more frequently than they had been, even though this seemed to indicate that some orderly system was being evolved which would be for their ultimate good — or the good of their successors, as Mr. Carter wryly added. Both Mr. White and Mr. Carter had been a long time in London, and were certainly due for promotion. But neither of them wanted to leave London, where they had bought homes and where their children were growing up and many friendships established. They had hoped to remain more or less permanently, and this speeding-up of diplomatic changes all over the world gave them nothing but cold shivers.

There was an air of restlessness over the whole Embassy. Diplomacy almost stood still, as it usually does in the Presidential election year. Mr. Phillips told us he did not intend to stay if Mr. Choate went, but would apply to go elsewhere, as he had made up his mind to enter the Diplomatic Service.

When we were not busy that winter, Mr. Carter enlivened me with speculations as to what he *might* do if he were superseded and given no promotion elsewhere. His first idea was to go into the second-hand clothes business and hire out uniforms to butlers and footmen and American diplomats — all about the same, you know! — and Americans who wished to go to Court — *men only!* How we laughed! But there was so little real future to it, he lamented! And B. J. Simmons, the professional who furnished costumes for all purposes, wouldn't care for it either! His children would go anywhere or live in America, he went on more seriously, and as to his wife, she was always content to do what the others wanted, though she had opposed his going into the Service in the beginning. But that was a long time ago!

The prospect of the coming changes was the main topic of correspondence between the various American Embassies, for everyone was anxious and eager to hear all the latest gossip about the new ideas that filtered from Washington; that the whole Service was to be regimented, that a few of the kindly misfits who flourished in obscurity at small capitals, where a good dancer was more in demand than a good diplomat, were to be eliminated, and — worst of all — that examinations for entrance to the Service were being considered. Not that anyone in London would have minded taking an examination, and could have passed it hands down — but Examinations! — which meant competing with a group of young college men — still 'wet behind the ears' — was laughable.

There was continued grumbling among the diplomats who felt themselves merely victims to be sacrificed every four years to make a Roman holiday for a new President. Why the whole Diplomatic Service all over the world had to be shaken up just because there was a new President in Washington was a mystery to me. The only bit of comfort turned out to be that as President Roosevelt was elected in November there might not be as many changes as if the new President had been a Democrat.

The resignations went forward, and Mr. Choate's was accepted, though he was told to take his time about leaving London. He had explained that he would like to remain to see the window installed which he had given to Southwark Cathedral in memory of John Harvard, who had been baptized there, and it was uncertain just how long that would take, for, although the old European glass had been sent to him a long time ago, Mr. John La Farge was not to be hurried.

After that the changes came thick and fast. The appointment of Mr. Whitelaw Reid as Ambassador was approved by the King and announced in Washington; Mr. White was appointed Ambassador to Rome, and in April Mr. Carter, to his own and everybody else's relief, was promoted to be Councillor in Mr. White's place. Mr. Wadsworth moved up to Second Secretary, and a Mr. Lewis Einstein was coming to be Third Secretary.

On the whole this was better than had been expected. The British Government's acceptance of Mr. Reid was most cordial, there was general rejoicing that Mr. White had been given the Ambassadorship that he deserved, especially at Rome, which had up to then been a political spoils post, and everybody, in congratulating Mr. Carter, considered Mr. Reid very lucky to have him as Councillor.

Until he left for Rome, Mr. White attended to many of the details of finding a house for the new Ambassador. With the aid of a special code sent over for the purpose by Mr. Reid, Mr. White had been carrying on a lively correspondence ever since his appointment had been mooted and, after a good deal of backing and filling, had leased Dorchester House for his occupancy. Dorchester House was one of the most beautiful houses in London, directly opposite to Hyde Park in Park Lane, a perfect example of Renaissance art, built by men who had been brought over from Italy for the purpose. It was a house which entirely met Mr. White's conception of what the American Ambassador's residence in London ought to be, and its prestige had been augmented in consequence of rumours that it would be bought in one day for a Royal residence.

The activity about the proper housing of his successor was naturally going on right under the nose of Mr. Choate, who, while making his own preparations to go, enjoyed the breathtaking preparations, and, when he and Mr. White occasionally encountered each other at the Embassy, Mr. Choate let no chance go by of catechizing him about his activities. Mr. White, naturally a little on the defensive at being so completely on with the new love before he was off with the old, was extremely embarrassed. At the skilful but merciless hands of one of America's most famous lawyers he was compelled to submit to a grilling examination of his doings, and details that he was trying to keep to himself were beguiled out of him. And when it was all over, Mr. Choate would say loudly and cheerfully so that he could not help hearing, 'Well, well, Harry's quite domesticated, isn't he? Who *would* have thought it!'

Mr. White left London suddenly in the end, so along with the ceremonies attendant on the departure of Mr. Choate, Mr. Carter inherited the making of the final arrangements for Mr. Reid's coming. Compared with the assembling of a household, the leasing of a house was simple. Mr. Carter had to engage a staff, and assist in getting horses, motors, and a functionary known as a 'donkey boy,' as well as make the official arrangements for the reception of the new Ambassador. He discussed with Mr. Choate every new cable from Mr. Reid and every new complication, and Mr. Choate was most entertained.

So those two months after Mr. White had gone and while Mr. Choate remained in London were very happy ones, though a little emotional too. There was a feeling of clutching at things that were slipping away, a desire to cement moments that would never come back, a consciousness of time rushing along all too fast towards something strange and therefore possibly to be feared.

I typed Mr. Choate's last addresses, the one given before the Bench and Bar of England, when for the first time in a hundred and fifty years an American was made a Bencher of the Inner Temple — and his farewell, delivered at the banquet given by the Lord Mayor of London at the Mansion House. The two speeches, equally brilliant, were entirely different. To the Benchers he spoke of legal matters, and told the sad story of the fantastic end of the impressive wig worn by a past Lord Chancellor. Mr. Choate claimed that it was purchased and exported to the coast of Guinea to be worn by an African warrior to make him more formidable to his enemies on the field of battle. 'Our pure democracy,' he said, 'would never accept such a manner of overawing the Court.'

But it was the writing of Mr. Choate's farewell that was the
hardest for me, and as I wrote, the tears almost blinded me:

> ... I have been asked a thousand times in the last three
> months, 'Why do you go? Are you sorry to leave England? Are
> you really glad to go home?' Well, in truth my mind and heart
> are torn asunder with conflicting emotions. In the first place,
> I will tell you a great secret. I am really suffering from home-
> sickness. Not that I love England less, but that I love America
> more, and what Englishman will quarrel with me for that? ...
> My friends on this side of the water are multiplying every day in
> numbers and increasing in the ardour of their affection. I am
> sorry to say that the great host of my friends on the other are
> as rapidly diminishing and dwindling away. 'Part of the host
> have crossed the flood and part are crossing now' — and I have
> a great yearning to be with the waning number....
> I have gone to and fro among the English people, coming in
> close contact with them, studying them at near range for the
> purpose of discovering the distinctions and differences, if any,
> that exist between us. I have endeavoured to make them better
> acquainted with my own country, its history, its institutions,
> its great names, for the purpose of showing them that really the
> difference between an Englishman and an American is only skin
> deep, that under different historical forms we pursue with equal
> success the same great objects of liberty, of justice, of the public
> welfare, and that our interests are so inextricably interwoven
> that we would not if we could, and could not if we would, escape
> the necessity of an abiding and perpetual friendship. I have no
> doubt now, and can have no doubt, about the permanence of
> peace which now exists between us. War between these two
> great nations would be an inexplicable impossibility....

That banquet must have included every great man of England, while in addition the Lady Mayoress, Mrs. and Miss
Choate, Mrs. Carter, and a few other ladies listened to the
speeches from the gallery. The toast of the King and Queen
was drunk, Sir Henry Campbell-Bannerman proposed the toast
of the President, and Mr. Balfour in his graceful way expressed
the thanks of the English people for the great work which

Mr. Choate had done. It was a splendid occasion, and Mr. Choate was very touched.

After that the rest of the time flew. We declined many invitations for Mr. Reid, for Mr. Carter was too experienced to be caught in any of the traps which are spread for a new Ambassador. Indeed, it is the responsibility of the Councillor to protect the new Ambassador and see that the wrong people don't get hold of him — whether these be English or expatriated Americans; for in every country there are many people who will attach themselves remorselessly to an unsuspecting official and have sometimes been the cause of much unpleasantness and even failure if the incoming Ambassador and his wife are not aware of the pitfalls. Long before May, of course, all the Embassy lists for the Court functions of the season had been filled, although, thinking the new Ambassador might possibly arrive before the last Court, Mr. Carter had reserved a few places for any friends he might possibly wish to include at the last moment. To add to the gaiety, the young King of Spain was coming on the visit that preceded his marriage to the King's niece, Princess Ena of Battenberg. The Spanish King, indeed, arrived the day before the Ambassador, so it was evident that if he and Mrs. Reid were to have any part in the 'doings' Mr. Reid must immediately present his Letter of Credence, get through as many of the ceremonial calls on the Royal Family and his fellow Ambassadors, as he could, for these must be done — or at least some of them — before he could be considered to be accredited to the Court.

That Mr. Reid took all his new duties very seriously was evidenced by a cable which came from him in mid-Atlantic. 'Silk or derby' it read. No one knew to what it referred and the special code gave no hint. A bright young man furnished the clue by suggesting it was probably only an enquiry as to whether Mr. Reid ought to step ashore in silk hat and spats. 'What does the well-dressed Ambassador wear while he listens to a salute of nineteen guns fired in his honour and, through the cheers and hubbub, hears the sweet words of the Address of Welcome tendered him by the Mayor of the City?' murmured this young man.

Mr. La Farge finished the window, so Mr. Choate was able to see it installed and consecrated. Now there was nothing more to keep him. So on the twenty-third of May he presented his Letter of Recall to the King and informed Lord Lansdowne that he had placed Mr. Carter in charge until the arrival of Mr. Reid.

Up to the last moment Mr. Choate was full of fun. On the day before he left he wrote references for his house servants, those who were not going back to America with him. He went down the list until he reached the very last, the 'Usher of the Hall,' a boy who waited on the servants' hall and did odd jobs.

'Well, George,' he said to this youth standing bashfully before him. 'I'm going to give you a very good reference because I feel that you've done all the work of this house.'

The boy shifted uneasily from one foot to the other, mystified.

'But only,' went on Mr. Choate, 'because there was no one else you could put it on to.'

And so Mr. Choate went back to America, after a sorrowful good-bye from us all and a superb send-off at the station given him by a large gathering of British and American friends and many officials. Mr. Phillips having already gone — leaving me a large package of signed blank cheques to pay his bills — there was no Secretary to go with Mr. Choate and send us back the news. The only thing that prevented us from brooding was the stimulus of the multitude of last-minute things still to be done before Mr. Reid arrived. During those few days while he was Chargé d'Affaires Mr. Carter also attended a Levee and two Courts, and at the second, which was the last

Court of the season, Mrs. Carter presented the Misses Mills, nieces of Mrs. Reid, who had come over expecting to be presented by Mrs. Reid herself, but who decided not to wait until the following year.

10

Arrival of the new Ambassador, Mr. Whitelaw Reid. The successful beginning of his Embassy. Mr. John Hay's last visit to London. Mr. Fritjof Nansen, the first Norwegian Minister to England, seeks advice as to Norwegian diplomatic uniforms. Mr. Elihu Root becomes Secretary of State.

1905

To be his country's Ambassador at London I understood was to have reached the apex of diplomatic achievement. Men belonging to the Diplomatic Service of countries which have a regular system of promotion were content to spend the best years of their lives in uninteresting capitals, wrestling with heat and cold and lack of comfort and boredom and separation from their families if they could look forward to rounding out their career as their country's Ambassador at the Court of Saint James's. For London, the heart of the British Empire, the gathering place of Britons from the ends of the earth, where the high traditions of the Anglo-Saxon race are carried on with an infectious gusto and sense of humour, is the most popular capital in the world. As a favourite song has it, 'We always come back to you, London, when there's nothing else to do.'

American diplomats also hoped that by the time they had served their country in many places and gradually risen in the Service they, too, might round out their careers as Ambassador at London. They knew full well, however, that there was about as much chance as there was of their becoming President — perhaps less. For the Ambassadorship at London has always been a political plum given for service to the party in power. It seemed to me a pity that there were no knighthoods or earldoms or other harmless honours in America, such as England uses to decorate her deserving, for at least the conferring of a title does not interfere with the conduct of foreign affairs as an Ambassadorship might do. No British Government would take the risk of placing complicated diplomatic affairs in the hands of inexperienced men, however successful they might have been in other directions.

The American Ambassador coming to England has a mission to fulfil which cannot but appeal to every fine instinct that he has, and it was no wonder that, as the day drew near when Mr. Reid's ship would dock, the Embassy felt that a new page was about to be opened and that we might be on the verge of momentous changes. A more impressive and elaborate setting was going to be used by Mr. Reid, and the question in everybody's mind was what effect this would have on Anglo-American friendship — whether it would accelerate its growth, or, as a mere passing ornamentation, be valueless in the long run. Would this demonstration of the wealth and power of the United States which Mr. Reid intended to give impress — or intimidate — the British Government as it was said the majestic trappings of British Ambassadors impressed — and possibly intimidated — other Governments? Had the United States suffered in the past from the simplicity with which its diplomacy had been conducted, as so many people believed? It was an interesting speculation.

The experience of representing his country abroad was no new one for Mr. Reid. Many years before he had been Minister to France, and more recently had twice been Special Ambassador to Great Britain, first at the Diamond Jubilee of Queen Victoria and then at the Coronation of Edward VII, both these latter, however, merely decorative appointments for a brief particular occasion.

When Mr. Reid went to Paris as Minister, a much younger

man, he was not the wealthy man he afterwards became, so, when his appointment was announced in Washington, there had been speculation whether he could afford to accept, the salaries of American Ministers being so pitifully small. But as it was well known that Mr. Reid's father-in-law, Mr. D. O. Mills, a Californian, known to his intimates as 'D.O.,' would gladly foot the bills, one of the wits is reported to have remarked that Mr. Reid would certainly go to Paris — D.O. volente!

This story and many others were not particularly reassuring, although we knew that Mr. Reid was a most eminent man and most anxious to come. An editor would be very different from a lawyer, and our loyalty to Mr. Choate made us unwilling to admit that anyone could ever fill his place. Newspaper men seemed to me hasty, gossipy, and superficial, and an Ambassador with that background would carry on the Embassy very differently from Mr. Choate's leisurely but completely satisfactory way of handling questions. The miscellaneous items of news were supplemented by Mr. I. N. Ford, the New York *Tribune* correspondent in London, long a friend and indeed almost an institution at the Embassy. Mr. Ford, an enthusiastic little man, openly rejoiced that at last an Ambassador who was a newspaper man of the best type was coming, and — even more important to Mr. Ford — 'had enough money to put the United States just where she belonged — "right at the top of the heap." ' Mr. Ford wanted nothing but the very best for the American Ambassador, and he said so much about it that I was quite resentful, for he seemed to be hinting that Mr. Choate and his predecessors had somehow let their country down by living in less than enormous palaces! But Mr. Carter said not to take Mr. Ford too seriously as he was one of Mr. Reid's employees.

Now, for the first time, exulted Mr. Ford, the American Ambassador would represent the United States in the way it should always be represented at London, so that Americans would be proud of their Embassy instead of being ashamed of

WHITELAW REID
1910

it. 'Back-street Embassies, modesty, dignity, where do they get us in this age of splendour? Isn't the United States the richest country in the world and getting richer every day? Well, then, be bigger and better than anyone else! America practises it at home and knows its value, and every American woman knows it. Why not dazzle the foreigner? It's good business, I tell you! People are impressed with the outward signs of prosperity and we know only too well that the United States is judged abroad by its Embassy buildings and its expenditures just as much as by its Ambassadors.'

There was also so much being written and talked about the marvels of Dorchester House that by contrast the poor old Chancery looked shabbier and shabbier. Mr. Reid, unlike Mr. Choate, would have lots of secretaries — this was my private worry — who would know so much more than I did that I should be supplanted — and I didn't want to be. The younger members of the staff looked forward to many a gay party. Mr. Carter's feelings were a mixture of regret for the old days, for he loved Mr. Choate dearly, and a sense of responsibility for a good beginning for the new 'reign.'

The day before the Ambassador's arrival was a nightmare of details. Mr. Hodson, boasting of how many Ambassadors and Ministers he had already met, started for Plymouth in the afternoon to be ready to meet the boat, taking an enormous package of mail and greetings to hand to Mr. Reid's secretary. Another stack of letters awaited the Ambassador in his room at the Chancery because we wanted to make Mr. Reid understand from the very first that the mail belonged there. Mr. Carter, having worked with me right up to the time of going to the train, dashed off for Plymouth near midnight, to be there when the ship docked in the morning, hugging two or three diplomatic Notes he hoped Mr. Reid would go over in the train.

'I don't know when I shall see you again,' said Mr. Carter, shaking hands as though he was going for a long time.

'Think of me wrestling with all these questions and trying to coax Mr. Reid to do things he probably won't want to do, and be a little sorry for me. And be a little sorry for yourself, too, for you won't be idle much longer.'

'Idle?' I laughed, pointing to my crowded desk.

'That's nothing. What you've done in the past is nothing to what will be expected of you in the future.'

The next afternoon I saw the remaining members of the staff leave for Waterloo to meet the Ambassador. The Embassy seemed subtly changed already. The new Embassy would be very different, with no Mr. Choate, no Mr. White, and no Mr. Phillips.

Everything finished and ready, I went gloomily home, for the Royal train in which the party were travelling would not reach London until nearly dinner-time and they would go direct to Dorchester House. I knew also that there was no need for me to be early on Monday morning, for the whole staff was to accompany the Ambassador to Buckingham Palace for the presentation of his Letter of Credence and a lunch party was to follow at Dorchester House. I nobly got to the Chancery, however, at ten, and to my surprise and delight — though I should have expected it — Mr. Carter came hurrying in shortly after to get the Letter of Credence from the safe and give me the news. He told me that Mr. and Mrs. Reid and their daughter had arrived and brought several other people with them. There was a private secretary, Mr. De-Lancey Jay, who he was certain I should like, for he was not only handsome, young, and friendly, but knew a great deal about England and diplomacy already as his father had been at the Paris Embassy and he himself had been partly educated in England. He and Mr. Hodson had fallen on each other's necks, for it seemed that when Mr. Jay was a little boy and came from France to England to and from school Mr. Hodson had been in the habit of meeting him, giving him his dinner and speeding him on his way.

There was also a Mr. Irving Blake, who had been brought from the *Tribune* office to be the Ambassador's stenographer; and Mrs. Whitelaw Reid had a secretary also, Miss Helen Rogers, very pleasant both of them, and several servants. Would Mr. Blake and Miss Rogers be at 123 Victoria Street I wanted to know? Mr. Carter assured me they would not. Mr. Jay, being the official Secretary to the Ambassador and ranking as a diplomat, was of course different. He would do his work at the desk in the Ambassador's room just as Mr. Phillips had done, and — Mr. Carter cocked his eye at me across the room — 'You remember what I warned you about much more being expected of you.'

After lunch Mr. Carter came in again for a few minutes to bring the official Note to the Foreign Office which had been written beforehand announcing Mr. Reid's arrival. This was now signed in Mr. Reid's large, distinctive, and somewhat straggling handwriting. There was also a cable:

> Arrived Saturday night. Carter had everything in perfect shape. Lansdowne waived call at Foreign Office. Received me instead at home and arranged presentation today at noon to His Majesty. Queen received Mrs. Reid and daughter at same hour. King expressed great cordiality and satisfaction at relations with United States, regret at losing Choate and very gracious as to successor. After presentation staff Embassy rejoined Queen and sent for me.

Mr. Carter told me that the reception had gone off splendidly, and with the utmost cordiality. The King had been in his happiest frame of mind, and had given Mr. Reid a splendid welcome. Mr. Carter seemed to feel that something very special had been attempted in the way Mr. Reid had been received. The ladies, too, had been almost overwhelmed. Apparently Dorchester House and all it implied had already made an impression!

Later in the afternoon Mr. Reid and Mr. Jay came down to the Chancery with Mr. Carter in Mr. Reid's smart electric brougham. Mr. Reid listened to Mr. Carter's explanations of everything, gave a cold, rather casual glance round, and shook hands perfunctorily with me. He seemed rather fragile with his thin face, beautifully trimmed short beard, and delicate body, very unlike the burlier Mr. Choate — more indeed like a Dresden china figure, petite and exquisite but aloof. He seemed weary and stayed but a few minutes. Mr. Carter left with him, but Mr. Jay remained. He looked so jolly, with his dark slicked hair brushed straight back from his forehead, that I fell in love once again — a continuous habit of mine ever since I had been at the Embassy. He was taller than Mr. Carter and a bit on the lanky side. Under his arm was the familiar packet of correspondence which Mr. Hodson had taken to Plymouth, bursting now with new additions. If I was to help with those I should not have to complain of lack of occupation for a long time! It appeared I was, so we were soon hard at work dividing possibilities from impossibilities, and deciding who was to answer which. As things came up in the correspondence, I gave him many indiscreet but necessary bits of gossip about some of the writers, and he responded with anecdotes about Mr. Reid and the trip over.

It was not until later that Mr. Jay told me his own story of those first busy days. Mr. Hodson handed him the mail at Plymouth and he spent his time on the train reading and sorting and making notes. But long before he got through, the train reached London and he drove with the others to Dorchester House for dinner, and then, not having been invited to stay, he went to be the guest for a few days of the daughter and son-in-law of Mr. Phelps, a former Minister. Going to bed that night very tired, he slept soundly until roused by the butler in the morning, enquiring,

'What suit shall I put out for you, sir?'

Mr. Jay turned over sleepily, 'I shall wear my evening suit this morning.'

'Beg pardon, sir, did you say your *morning* suit?'

'No, my evening suit.'

So, crumpled from the way he had thrown it down the night before, he put it on and wore it all that day, going in it to Buckingham Palace and returning to Dorchester House for lunch. After lunch he worked with me and went directly back to Dorchester House for dinner and again got home very late. Judge of the horror of the butler the following morning when he was again told to put out the evening suit, for that morning the King of Spain was giving a reception to the Corps Diplomatiques! Once more, then, he donned the evening suit and wore it all day, running from place to place, trying to get decisions on invitations and appointments, etiquette of this and that, and finally retired once more to his bed in the small hours of the morning, tired, but extremely thrilled. The first rush was over and tomorrow, he reflected, he would be able to return to his ordinary clothes, and not look as though he had been out all night. He fell asleep, and next morning his evening suit had been put ready for him, the butler having apparently given up the struggle in despair. If Americans chose to wear evening dress in the daytime it was all the same to him!

Mr. John Hay was in London when Mr. Reid arrived. He had sailed with Mrs. Hay in March to try to regain his health at Bad Nauheim, and Mr. White left London to meet him. But even in that peaceful spot he had not been able to secure quiet. The German Emperor and other sovereigns invited him to visit them, and King Leopold of the Belgians went them one better by appearing for an interview unannounced, an interview which Mr. Hay would doubtless have avoided if he could, for the doings of Leopold in the Congo stank in the nostrils of civilized people, and his personal habits were such that King Edward VII would not receive him in England! The University of Cambridge had also voted to give Mr. Hay an LL.D. and wanted him to come for it.

But Mr. Hay was not strong enough to go to Cambridge.

On June 2 he crossed to London from the Continent, and went to Claridge's Hotel where Mr. Carter had arranged for his stay *incognito* and where he hoped to have a few days' rest before sailing for home. Apart from a few brief calls from Mr. Choate and the friendly interest of Mr. Carter, who spent as much time as he could with him, Mr. Hay saw only his very closest friends, lunched at Dorchester House the day after Mr. Reid's arrival — for they were old friends — and had a brief interview with the King. This last had not been planned, but when the King discovered Mr. Hay was in London he told Mr. Carter he wished to see him. Mr. Carter explained that while Mr. Hay appreciated the honour he could not climb the stairs at Buckingham Palace, so the King, not to be put off, came downstairs instead, and the interview took place in one of the rooms on the ground floor — the last time the two met.

I had been hoping to see Mr. Hay, but he did not get to the Embassy. But I felt I knew him from the stories told about him by Mr. Hodson and Mr. Carter. One that I specially enjoyed was when he informed his open-mouthed audience at a Fourth-of-July banquet in London that the national American flower ought to be a violet — the emblem of modesty and self-effacement — on every day of the year except Independence Day; but on that particular day he agreed with Walt Whitman in feeling that Americans had a perfect right to 'sound our barbarous yawp over the roofs of the world.' Mr. Carter, like everybody else, had been much worried at Mr. Hay's lack of strength, but was encouraged, when he saw him off, at the improvement in his health. But it did not last. He went to Washington almost as soon as he landed and remained a few days, but on July 1 he died.

Mr. Hay's death was a profound shock to everyone. The Fourth-of-July reception was postponed until the eighth, and the Embassy did not attend the State Ball of the seventh. An impressive and beautiful memorial service was held at

Saint Paul's Cathedral at which the King was represented, the entire Diplomatic Corps was present, and the rest of the Cathedral packed with Mr. Hay's American and British friends and admirers, the ladies in deep mourning and the diplomats with black bands on their sleeves. The funeral service and the Gregorian chanting of the choir in the Ninetieth Psalm were most moving. The Embassy flag remained at half-mast for many days and we used black-edged paper for everything.

There was some changing round of rooms at the Chancery. Mr. Wadsworth came downstairs and took Mr. White's old room. This being much larger — and therefore more suited to the dignity of the Councillor of Embassy — I wondered whether Mr. Carter would take it. But he said he preferred his own cheerful room, so near to the Ambassador's. Perhaps then he would prefer to have it to himself! But he wanted no change at all! He was not the sort of man who needed impressive surroundings or to dress his new part, for even had he been quartered in a cellar he would have inspired the proper respect. So he kept the old room and I stayed, too, which made me very happy — and incidentally, of course, added to my prestige — so I dare say I gave myself airs, for someone said that he supposed the next thing would be that I should have on my visiting cards, 'First Secretary to the First Secretary of the Embassy of the United States to the Court of Saint James's.'

Mr. Wadsworth thoroughly enjoyed his new room and his new dignity as Second Secretary and went about looking solemn. Mr. Einstein made only a very brief stay, for he was soon appointed assistant to Mr. Henry White at the Algeciras Conference, which must have been more interesting to him than being Third Secretary at London. He was a big man, a little on the awkward side, and his wife had the prettiest teeth I have ever seen. He did a good deal of writing on historical subjects.

The campaign to persuade Mr. Reid to make the Chancery

his official headquarters was successful. He came to 123 every morning, but unless there was something urgent his afternoons were spent at home.

Very shortly after Mr. Reid came and just after the formal separation of Norway from Sweden, the marriage took place of Princess Margaret of Connaught to Prince Gustav Adolf of Sweden. This as usual was announced as a love match (every Royal marriage is conventionally a love match) and everybody was delighted, for Princess Margaret was very popular. The wedding took place at Windsor, and I remember that Sir Rennell Rodd, British Minister to Sweden and Norway, present in his official capacity, wrote that the ceremonial reception, with the escort of Life Guards and the State Entry to the Castle precincts in the splendid June weather, offered in his opinion an experience no other country could equal.

Mr. Fritjof Nansen, the great explorer, came to London soon afterwards to be the first Minister from Norway, and one of his first difficulties being to devise a uniform for himself at twenty-four hours' notice for the official reception by the King, he came to the Chancery to ask advice. Naturally he did not wish to wear the uniform which had been worn by the Scandinavian diplomats, and indeed was not entitled to, and the Norwegian Government had not got round to deciding what their diplomats should wear.

But Mr. Nansen had to have something, so, with vague ideas of a simple garb on the lines of the American uniform, he called to know what the Ambassador or Mr. Carter thought about it. Mr. Reid was out and so were both Mr. Carter and Mr. Wadsworth, so Mr. Jay offered his services, although he made it clear he had no authority and very little experience. 'You will probably do just as well as anybody else,' said Mr. Nansen. He explained his difficulty, and Mr. Jay commented that, although it was most flattering that he should think of imitating the American diplomatic dress, that uniform commended itself to nobody else — and certainly not to the American diplomats themselves. But of course if that was what he had set his mind on, it might be possible to evolve something.

'Why not,' suggested Mr. Jay after profound thought and much idle scribbling on a pad, 'instead of an ordinary black suit have one of very dark blue, that lovely midnight blue, which doesn't look rusty when it has to be worn in the daytime — which happens sometimes — and at night will make everybody else's suit look seedy? And, why not, instead of a black waistcoat and white tie, reverse it and wear a white waistcoat and black tie? And — while you are about it — gold buttons on the waistcoat. Later you could have the Norwegian flag or coat of arms put on them.' Mr. Nansen, who seemed to think the idea a splendid one, wore this demi-semi-uniform for a time, but later the Norwegian Government decided on a more conventional diplomatic uniform with gold embroidery and high collar — more like the British.

Some Japanese princes came to visit the King that summer, just when the *Mikado* was at the height of its first popularity and was being played everywhere. To be on the safe side and make sure that nobody's feelings might be hurt, orders went forth that its catchy music should be absolutely eliminated from any programs offered before the Royal visitors. But when the Japanese ship steamed into Gravesend with the princes aboard, the strains of the *Mikado* were heard floating across the water from its decks!

The usual invitations poured in thick and fast on the Ambassador to attend concerts, go to galleries, and sponsor everything that any American was doing in England. Mr. Reid was also continually obliged to deny that he took an active part in the running of the New York *Tribune*, and after a time became very touchy about it when people came to ask whether some editorial concerned with Anglo-American affairs represented his views. Mr. Ford came in perhaps a little oftener, openly purring about the prestige he believed was ac-

cruing more and more to the United States, and the other
newspaper men seemed equally impressed, though they did
not find it any easier to get news. Indeed, I think they found
it more difficult, for Mr. Reid was inclined to be hard on them,
and the free-and-easy access of the old days was gradually
tightened up.

Mr. and Mrs. Reid leased a beautiful estate in the country
that autumn, Wrest Park in Bedfordshire, the property of
Lord Lucas, where they were to spend many of their week-
ends and entertain large parties. They soon became very popular. Although the warmth of the King's greeting had been
very marked, the English people held back a little at first, but
soon they succumbed. As to Mrs. Reid, it was Henry James,
I think, who said that during Mr. Reid's administration the
Embassy of the United States, because of her, was not *an* Embassy but *the* Embassy of London.

Of more political moment was the appointment of Mr.
Elihu Root to succeed Mr. Hay as Secretary of State, an appointment which it was felt at the Embassy might make Anglo-American relations a little more official, but might make
them easier to handle on the American side of the water,
where the Senate's dislike of Mr. Hay had blocked everything
he tried to do. But with the Newfoundland Fisheries question
awaiting settlement, and Mr. Lodge doing everything to foster ill-will to please his Irish constituents, and President
Roosevelt intent on getting the best of every bargain, the sky
was not without clouds. Mr. Root, himself, it was rumoured,
had once gone so far as to deny Newfoundland's right to 'interfere at all, whether reasonably or not, with the American
rights of fishing.' This sort of talk was too much like Mr.
Roosevelt's bullying attitude in the Alaska Boundary Arbitration to make the Embassy feel comfortable. The Fisheries
question was a thorny one, but there were two sides to it.
After lying dormant for several years, 1906 saw the beginning
of new regulations imposed upon American fishermen by the

Newfoundland authorities, and this we realized would mean trouble.

There were political changes in England too. The Conservative Government which had been in power so many years gave way to a Liberal Government, with Sir Henry Campbell-Bannerman as Prime Minister and — important particularly to the Embassy — Sir Edward Grey as Foreign Minister in place of Lord Lansdowne. The resignation of Lord Lansdowne saddened the Embassy, for he had been a most courteous official with whom to deal. Of Sir Edward Grey little was known except that he was a quiet, genial man of wide interests including a love and knowledge of nature. Would he be as good a friend as Lord Lansdowne? A great deal depended on that for the safe conduct of Anglo-American diplomacy.

11

The first steps towards the establishment by the United States Government of a 'career' Diplomatic and Consular Service. The visit to London of Mr. and Mrs. Nicholas Longworth, and a second visit by Mr. Bryan.

1906

THERE being nothing immediate on the diplomatic horizon on their return from the United States early in 1906, Mr. and Mrs. Reid were able to begin at once to interest themselves in the responsibilities of their first London season, and in the official record kept in the Embassy's Red Book, written in Mr. Carter's own handwriting, appears this entry:

> The Hon. Whitelaw Reid appeared for the first time in his official capacity at the Levee held by His Majesty King Edward VII on the 20th February 1906. Captain J. H. Gibbons [Naval Attaché], and Mr. DeLancey Jay [Secretary to the Ambassador] also appeared for the first time at this Levee, though previously presented to the King in private audience in January 1906 [by Mr. Carter] and June 1905 [by the Ambassador] respectively.[1]

It was, however, a busy spring for me, doing things for everybody and ambitiously reading international law from the volumes of Moore's Digest in the Ambassador's room. One day I did a bit of shopping for Mr. Choate, who was apparently feeling the chill of the American winter, for, looking up from a letter, Mr. Carter asked me whether I would mind going to some shop in Regent Street and getting Mr. Choate

---

[1] See Appendix for List of American Presentations at Court, 1903-1914.

some — er — er — belts — you   know — er — belly-bands. 'You can guess the size just as well as I can,' he added in answer to my enquiry.

Mr. Carter and Mr. Wadsworth were occupied with the usual troubles in connection with the coming season, and indeed it made much extra work because Mr. Reid had his own ideas which didn't always correspond with Mr. Carter's. Mr. Grant-Smith, the new Third Secretary, who had been transferred from Constantinople to succeed Mr. Einstein, was a dapper young man with a lovely waxed moustache which he twirled nervously as he talked, full of the deeper significance and mysteriousness of the diplomatic profession — and *most* amusing. He attended to many visitors and in between times tried his hand at a few reforms which he felt to have been long overdue. He also told tales of romance across the roofs of Oriental palaces in which he tried to make me believe he took part. We all liked him and listened to his stories with interest, but had no intention of being reformed, for every new Secretary wanted to change something and it was just as well not to encourage him.

That spring saw the first steps towards a momentous change in the Diplomatic and Consular Service of the United States, the actual birth of the Foreign Service as a profession, although the complete organization was not effected for many years, and indeed is not perfect yet. As a usual preliminary cautious step was always to ask for assistance from countries with more experience, a routine Instruction asking us to secure full information about pensions given to British civil servants, caused a good deal of interested speculation. It began to look as though something might possibly be going to be done about at least one of the subjects so near and dear to the hearts of all Americans in the Foreign Service, that of pensions, *if* the Foreign Service was to be considered part of the Civil Service, which was not at all certain.

The Foreign Office forwarded enough data to make out a

good case for pensions, and everybody began to be hopeful. A retiring allowance would be even more useful than to a man at home — indeed, a veritable life-line to one finding himself superseded through no fault of his own and because he had lived abroad for years, out of touch with conditions at home, the responsibility of no one in particular, and — with younger men in the field — not very likely to find satisfactory opportunities in a new career.

Some day there must also come organization, permanence of tenure, and orderly promotion, for the United States could not afford to go on now in the old haphazard fashion of protecting her interests abroad. These must come, too, if the Foreign Service was not to be composed entirely of wealthy men — a most undemocratic business — though it seemed to me it would have been difficult to improve the London Embassy of those days. Indeed, perhaps a rigid Civil Service, if it was to include the Foreign Service, would have disadvantages in a profession where personal relationships and personality count more than high marks in an examination.

While most thinking people seem to believe in examinations as the most democratic way of deciding fitness for office, I cannot help thinking, as I look back now at the three Ambassadors I knew in London — all of them 'spoils' Ambassadors — that there is something to be said for sending men who are not trained diplomats to posts where other qualities are equally necessary. A few of the career diplomats — and I don't mean to hurt them — tend perhaps to become stereotyped and to lose some of their sharp outlines from the weighing of many differing points of view; and a few of them become so international in their thinking and way of life that they could just as well be part of the Foreign Service of any other country. On the other hand, when occasionally I met 'spoils' Ambassadors and Ministers who lacked the essentials of the well-brought-up man, I decided that a middle course was best — a few 'spoils' Ambassadors, provided they are the best type of Americans, but the majority career men. The latter would make no errors of judgment, whereas the judgment of the 'spoils' Ambassador might be worth less than the paper it was written on — unless he had an astute career Councillor to protect and guide him — a precaution usually taken by the Department of State in appointing an inexperienced Ambassador. However, this was only what I observed in other capitals. London has always been particularly fortunate — although I have heard that even there one or two of the post-war 'spoils' Ambassadors have left something to be desired!

In April, 1906, an Act was passed setting up new rules for eligibility for the Consular Service, and the light having now been turned on all the men living abroad in the interests of Americans at home, the time seemed propitious for the further necessary changes. The American Government had also begun to find a growing competitor for the services of its diplomats. Business had discovered that their knowledge of world conditions made them valuable and tried to tempt away the best. It was not until 1909 that the Diplomatic Service was included in the reforms.

May soon came, time for the London season to begin. Mrs. Reid was to make her first appearance at a Court as the Ambassadress, to present not alone her only daughter, Miss Jean Reid, but Mr. Carter's only daughter, Miss Mildred Carter, and Mrs. John H. Gibbons, wife of the Naval Attaché. There were in addition several ladies to be presented by her in the General Circle, who had given Mr. Carter a fair amount of trouble because of changes in their sailing dates and other complications. As was perfectly natural I was more interested in Miss Carter's presentation than in that of any of the others. Miss Reid and Mrs. Gibbons were strangers, but Miss Carter, a school-girl when I first met her, had grown up into a most lovely and popular young woman. I remember her so well that year with her piquant little face, the charming manners of her father, and the lovely peach-like complexion and blonde hair of her mother, set off to perfection by a series of dresses of many pastel shades, all made exactly alike. 'She's very sweet,' I said to Mr. Carter, 'and so beautiful that she will marry at least a Duke.' Mr. Carter laughed. 'Oh, no, she won't,' he said. 'She'll marry an American.'

Of other distinguished American visitors Mr. D. J. Hill, American Minister to The Hague, and Mrs. Hill, were presented at the Court of June 1, and a few days afterwards Mr. and Mrs. Nicholas Longworth, recently married, arrived on a visit to Dorchester House. Some of the American papers, referring to Mrs. Longworth as 'Princess Alice,' gave some purely imaginary accounts of things she was supposed to be doing in London — roused from sleep by trumpeters, walking down the main staircase through rows of bowing flunkies in powdered wigs and embroidered coats, etc., etc. According to these many entertainments of more than royal splendour were given in her honour. Some of this may have been more or less true, for, as the daughter of the President and a popular young bride, she was of course made as happy as possible. But she must have been quite a responsibility for Mrs. Reid....

With so many entertainments and so much dining and dancing, the Embassy Secretaries came down in the mornings more than ordinarily grumpy, inclined to see their honoured profession with a jaundiced eye. One peevish young man told me that his whole salary went for dancing shoes, and when I replied that such a heavy treader would never make a good nurse, and then tried to make up by saying how nice it must be to dance with so many beautiful ladies, he said, 'Young ladies be hanged.'

'Don't let anyone hear you say that,' I reproved him. 'Or you may be sent to some capital where there is nothing to do but protect the interests of the United States with correspondence. How would that appeal to you?'

'Well,' he conceded, 'I suppose I might be worse off, but I do wish they didn't have parties every night of the week.'

Soon after the Longworths had gone, Mr. W. J. Bryan, this time accompanied by Mrs. Bryan, made his second visit to England returning from a trip round the world, and was at once invited to make the principal speech at the American Society Banquet on July 4. Again he made a most stirring speech, but not quite so complimentary this time, protesting against the arrogance of imperialistic nations. Mr. Bryan's magazine *The Commoner*, in reprinting this speech, added Mr. Bryan's views on British rule in India, which were so critical as greatly to embarrass the Embassy. He seemed to be the same old 'hot potato'!

Although Mr. Reid did not like Mr. Bryan, he and Mrs. Reid invited the Bryans to spend their first week-end at Wrest Park, and gathered a distinguished group of English and Americans to meet them at dinner. Mr. Bryan was in his element and enjoyed himself thoroughly, not at all disturbed by criticisms he had made of the British Government. That his observations had been of the most cursory nature did not restrain him from talking at length, and the Englishmen plied him with so many questions and drew him out so completely that Mr. Reid could not escape the conclusion that they were 'stringing' him. So he tried to stem the floods of oratory, or to change the subject. But it was impossible to interrupt Mr. Bryan, and indeed he was so simple and so friendly that in spite of everything he charmed and disarmed them all. But Mrs. Bryan, sitting impatiently farther down the table, didn't approve, so, as she passed out with the other ladies, leaving the men to their coffee and cigars, she tapped him smartly on the shoulder with her fan and said, 'William, don't talk so much.' After the ladies had gone, Mr. Reid moved and sat down next to Mr. Bryan, and showed so unmistakably by his attitude that he considered Mr. Bryan a most distinguished guest, that the rest of the evening was devoted to friendly conversation instead of listening to Mr. Bryan exploring the universe. Sir Edward Grey, one of the guests, asked later his opinion of Mr. Bryan and possibly still smarting a little under his frankness, is said to have replied merely that Mr. Bryan seemed to have done a good deal of travelling and talked a good deal about it.

Mr. Bryan's visit coincided with the annual meeting of the Inter-Parliamentary Union — an international peace group. This body, which included not only members of the House of Lords and Commons, but leading statesmen of many countries, and met in the Royal Gallery of the House of Lords, invited Mr. Bryan to address them on July 26. His speech on that occasion was judged to be one of the most distinguished of his whole career, and enhanced his political position in the United States considerably. It was especially memorable because in it he announced his plan for treaties of peace among the nations to stop the spread of war, the plan which was incorporated in the peace treaties made with thirty-two nations when he became Secretary of State in 1913. It called for investigation and delay before taking up arms, thus giving time for hot tempers to cool.

Mr. Jay, who used to retail many of the incidents that happened at Wrest Park, told me how he had been put in charge of Mr. and Mrs. Bryan the week-end they were there. He, like everybody else, enjoyed Mr. Bryan, though he did not approve of everything he did, and was most amused when that gentleman confided to him, during a walk they took together down the country lanes on Sunday morning, that he had started his career by being a bill collector for a saloonkeeper.

Mr. Jay must have made an equally favourable impression on Mr. Bryan, for when he became Secretary of State a few years later, he gave tangible evidence of it. Mr. Jay's brother, Mr. Peter Augustus Jay, a career diplomat, had been appointed by President Taft during the last year of his Presi-

dency — a strictly emergency and temporary appointment —
to be Diplomatic Agent and Consul-General at Cairo, a post
outside of the regular routine of diplomatic advancement
which by that time had been set up, and subject to a 'spoils'
appointment.

So when, on the election of President Woodrow Wilson,
the Democrats came into power, a Democrat was appointed
at Cairo and Mr. Jay was dropped. His brother went to
Washington to see if anything could be done. He was not sure
whether Mr. Bryan would remember him, but he did, and
received him immediately with great cordiality, recalling
their former meeting in England. Mr. Jay explained his
brother's predicament.

'I see,' said Mr. Bryan. 'But Cairo is not a diplomatic post,
and we thought it might as well be filled by a Democrat.
There's no Mission vacant, I am sorry to say. What would
you like me to do?'

Mr. Jay considered a moment. 'My brother wouldn't mind
dropping back to being a Councillor of Embassy if by so doing
he would bring himself back into the Diplomatic Service
again,' he said.

Mr. Bryan nodded and rang his bell. 'Bring me the list of
diplomatic vacancies.' It was brought. Mr. Bryan ran his
pencil down the page. 'Rome is vacant. What about that?'

Mr. Jay smiled. 'It would be perfect.' So Mr. Jay was appointed to Rome as Councillor, and remained there through
the World War, doing excellent service, and was afterwards
advanced to a Minister.

The King expressed a wish to see Mr. Bryan, to the Embassy's relief, as they had not wanted to make a special request
on his behalf. The Ambassador took him to Buckingham
Palace and introduced him. I heard that he made the same
good impression on the King, but the Embassy never got over
the 'hot potato' feeling, always uncertain what Mr. Bryan
might say or do next.

The Embassy Messenger, Mr. Charles Hodson, passed away on August 3. He had been at the Embassy thirty years, served under eight Ambassadors and Ministers, and had done many pieces of semi-diplomatic work excellently. The day he died the *Evening News* said of him: 'Mr. Hodson was one of those really great men in the Embassies of London who are little known to the general public, but who in their time do great work. To no one will his death be a greater blow than to Mr. Choate whose "leave it to Hodson" was a common remark.' Mr. Carter was very sad, for 'His Excellency,' as Mr. Carter always called him, had been one of his greatest admirers, and there had been a warm friendship between them for years.

Mr. Hodson was not only a real personage, but also, I fear, something of a martinet. I remember his telling me how he had forced the unwilling Ambassador Bayard into a cab one day when he had been looking forward to a leisurely ride in the front seat on top of a bus with jovial converse with the driver, saying that Ambassadors shouldn't ride in busses. I said I didn't see why an Ambassador shouldn't ride in a bus if he wanted to. Everybody else did. But Mr. Hodson replied that I should understand when I was older. Perhaps I shall! Frank succeeded his father, and his brother Edward came to be his assistant. Edward was a rather morose individual, a little jealous of his smiling elder brother. Neither of them had the ability nor distinguished appearance of their father, though both served the Embassy faithfully as long as they lived. They were the last British subjects employed at the Embassy in any position of trust.

Mr. Jay resigned in December to go into a law practice in New York. Everybody was sorry to lose him, as he was so jolly and able, and in addition was very thoughtful about little things. It had been his habit to keep the Ambassador supplied with a special sort of stylo pen — the only pen I ever knew Mr. Reid to use — so whenever Mr. Jay sent for a new supply he would get an extra one for me, and once, when I was in mourning, he wrote to his mother in Paris to send me a suitable brooch. He was just as thoughtful with everybody else, and with his dependability and good sense must have saved the Ambassador many annoyances. He made me promise to write him 'everything.'

The Military Attaché changed, too. Major Beacom resigned and Captain Sydney Cloman came in his place, to arrive January 1. It was reported that he had just married a wealthy lady known as the 'turquoise widow' because she owned turquoise mines; both of them were very popular. But Mr. Reid was not pleased. He would have preferred a bachelor. Indeed, he would have preferred an entirely bachelor Embassy. He had no patience with so many wives who had to be invited on official occasions. He wanted bachelors who could help look after the girls and give them a good time.

There was a change, too, in the British Ambassadorship at Washington. Sir Mortimer Durand was not a success, and President Roosevelt was rumoured to have said that he was about as much use as a family portrait, and this coming to the ears of Sir Edward Grey there was nothing to do but recall him. Mr. James Bryce was appointed to succeed him. The Embassy did not especially approve of such an outside appointment — though they did not advertise the fact! They felt it was too bad for the British Government to be letting down the diplomatic bars and appointing a man outside of the Service (even such a friend of America as Mr. Bryce) at a time when so much of the thinking in Washington was directed towards putting the American Foreign Service on a professional basis. In the end, however, this departure from precedent was not as successful as had been expected, and the British Government went back to appointing Ambassadors at Washington from their regular Diplomatic Service.

Mr. Grant-Smith, who had talked us all to death about the deviltries of spies who seek to steal passports and cipher codes, and was seemingly vindicated when the Brazilian Ambassador informed us that someone was trying to sell him the American code (it turned out to be an old one quite out of date), managed to put through one reform. He didn't like copying by hand the official correspondence of the Embassy. He thought it stupid when it could be typewritten so much more easily, so on December 31 he laid down his pen and on January 1, 1907, I gleefully added to my other duties the making of typewritten copies for the permanent files. I was a glutton for work! Thus was one more time-consuming job lifted from the bowed shoulders of the Third Secretary and laid on mine!

Speaking of codes reminds me of a call we had from the police one day, who told us that a man was walking about the streets of London entirely out of his mind. They believed him to be an American consular officer, and he had a book clutched tightly in his hand which they had reason to suspect might be his code. The Embassy sent Frank Hodson along with the policeman, and with a little persuasion they brought the man to the Embassy, where he was induced, on seeing the Eagle above the safe and the rest of the Embassy paraphernalia, to deposit the code inside — for he *was* a Consul and it *was* his code. It appeared he had been for several years on the west coast of Africa and was on his way home for a rest, as the climate had been too much for him. In spite of everything his poor diseased mind had retained the warning that his code was his most precious possession, to be guarded every moment, and he had accordingly carried it in his hand wherever he went. He sailed, much relieved to be rid of it. I hope his visit home cured him. We never heard.

┌─────────────────┐
│ ┌─────────────┐ │
│ │   12   │ │
│ └─────────────┘ │
└─────────────────┘

An Independence Day Reception by the Ambassador. Last visit to London of Mark Twain. The Second Hague Conference; Mr. Joseph H. Choate and General Horace Porter, delegates from the United States, in London. The Consecration of the Harvard Memorial Chapel in Southwark Cathedral.

1907

T HE Ambassador's Independence Day Reception was then (and probably still is) the greatest annual gathering of Americans in London, for on that day he apparently entertained every American resident in or visiting London and a few hundred English and Canadians for good measure. The friendly, hospitable and mainly American receptions of Mr. Choate's time grew in splendour with the coming of Mr. Reid, for everybody sought an opportunity of seeing the interior of the magnificent and spacious Dorchester House, and this was the only occasion during the year when it was opened to a large miscellaneous group.

In Mr. Choate's time every American was welcome to attend his Independence Day Reception without any sort of card, but when Mr. Reid came it was decided — to protect the house and keep some check if possible on the numbers — to issue invitations, and on me fell the task of seeing that everybody who ought to be there was invited and nobody who ought not to be there received a card.

Invitations were sent to every American we could find, but the hundreds of requests from people we had never heard of and who seemed to have no claim were disregarded. No one could blame Americans for making sure of an invitation, for the Fourth of July was an inspiring occasion — albeit a bit outmoded — and they enjoyed meeting their Ambassador and making the Eagle scream.

Most of the English people looked upon the Fourth as a mere survival of an unfortunate misunderstanding, but Ambassador Bryce, a rather ponderous individual, took the celebration very hard. 'So far from being a cause of rejoicing,' he announced, the rupture between Great Britain and her Colonies appeared to him to be 'one of the great misfortunes of world history.' He did not believe that the severance between Britain and America had been inevitable. That it should have been allowed to occur at all was to him a great calamity, leaving behind it so much bad blood and poisoning quite needlessly for many generations, relations which otherwise might have remained sweet and wholesome. Apparently other members of the British Government did not feel so badly, for they came in numbers and seemed to enjoy themselves. Perhaps they realized that a quarrel at least presupposes a link — which may be repaired in time.

For this reception the impressive range of handsome reception rooms leading one into the other on the second floor of Dorchester House was transformed into an enormous bower of flowers, and the garden at the back, entirely covered in and decorated with ropes of crimson ramblers, became the buffet. The windows were taken out, and staircases covered with crimson carpet were built into the openings, out of which went the thousands of people on their way to the refreshments. Strawberries embedded in Devonshire cream, delicious cakes, sandwiches of all sorts and drinks were well patronized. I remember once seeing a greedy but plucky lady — cup of tea in one hand and squab rolling about on a plate in the other — staring round for a place to sit down. I turned my back, so never knew whether she found one, or, if she had to part with one of her two treasures, which one she gave up! There was no trouble with American appetites — nor English either for that matter — and the complaint that Americans eat their Ambassador out of house and home seemed to have a fair amount of justification.

The Ambassador and Mrs. Reid received at the top of the main staircase, and if one got there early enough, as I always tried to do, one could walk round the balcony square and watch the other guests coming up and hear the butler announce the names. I would see all the leaders of Anglo-American society advancing up and up, the women's dresses trailing on the ground, with huge befeathered hats on their overdressed heads and parasols self-consciously tilted in their hands, escorted by men in fashionable morning coats, their silk hats in their hands. Mr. J. P. Morgan would step briskly up, and among the others I knew would be Mr. R. Newton Crane, the Despatch Agent, the Consul-General and his wife, various newspaper friends, Mr. and Mrs. J. Arthur Barratt, several visiting American diplomats with their wives, Lord Strathcona, the Canadian High Commissioner, Count and Countess Benckendorff, and indeed most of the members of the Corps Diplomatiques. I knew many of the men at least by sight, but the women were mostly strangers at first. Some of the men would come along and introduce their ladies and I would try to think of something more original to say than 'lovely house' or 'more people than ever.' But most of the guests were strangers, many tourists and a good many obviously not Americans at all. It was alarming to see such crowds who had no right to be there, responsible as I was for the issue of the invitations. But I suspected that everybody else at the Embassy surreptitiously included a few invitations to their own friends.

The only disagreeable incident I ever recall was when a newspaper man, who had been banned by Mr. Reid from ever entering his house again because of some breach of newspaper trust, received a ticket and presented himself with an ingratiating smile at the head of the stairs quite unmoved by the Ambassador's glares, knowing well that Mr. Reid's politeness would protect him. So it did at the time!

A band played upstairs, and outside in Park Lane the traffic was either in an uproar or at a complete standstill because of the stream of cars which cut across it coming in and out. Park Lane, because of its narrowness, was one of the worst streets of all for parties. Even on ordinary days it was filled with busses, and in the season choked with private cars as well.

Mother sometimes came to some of the receptions, with a faintly suspicious attitude of being lured into a menagerie filled with strange animals, who, although they would not bite, might be dangerous in other ways. With me to stand by her side she was well protected and in spite of her diffidence she really thoroughly enjoyed herself, though she would never admit it. She was always on guard, and Mr. Laughlin, Councillor of Embassy at a later date, confirmed her worst suspicions of the queerness of Americans when he came up to be introduced, saying he was most anxious to meet 'the Mother who produced this' — pointing at me. I knew at once that this was shyness induced by Mother's cool appraisal, but Mother did not appreciate his humour. Indeed, her feeling about Americans was that they were always unpredictable. She didn't see them as I did, as men doing a creative long-time piece of work in a foreign land with great ability and patience and understanding. She admitted how kind and generous they were to me, but — they were strangers to her. So, after a few experiences, I did not invite her any more. She could stay at home, I decided wrathfully.

The last time that Mark Twain visited England — it must have been in 1907 — he reached London actually on the day the famous Ascot Gold Cup was stolen — a most spectacular and outrageous theft which caused consternation throughout the British Isles — and the newspapers of that afternoon announced the two events in suspicious juxtaposition, 'Arrival of Mark Twain' at the top, with 'Ascot Gold Cup Stolen' underneath. Not to be outdone in this exchange of pleasantries, Mark Twain prefaced every speech he made by telling his audience in sepulchral tones that he not only had the Cup but intended to keep it! It was during that visit that the Ambassador gave a large dinner in his honour, and, assuming that he would be called upon for a speech, he not only prepared it, but thriftily sold it in advance to a news agency in the United States for a good round sum. Judge of his feelings when he found no speech was expected. Though it duly appeared in the American papers, it was never delivered.

The Pilgrims also gave a lunch for him, each guest receiving a souvenir of a picture of the humourist in bed writing his autobiography, with this verse:

'He lit our life with shafts of sun
    And vanquished pain.
Thus two great nations stand as one
    In honouring Twain.'

To which he gracefully replied that 'under the British flag I am no alien.'

To go back to the beginning of 1907 — the Ambassador had returned from the United States in January, but Mrs. Reid remained until March. Mr. Carter went away for a few days on the Ambassador's return, leaving instructions to Mr. Grant-Smith to do what he could for an American lady whose daughter he had just learned had died. Mr. Grant-Smith and Frank went to see the poor old lady, who was about eighty and all alone in a lodging-house, sitting almost distraught by her dead daughter's bedside. They attended to everything, and afterwards helped the old lady to return to the United States. Both of them were much moved by her despair and loneliness. Why is there something so pitiful about dying in a foreign land? Everybody seems to feel it. All of us want to die at home, and the Embassy often helped to hurry off American travellers who had been taken ill in England and couldn't get back fast enough.

It was two years since we had seen Mr. Choate, so when it was announced that he would be the chief delegate sent by the United States to the Second Hague Peace Conference, and would go *via* London, we were much excited, for there would be much to tell him, and we wondered what he would think of the new Embassy. It was only a hurried visit, however, and after a few days of talks with the Foreign Office and the Ambassador about the program of the Conference, he left for The Hague, not very sanguine of results, but hopeful.

There was always a certain pathos about the visits of former members of the staff. They remembered so vividly the small happenings of human interest and seemed to have entirely forgotten most of their diplomatic troubles. They noticed if the place had been painted, or if the arrangement of the furniture had been changed; and if they were ex-Ambassadors they always wanted to look at their portraits hanging over the mantelpiece in the Ambassador's room, something they never saw until then. They resurrected and laughed at all the old jokes, and enquired for old friends. To each of them his years in London brought back many memories, and it was but natural to want to revive them with a sympathetic audience.

'Do you remember the day,' began Mr. Choate, smiling at me, 'when a box came for me that rattled, and we thought it was a bomb, and it turned out to be a miniature Plymouth Rock? Frank was green about the gills, and I wasn't specially comfortable — but *you* — you were as brave as a lion — a British lion!... And that place where Billy Phillips and I used to lunch, where the girls lived on cream puffs and drank tea so strong that it makes me shudder even now.... And that poor woman who used to write pages of gibberish almost every day? Dead, did you say? Much, much better for her and everybody else.... And the people who criticized us, and the

(*134*)

lady who said that George Washington was a woman, and tried to prove it, and the ones who were going to complain to Washington of our various villainies? Still going strong? I thought so. They are like the poor, always with us. It is sad that even in this short time so many of the old friends have gone. But, thank goodness, London itself hasn't changed at all. It smells the same and looks the same, and I can still find my way about without a guide.'

The invitations to the Second Hague Conference had been sent out by the Czar of Russia some months before, and had brought acceptances from forty-six Powers, though several of them made reservations as to the program. But, long before the Conference met, the seeming hopelessness of discussing limitation of armaments had become apparent to the diplomats. With so much caution and so many mental reservations little was accomplished, though machinery was set up for the further consideration of specific points that had developed in the Conference.

Writing about it afterwards, General Horace Porter, a former American Ambassador to France, and a co-delegate with Mr. Choate, expressed his opinion with some pessimism:

At the Second Hague Conference, which was the first great international peace assembly in the world, the first one at which every nation in the world was represented and represented by very able men, we laboured in the interests of peace for four months and a week, in season and out of season, by day and by night. What did we accomplish? Why, before we got there, we were notified in writing by the great Powers that if the question of reduction of armaments was mentioned, they would leave the Conference. Russia at the Conference eight years before had made that one of the paramount topics to be discussed, but now it may not be mentioned. And after our labours we had hardly turned our backs when this flame of war [the Balkan War, I presume] was begun. Well, this taught us many things. It taught us that in the great emergencies the nation can be saved by guns but never by tongues.

The Harvard Memorial Chapel at Southwark Cathedral was now completed. Before Mr. Phillips left London he had drafted an appeal for help. Mr. Carter sent it out, and soon cheques began to pour in, testifying to the interest of Harvard men. I kept Mr. Phillips and Mr. Choate informed of the progress of events and took charge of the money. But it didn't come in fast enough for me, so I took it upon myself to send the appeal to a few other men, who, though not Harvard men, had friendly relations with the Embassy, among them Mr. Carnegie, a fairly frequent visitor for many years. The strutting little Scotchman used to come in often to see Mr. Choate. He was always very conscious of himself, and treated the exuberant Frank as though he was a piece of furniture. However, he had money to give away, and the Embassy had been useful to him on many occasions, so I did not think there was any harm in trying to get a little for the Chapel. He responded at once with generosity, promising the last five hundred pounds, so, of course, that made us redouble our efforts, as we did not want anything to 'happen to him' before we collected.

Mr. Choate could not leave The Hague, even for the short time necessary to race to London and back, so the Chapel was dedicated in the presence of Ambassador Reid and a large congregation. It was one of the longest services I ever attended, and at the end poor Mr. Reid looked as though he had gone beyond the limit of his strength, though he was as gracious as ever.

The Ambassador and Mrs. Reid again sailed for their Christmas in the United States, leaving Mr. Carter in charge, and his first official act as Chargé d'Affaires was to attend the memorial service in honour of the King of Sweden. Mr. Carter was not much in the habit of attending weddings, memorial services, and the like. He had no time, so Frank would go to the church instead to tell the newspaper men he was there so that his name would be included among those present. The newspaper men used to tease Frank, for they knew Mr. Carter was not there, though they good-naturedly reported that he was. Sometimes also, when Frank was particularly expansive, he would enlarge his clientèle and tell the newspaper men — listening tongue in cheek — that the other Secretaries were there, too. These Secretaries, reading in the paper next day that they had attended a wedding to which they had perhaps not even been invited, were wroth. But Frank was quite sure that it was always an honour to have the Secretaries of the American Embassy at weddings and funerals, and certainly I never heard anyone remonstrate.

13

The beginnings of the struggle of the House of Commons with the Lords over the control of budgets. The wedding of Miss Jean Reid. Mr. Grant-Smith. Social trials in connection with Court presentations. Mrs. Ronalds's Sunday musicales. The International Naval Conference at London.

1908

T HE spring of 1908 saw the beginning of a great constitutional change in England when the struggle of the House of Commons began to curb the power of the House of Lords. This was to continue until the World War turned men's attention to questions of survival instead of methods of government. Mr. Lloyd George, Chancellor of the Exchequer, brought in his old-age pension scheme which was duly passed into law, and the following year asked in his budget for fourteen million pounds to pay for health and unemployment insurance, which sum he proposed to find by an increase in the income tax, by super-taxes, by death duties and taxes on undeveloped land. The House of Lords rejected this outrageous budget by a large majority and a general election followed to test the authority of the House of Lords to interfere with the financial arrangements set up by the House of Commons. The election was won by the Liberals, and a definite program for a peaceful social revolution was set on foot which resulted in strengthening the democratic processes in England by taking some of the sting out of sickness, old age, and unemployment.

How my family hated Mr. Lloyd George! We should all

be ruined; there was no doubt about it! And where was the money to come from?

The spring of 1908 also brought an increase, by nearly twenty per cent, of Germany's naval estimates, she having rejected a proposal made by the Liberal Party in England for a reduction. It had been the custom in Europe that a country could either be naval or military, but not both. England having a large navy was content with a small army, and Germany had a large army and a small navy, but now she wanted a big navy as well, which English people were sure was directed ultimately against England.

On the social side the spring of 1908 was memorable to the Embassy because of the wedding of the Ambassador's only daughter, Miss Jean Reid, whose engagement to the Honorable John Ward, brother of the Earl of Dudley, was announced in April. As there had not been an Anglo-American Embassy wedding for many years — I could not remember that there had ever been one before — everybody was more than delighted at this new international link between the daughter of the Ambassador and a man of high position at the British Court. From the day of the announcement until the wedding day the Embassy was busy answering enquiries about it from the most outlandish sources. Why strangers should want to know about it, or what interest they could possibly have, we did not understand, except that there are seemingly thousands of people with nothing better to do than live off other people's lives and get their experiences and thrills at second hand.

Miss Reid's wedding took place in June. A letter written at the time records my impressions:

You have heard of all our excitements from the newspapers, of course. The wedding of Miss Reid was very, very smart, and we all felt proud, as though, in sooth, it was an Embassy accomplishment. She had many beautiful presents; a diamond tiara — five hundred diamonds in it; bracelets from the King and Queen, diamond dog collar — she has one of the long American necks — and hundreds of other things. There must have been about three dozen small clocks and fans, and the favourite small gift seemed to be a jewelled parasol handle, of which she had more than enough to last her lifetime.

The wedding itself was very grand, and as it was celebrated at the Chapel Royal, which only holds about a hundred people, the family and Royalty and a few intimate friends were all that could squeeze in. Afterwards there was a small reception at Dorchester House, to which I was invited. This was also most select, as it included the King and Queen, the Prince and Princess of Wales, the Duke of Connaught, Princess Patricia of Connaught, and many others of the Royal Family. I was as smart as anyone else, in a white Liberty dress embroidered with pale blue roses appliquéed round the hem and on the bodice, and a most roguish hat. Can you see me looking roguish?

I was afraid I mightn't reach the house until the reception was all over, for the train simply crawled. At Victoria Station I took a cab, and that also loafed along and stopped dead — apparently forever — near the beginning of Park Lane. The traffic was entirely blocked, owing to the multitudes waiting to see the King and Queen. They had seen them go into the house, but they must wait to see them leave! In time I was deposited at the front door, but it was too late to see the bride in her wedding dress. The butler whispered that she had gone to change. Just as I got inside I caught sight of Mr. Blake, looking a bit forlorn, and he very kindly took me to tea in the tent at the back. My dear, what food! Upon our return to the front hall the butler (always be friends with the butler!) suggested that if we waited there we should see the King and Queen who were in the library taking tea. So we planted ourselves at the foot of the stairs and glued our eyes on the library door. Alongside of us stood Mr. Balfour, his six feet four or so towering above a bevy of ladies who were hanging on his every word. As he talked he twisted his hat into a number of new styles, to the amusement of his giggling audience, who encouraged him to more and more grotesque exhibitions. He seemed quite human.

Presently out came the Ambassador with the Queen on his arm, followed by the King by himself, then Mrs. Reid, the Prince and Princess of Wales, and some others, all in a friendly group. The Queen wanted to see the tent, so to get to it they passed right in front of us. As the King came along, ladies who

wanted to be noticed curtseyed deeply. Then he would stop
and speak a few words. The lady next to me seemed to be a
friend of his, and he talked with her some minutes. I was
hemmed in so tight I couldn't move, much to my outward embarrassment but inward glee. His Majesty glanced casually at
me several times — it was probably that hat! Should I curtsey?
I wanted to — Oh, how I wanted to! But I wasn't sure. Mr.
Reid was opposite, so I didn't, and therefore missed a chance of
talking with His Majesty, for the King undoubtedly would have
acknowledged the curtsey. Being employed by a foreign government I didn't seem to know just where I belonged or what
the etiquette of such a moment was!

All this time the King was blocking up the passage with his
portly person. But after a few minutes the impatient Princess
of Wales decided to wait no longer, and gave His Majesty a
shove that made him swerve out of her way. The look he gave
her was certainly not friendly! It was a hot, sticky day, and
perspiration poured off everybody. The make-up on some of
the dowagers' faces had begun to run, and the King, in his heavy
coat, seemed uncomfortable. I must admit that such a near view
of Their Majesties was rather disillusioning. It was better to
think of them as symbols — for a more dowdy crowd I never
saw. Most of the guests far outshone them, especially the
Americans, with their slick figures, perfect hair, thin necks and
small heads. But the Americans were too perfect, too cold, too
critical, like machines. I liked our King and Queen better. I
had a lump in my throat that the most perfect American could
never give me.

After a long wait the bride and bridegroom came downstairs
ready to go, and on discovering that the King and Queen were
still in the garden they went out there to say good-bye, and
presently everybody came trooping back, and after much kissing
and throwing of rice they left. One of the little bridesmaids, a
daughter of Lord Dudley, kept calling out, 'Good-bye, Aunt
Jean,' in her childish treble, until, looking round and finding
her close to him, King Edward put his hand under her chin and
said, 'So this is the young lady who is making all the com-
motion.'

As soon as the bridal party had left, the Royal Family, with
lengthy good-byes, much curtseying and bowing, followed suit,
and as I returned to have a second cup of tea I heard the roars of

the crowd outside. The Park was jammed with people, and the traffic down Park Lane entirely stopped for hours, but nobody minded so long as they saw the King and Queen in the end.

Immediately following on the wedding came the Fourth of July, with the usual reception. We sent the bride and bridegroom an invitation to Ireland to show they were not forgotten.

Mr. Carter was his friendly and popular self at the wedding, rushing about doing the many little pleasant things that no one else ever seems to think of. He looks very tired, but as he is sailing for America soon, I hope he will get a rest. His daughter is lovelier than ever, a real belle, and Sargent has just painted a charming picture of her. She'll never be an old maid, I can see that. . . .

There were more Americans than ever in London that year, and all the four Courts had been completely filled so far as Americans were concerned months before. The American list for Ascot was also quite imposing, including not only the Ambassador and Mrs. Reid, but Mr. Ogden Reid also, who had come over for his sister's wedding, and Miss Muriel White, who had come from Rome, all the Carters, Gibbonses, Clomans, indeed the entire Embassy, and in addition Mr. D. O. Mills, Mrs. Reid's father, who was staying at Dorchester House. Mr. Grant-Smith said he had better go and take a long last look at the noble steeds, just in case! I think he had an inkling that his days in London were numbered and may have known just when and where he was going. But he loved to be mysterious!

It was not long afterwards that, to our great regret, he was appointed to Santiago, Chile, as Second Secretary. I don't know whether he was sorry to go or not. One day he would say he was, but the next he would shout how glad he was to be leaving the blasted British. But that was only when I had annoyed him.

I used to wonder whether any of his friends who had not been to London before might turn up one day and make a scene, for it had been his amiable habit to send out widely in the United States a photograph postcard of the Houses of Parliament, complete with Big Ben, Westminster Bridge, and the Victoria Tower, and write underneath — 'Our Embassy at London!'

He had other amusing qualities that we should sadly miss, for, a gentleman of the Oppenheim School, he apparently lived in a world of wild intrigue. He was all for secrecy, mystery, and the tiptoe method of conducting business, and I should never have been surprised to find a solid front door with a small peephole installed through which a visitor could be inspected before being admitted. Among his achievements was the purchase of an enormous safe into which were crammed all the bulky books and documents that such suspicious people insist be kept under lock and key. When I first went to the Embassy there had been only one safe the size of a small refrigerator, but the efficiency of various Secretaries resulted in one about the size of a small house, and this became so filled up that when anything was needed in a hurry it took the wizardry of a detective to unearth it.

Poor Mr. Grant-Smith. How they teased him and how he enjoyed it! I remember Mr. Carter saying to him one day,

'Well, Grant, if anything should unfortunately happen to you, I suppose if I cable "Smith America" your relatives will receive it?'

'Oh, dear, no,' replied Mr. Grant-Smith solemnly. 'There are millions of mere Smiths, but only one Grant-Smith. A cable "Grant-Smith America" will relieve you of all responsibilities. To ease your mind, however, which I must say seems to be concerned with far-flung fears, I will put my last wishes in the safe.' So I typed for him a most impressive document saying that if he died in England he did not want his dead body carted across the Atlantic, but interred economically in the nearest churchyard. This may still be in the Embassy safe for all I know!

Another subject of idle conversation was the reason why

their ancestors had gone to the United States in the first place. Mr. Carter thought his ancestor, Lord Baltimore, had a fair record for those times, though if there had been any little misdemeanour, it might have been sheep-stealing. In return Mr. Grant-Smith claimed that there were a few minor massacres and quick get-aways in his background. The Civil War was still another topic of perennial debate. Between Mr. Carter of the Carters of Virginia representing the South, and Mr. Ulysses Grant-Smith, a nephew of General Grant, the North, there were some lively exchanges. Mr. Carter shocked me by telling me that the wicked Yankees had buried their soldiers in the grounds of one of the most beautiful of the Southern estates near Washington called Arlington. 'Oh, dear me, no. They didn't take it from us. They wouldn't do a thing like that. But who wants a cemetery in one's garden.'

Mr. Grant-Smith made a face, but would not be drawn!

He did one of the most disagreeable jobs I remember, when he was sent to ask King Edward VII to cancel the presentation of an American woman because it was discovered afterwards that she was not eligible.

This lady was the recently married wife of a successful American business man living in London. I think it was Mr. Carter who vouched for her, as he had known her husband a long time. And, indeed, as the couple were to live in London and promote American interests, it was only fitting that she be introduced through the Embassy. So both of them were presented, and their house became a pleasant rendezvous for smart Londoners.

But it happened one day that, lunching at the Ritz, the lady waved her hand gaily across the room to one of the Embassy Secretaries lunching there too, with an American recently arrived from Washington. This man stared across at the woman.

'Who is that?' he asked. 'She looks familiar.'

'Does she? She is Mrs. J. K., the wife of J. K.'

'You know who she used to be, don't you? I knew her years ago and ——' It was not a pretty story.

Soon after that an American former diplomat called at the Embassy and informed Mr. Carter that a terrible mistake had been made in presenting the lady. Mr. Carter, startled, would not — could not — believe it. Anyhow, he said, she was now married to a fine man, so why rake up the question at this late hour? Let the poor woman alone! But the former diplomat said that that could not be done. He was not the only man who had recognized her and the story would soon be all over London. He thought that the authorities were bound to find out, sooner or later, and that the Embassy would be embarrassed if the cancellation of the presentation were to be officially requested. He advised Mr. Carter to forestall this by having it quietly cancelled. Mr. Carter agreed to think it over. He felt pretty sure the husband didn't know. He was terribly distressed — though rather angry, too.

The former diplomat, dissatisfied at any thought of delay, called on Mr. Reid at Dorchester House and told him also. To his amazement and chagrin Mr. Reid was cold. He intimated that he would think it over and dismissed him.

But he would not be dismissed. 'Think it over! You must act at once, for if the King finds out from someone else, it will be serious.' To make his meaning clearer he reminded Mr. Reid that some years previously a lady had been presented to Queen Victoria by the American Minister under express instructions from the Vice-President of the United States, and when it was found out later that she was not eligible to go to Court, the Prince of Wales, later Edward VII, was so incensed at this insult to his royal mother that he demanded of the Foreign Office that the United States be asked to recall the Minister, and the matter was only smoothed out after a great deal of trouble and many apologies. Mr. Hay also, he reminded him, had had embarrassments of the same sort when he was Ambassador to England.

Mr. Reid was stirred. 'What do you suggest, then?'

'You must explain the whole matter at once to His Majesty.'

'But the King is at Marienbad.'

'That doesn't matter. Send someone to Marienbad. The main thing is to tell him before anybody else does.'

So Mr. Grant-Smith, leaving on vacation, was delegated to go by way of Marienbad. When he arrived, he reported the matter to Sir Sydney Greville, one of the King's *entourage*, expressed the Ambassador's regret, and emphasized that Mr. Reid's anxiety had been so keen that he had gone to the length of sending his messenger half across Europe to explain. Sir Sydney informed the King. The King was gracious, and, saying that the matter would be adjusted at London, Mr. Grant-Smith was free to begin his holiday.

That was the end so far as the Embassy was concerned, but its reverberations brought tragedy which they were powerless to prevent. Soon the story, and all it implied, leaked out and was a nine days' wonder. The woman left her husband and he remained in London a broken man. She returned again a few months later, but when she left the second time, this time for good with another man, she took with her most of his money. He died a few years afterwards a drunkard, at one of the Continental resorts.

There was another woman, too, of whom the Embassy was suspicious who bombarded the Embassy to present her. She came to London with letters of introduction from prominent American officials, and also had one from an Englishwoman who — at a price — was often helpful to socially ambitious Americans in London. The following year, as she was not successful, she sent letters from other officials, but again was told the lists were full. Then her husband applied for her and tried to use threats!

During this time the Embassy was flooded with anonymous letters about the morals and manners of several other American women in London, and had begun to suspect this woman of being the author. I kept the letters in my desk, and used to be horrified that one woman — we all knew it must be a woman because of the accusations made — could be so hateful. The handwriting, though disguised, was distinctive, so, as I wanted to help Mr. Carter, I took the opportunity one afternoon when she came to call on him and he was out to pin her down. I told Frank that I would see her, and going into the reception room suggested that if she cared to write him a brief note I would see that he got it immediately on his return. I put a sheet of Embassy paper in front of her and handed her a pen, and before this insistence she succumbed. The note was sent, along with some of the anonymous ones to an expert who pronounced them written by the same person. As I remember, Mr. Carter, desiring to keep the matter quiet, tipped her off casually about the penalty incurred in writing anonymous letters, and that particular activity ceased.

But of all the presentation troubles the one that annoyed Mr. Carter the most was to be told by an American gentleman that the day his wife was presented he would find a credit of twenty-five thousand dollars at Cartier's. Someone had only to mention it to make him extremely irritable.

This disagreeable subject reminds me of an exhibition of social cruelty I saw one afternoon at Dorchester House. It was a large reception, and many groups were talking to the accompaniment of a stringed orchestra. Into the room came an American from another capital, well known to all of us, with his wife, a most charming lady who was not received in London society, although the man himself was. As the butler announced them, there was a sudden hush. They crossed the room and spoke to the Ambassador and Mrs. Reid for a few minutes until someone else was announced, and then turned to the rest of the company. But all of them were suddenly immersed in conversation, many of them turning their eyes another way. There they stood alone, not knowing just where to go, the man seemingly nonplussed, but the woman calm and collected as she coolly surveyed the scene. Out of all that gathering, mine was apparently the only friendly face, so he came straight over to me and introduced his wife. As I made a few obvious remarks, I was conscious of unfriendly eyes, and a grin on the face of one of the young diplomats for which I would make him pay sometime! Surely I didn't also see a quick glance from Mr. Carter as he again determinedly turned his back? Finally the two moved on, and when I glanced up after a minute or two they had gone. The hurt in the man's eyes haunted me. It was one of the most distressing moments I have ever experienced, and the rest of the guests seemed like a host of vultures watching rather gleefully the death struggles of two other defenceless animals. So that's what civilized people did to others who had broken the social code? I shivered.

I remember another woman, an American — not presentable at Court — married to an Englishman who had done so well by his country that he was offered a title. As the wife of a Knight the lady herself would naturally be presented at Court — though, as a British subject, not through the Embassy. As she was probably unaware of the dangers, and the Embassy was not sure whether the husband knew of his wife's past, they decided to warn her. A man who had known her in the past called, and when they were alone he told her she had better not think of going to Court, for if she did someone would be sure to find her out, and that under the circumstances it might be wiser for her husband not to take his title, as if he did and his wife was not presented, that would cause talk. He explained to her fully what had happened on other occasions, and what such a disclosure would mean to her husband and his career. The husband refused the title.

But there were many very notable Americans in London who added gaiety and friendship to the social scene. Perhaps one of the most charming as well as the most prominent was

Mrs. Ronalds, the former Fanny Carter of Boston, whose musical parties were one of the delights of the Edwardian period. Mrs. Ronalds had a beautiful voice, and was always most generous to musicians in helping them with money and a chance to show their ability. Tosti, whose famous 'Good-bye' has since been sung all over the world, was one of them. The week-end out of town had not become prevalent then, so for those who remained in town Mrs. Ronalds's Sunday afternoon musicales provided the smart place to go. Her house was small, so not only would the rooms upstairs be crowded to capacity, but a substantial overflow sat up and down the stairs. One Sunday afternoon a charming little incident occurred. Sitting together in a crowded corner were Mr. J. P. Morgan, Sir Ernest Cassell, Mr. D. O. Mills, Mr. Alfred Rothschild, and Ambassador Reid. When Mrs. Ronalds came up to speak to the group, Mr. Morgan took something out of his pocket and handed it to her. It was his invitation to her wedding almost forty years before which he had treasured all those years. 'You were a lovely girl, my dear,' he said, 'and also a very unselfish one, never thinking of yourself. Of course you are just as sweet now, but the years do horrible things to us, don't they?'

One occasion when Mrs. Ronalds's lovely voice was heard to special advantage was the year when she was a guest of the Prince and Princess of Wales and the King and Queen of Denmark at Cowes Regatta. On their way home in the Royal Yacht surrounded by many other vessels, everybody tired after a strenuous day's racing, the King of Denmark asked her to sing. So with the moonlight streaming over the dancing waves they drifted dreamily to shore, the familiar strains of that heart-warming old ballad 'Home, Sweet Home,' a fitting finale to the day.

My youngest sister, Millie, came to be secretary to the Military Attaché about that time. She had just finished helping with a bye-election where her employer, Mr. Stuart, Secretary of the Postmen's Federation, had put up against Winston Churchill at Dundee. Millie went up to Dundee to help Mr. Stuart and the Labour cause, armed with a most gorgeous red hat made for her by another sister, Winnie, and claimed afterwards to have shaken hands with every adult and kissed every baby in the constituency. Feeling very suspicious about this taking Millie so far away (for there was no Mrs. Stuart), I called on Mr. Stuart to enquire where my sister would be housed, and the irate Mr. Stuart informed me that she would be a guest of a family prominent in Labour circles, that they would write to Mother and invite her, and then asked sarcastically if I would also care to have a certificate of good behaviour for him also!

Notwithstanding all this expenditure of energy Mr. Stuart was defeated. Assisting her son against him was the former Lady Randolph Churchill, who, in what may be considered to have been the decisive speech of the campaign, fought on tariff reform versus free trade — the Free Traders claiming that a tariff on food would increase the cost of living — she said archly: 'I don't know *anything* about dear bread or dear butter or dear meat. What I say is, "Vote for dear Winnie."' And of course they did!

Millie was not altogether pleased to substitute the delights of politics for diplomacy, but at my insistence agreed, as the short hours gave her more time for the music which was her chief interest. I didn't see much of her, as she worked upstairs, although when I was away she helped out downstairs — whenever her jealous employer would let her — and enjoyed the storm which her trying to be in two places at once occasioned.

Her first battle was a crusade against the cuspidor which was part of the furnishings of her office — a fine manly note! But she couldn't see why, if diplomats didn't need cuspidors downstairs, military officers upstairs did. English offices didn't have them and she didn't see why she should have to put up with that! So she hid it far back in the cupboard and awaited developments. It was a war without words, and Millie won it!

The International Naval Conference set up by the Second Hague Conference to revise the rules and usages of naval warfare met at the Foreign Office in December. Sir Edward Grey received the delegates and opened the Conference, and Mr. Carter accompanied and introduced the American group. Thereafter the American delegation, consisting of Captain Stockton, former Naval Attaché, and Mr. George Grafton Wilson, with the handsome Ellery Stowell as secretary, made their unofficial headquarters in the Naval Attaché's office whenever the Conference was not in session, and very noisy and jolly they were. The quarter-deck tramping back and forth and the shouts to each other as though across miles of roaring ocean forced the Ambassador's hurried retreat to Dorchester House for peace.

The representatives of the Conference — delegates from maritime nations only — worked for several months trying to frame a code under which naval warfare should be conducted, afterwards known as the Declaration of London. But it did not meet the approval of the English people. They felt the important concession to German opinion in the matter of blockade was a sop offered to Germany by the Liberal Party, and were afraid that if it should ever be tested out in time of war between Germany and England, it would ensure a food supply for Germany while it imperilled their own. In the end, it may be remembered, the House of Lords in 1911 promptly rejected the Declaration.

As I recall, Germany, but no other Powers, signed it.

This outcome of the Second Hague Conference then lay dormant until, at the outbreak of the World War, the efforts of American diplomacy were directed towards trying to persuade the belligerents to conduct their naval warfare according to its rules — which would have permitted shipment of goods to Germany. This England would not agree to, so the United States was forced to abandon the Declaration for the time.

As a change from official duties the New Year brought me a different job — that of Cupid's messenger — when in a letter from Mr. Jay, heavily sealed and mysterious, he wrote:

> There's no denying the fact that the primary object of this letter — though not the only one — is to ask you to do me a favour. I ask you, as I don't want anyone to know about it, for though it isn't very interesting I'm hanged if I want to be teased about it, and I feel shy about asking Mr. Carter, as I fear his diplomatic mind would put too much importance on the errand I am going to ask you to do.
>
> I enclose a cheque for five pounds. Could you buy me some of the very best lilies-of-the-valley that you can get — also some violets — a good big bunch of them both — and have them sent with the enclosed note to the address on it? They are to arrive on the *18th of January*. I suppose parcels post is the quickest way to send them? Anyway, if they took the night mail train from London on the 17th they should reach Dublin early in the morning of the 18th. Navan is about 1½ hours from Dublin, and Philpottstown, the Morgan place, about four miles from Navan. Probably there is only one delivery of mail from Navan — if any — to a place like Philpottstown 3 or 4 miles out. Perhaps it would be better to send them on the 16th and then they would surely be delivered either the morning of the 17th or the morning of the 18th....
>
> In order not to unduly excite your feminine curiosity I may say that January 18th is little Miss Morgan's twentieth birthday; that she is very pretty and charming; that I have known her since she was a child and looked after her in the hunting field; that I have, however, never 'whispered any sweet nothings' in her ear; and, for that very reason, perhaps, we are very good friends and I always try to remember her birthday....
>
> Be sure to seal the note before putting it in, and if you tell Mr. Carter I'll kill you....

I did not tell Mr. Carter, nor anyone else, and at various times thereafter sent other flowers, books, etc. But even I — slow British that I am — was not deceived by what he termed in some other letter 'the affection of an elderly bachelor for a beautiful girl.' They were eventually married.

14

Mr. William Howard Taft becomes President. Mrs. Whitelaw Reid as a fairy godmother. Changes at the Embassy. Mr. Carter is appointed Minister to Rumania and Mr. William Phillips returns to the Embassy as Councillor.

1909

IN DECEMBER of 1908 President Roosevelt started the United States fleet from Hampton Roads to make its grand cruise round the world, an announcement to whom it might concern — particularly Japan — that it might be injudicious to pull Uncle Sam's coat-tails without carefully considering the cost beforehand. Just before he left Washington, after the inauguration of Mr. Taft, ex-President Roosevelt, who intended to sail within a few days for a hunting trip in Africa leaving the stage to his successor, was reputed to have invited a famous English big-game hunter, who happened to be in the United States, to come to Washington to give him some pointers for his own trip. After a two-hour conference at the White House, during which the two were not disturbed, the Englishman came out.

'And what did you tell the President?' asked a curious by-stander.

'I told him my name,' said the wearied visitor.

On March 4 Mr. Taft became President. Mr. Philander Knox became Secretary of State, a lawyer who knew little about foreign affairs, having been more occupied with corporation law. Such an appointment of an outsider always caused anxiety to the men in the Service, for they had good reason to know how much chaos such a man could make. The guillotine therefore hovered over the Embassy all that winter and spring, for President Taft was very slow to commit himself in regard to what he intended to do to the Foreign Service. It was assumed in London — I don't know why — that Mr. Reid would remain. To make certain of this the King urged Sir Edward Grey to remind the American Government of the increased cordiality that had grown up between the two countries during Mr. Reid's term of office, and the desirability of retaining him at London. Sir Edward Grey accordingly took up the question with Ambassador Bryce, but, while sympathizing, Mr. Bryce felt it only fair to warn the Foreign Office that there were probably many of his supporters whom Mr. Taft might wish to put in office, and that, after all, Ambassador Reid had had his turn. So the British Government let the matter drop.

Mr. Bryce must have said something, however, for the King's wishes were not forgotten in Washington, and later in the spring Mr. Reid was informed that there would be no change in the Ambassadorship at London and that, so far as Mr. Taft was concerned, he might consider himself a permanent appointee.

This was very pleasant news for us. At first we had found Mr. Reid so different from Mr. Choate that we hardly knew whether we liked him or not. It was never easy for people to get to know him, and most of us stood in great awe of him. But in time we grew more used to him and his ways, and as soon as he discovered that his every word was listened to with attention and respect and that everyone was sympathetic and helpful, he began to unbend, too, and was not so reserved and cautious. But he never acquired the easy friendliness of Mr. Choate.

Mrs. Reid always had a certain childish love of her part of the Ambassadorship and a thorough enjoyment of it. It was true that she did little in those days without first consulting her men-folks, but when their approval had been won, she spent money with a cheery good-nature and abandon that was most infectious and even startling. There must have been hundreds of struggling young Americans who found a saviour in her, to say nothing of almost as many English. Never in all my life did I know of anyone so generous as she, with an open-handedness and open-heartedness that seemed like a fairy story. Little interested in academic theories, with no finicking ways or ideas, she was a mixture of common-sense combined with the outspokenness of the woman who has never had to mind her *p*s and *q*s. She reminded me of Queen Victoria, the same somewhat deceptive motherly appearance and manner.

Short and stout, she wore her hair towering on the top of her head in perfect waves. Only once was one of her dresses for Ascot so stately that even the blasé Secretaries remarked on it. It was, as I remember, plum-coloured with some mixture of heliotrope about it, with hat and sunshade to match, which became her remarkably well. But whatever she wore, wherever she went, she was a real personality, and all those who like honest, outspoken, occasionally Malapropish, generous people loved her. One knew where one stood with her. She had a homely sincerity that was especially refreshing in the careful, almost superrefined diplomatic environment. Her remarks about the junior members of the staff would have given them apoplectic fits, but fortunately they did not hear them, and I found out just what she thought of me long afterwards when she said one day *à propos* the Embassy in general:

'Whitelaw always liked you. *I could never understand why!*'

She must have been difficult to work for and with. She was unexpected. She could ferret out the one question to which one did not know the answer. She was hasty, her judgments not always sound, and she therefore stuck to her ideas all the closer, and she would condemn a person forever for one piece of stupidity. She had that satisfied air of having been born a

Republican, of being absolutely certain that that party could do no wrong and that it was the only party to which any intelligent person could possibly belong. She was also sure that she graced the world becomingly and that she was doing her duty in that state of life to which it had pleased a discriminating God to call her. She represented all the certainties of her generation.

But it was always her marvellous generosity that stood out. The hundreds of lovely things — unexpected things, too — that she did for endless numbers of people, the abounding human kindness of her, was something to bring a lump in one's throat. I even suspected that she would have done more — if that were possible — but for the restraining counsel offered by more long-headed ones. Occasionally she was willing to be guided, for although she was sure of herself as a woman she was not always sure of herself as an Ambassadress, and perhaps a little alarmed sometimes that she was going further than prudence might dictate. But the slight dampening-down process occasionally administered had no permanent effect on her kindness, and there was no one at the Embassy who had not been the recipient of handsome gifts from her.

When on Christmas Eve or other anniversaries we opened boxes and ran our hands down through the billows of tissue paper to come on some charming piece of silver, it made us rejoice that here was one woman who actually loved to give. She acted as though her money came from a bottomless pit, apparently never hesitated to buy anything she wanted, spending gloriously, rapturously. Everybody who served her was overpaid. The men who escorted her to trains, looked after her luggage, and did the usual duties of travel considered her a fairy godmother. I have known her to give a man five hundred pounds to buy tickets and attend to many little things, and when he was about to give an account of his stewardship and return more than half of it, she would wave her hand and say, 'You did everything perfectly. Never mind about the change. I am sure you spent most of the money.' The young man, conscious of the many things he needed that that would buy, and overwhelmed, would murmur something, and she would smilingly go on with her conversation and forget all about it the next moment. Whatever one may think of the disintegrating effects of indiscriminate charity, there is no question that she brought into the drab lives of the little men who managed to serve her an amount of glamour they had never known before.

She used to retail amusing stories about her comings and goings. One I remember when she was seen off at the station by Mr. Irving Blake, that most discriminating, quiet, orderly man with a proper sense of the proprieties. Just as the train was due to go, and he was standing by the window waiting to see it start, she recollected that she had nothing to read. Mr. Blake immediately rushed down the platform to get something — anything — and returned panting, just in time, clutching in his hand — so she said — a copy of 'Saucy Stories'!

Dorchester House and Wrest Park certainly did their part to promote Anglo-American friendship. Both were the gathering places for the cultivated people of many countries, and Americans were proud to meet, in the home of their Ambassador, the foreign proponents of every school of thought. Some of the world's greatest singers entertained the guests at dinner parties, and I have among my autograph collection many letters from Caruso and other singers, from which I gathered some hint of their relative importance in the field of music by the sums they charged to come and sing! Mr. and Mrs. Reid used their homes, their personalities, and their money to demonstrate their friendly feeling towards the English people. They felt that bringing people together smoothed out differences and furthered mutual understanding. At their receptions English and Americans wandered together through the great rooms, mellowed by appetizing food in a gracious setting.

From a painting by P. A. Laszlo

MRS. WHITELAW REID

Insignificant citizens were given a taste of luxurious limelight, ordinary tourists were treated as honoured guests.

Two hundred and fifty Naval Cadets who had dropped anchor at Gravesend on a practice cruise were all invited to come up to London one afternoon and dance with a group of girls — not nearly enough, unfortunately — who had been hastily recruited by telephone. They came up two hundred and fifty strong, had such a meal as but seldom falls to the lot of midshipmen at sea, and danced as long as the girls could hold out, returning to their ship deeply impressed that their Ambassador and his wife had deigned to notice such as they. Mr. Reid was a most distinguished man, but without Mrs. Reid his Embassy would have lacked its unique flavour. It was she who was the spice of every banquet, the spoiled sovereign queen before whom they all bowed, while the Ambassador smiled on her, talked convincingly, and seemingly enjoyed himself.

During the summer of 1909 the King visited Wrest Park, and this party was one of the triumphs of Mr. Reid's embassy. I don't know whether King Edward realized that his presence there was used by Mr. Reid's critics as a reason why he should not be retained at London, because they thought his method of conducting the Embassy did not smack enough of democratic simplicity! Not that any of the gentlemen who officially believed in simplicity ever refused any of Mr. Reid's invitations. Not even Mr. Bryan went that far! I have the photograph taken at the party when the King was guest of honour, a picture which still breathes the atmosphere of those years, the large hats of the ladies and their ample flowing skirts, and the Homburg hats of the men. The King sat in the middle of the front row, with Mrs. Reid on his right and Georgiana, Countess of Dudley, on his left.

Mrs. Reid remained an energetic member of society until the day of her death. When the World War came, she threw herself into it with unselfish devotion. Her house in New York became the headquarters for the preparation of bandages while she herself was either in England or France looking after many other matters. But she never allowed her enterprises to dehumanize her. She took time in Paris one day to attend the funeral service of the first Y.M.C.A. worker who died in France. 'God did not choose a man to be our first martyr,' said Doctor Freeman, who conducted the funeral service. 'He chose a little woman.' When I saw her in the church, my heart warmed for a great lady who would so honour another member of her sex, one she did not know personally, but one who had lost her life in the cause in which they were both engaged. She also gave a beautiful house on the left bank of the Seine for an American officers' convalescent home, and there I went to see Mr. Jay, who was recovering from a wound. There must be many lovely chapters of her benefactions, and how they sweetened life for thousands, that deserve to be preserved, but I leave that to those better informed. To me, little as I knew her, she was one of the greatest of women.

The fate of Mr. Arthur Orr, the new Third Secretary who had been hurried from Berlin soon after Christmas to take up the work that Mr. Grant-Smith had laid down — and who was straining every nerve to get sent back to Berlin — remained unsettled. Mr. Carter also had begun to resign himself to the fact that he could not hope to remain much longer in London, though he consoled himself with hopes that he *might* be spared. Mr. Wadsworth had his moments of pessimism too, and Mr. Orr, commuting back and forth to Berlin, where he had left his wife and had foolishly leased a house, didn't know *where* he belonged. For the State Department made no move to relieve his anxiety, probably thinking a little discipline would do him no harm. It was due to me in the end that his fate was settled, for sympathizing with his uncertainty I wrote to Mr. Phillips, who had recently become Third Assistant Secretary of State, a powerful friend in need, and told him of Mr. Orr's predicament. On February 7, therefore, the State Department cabled that if he would not feel the financial hardship he might remain in London, to which Mr. Reid replied crossly that, having now taken a house in London and brought his wife from Berlin, a return there would be the greater hardship. Mr. Phillips wrote to me: 'I think you may consider yourself responsible for Mr. Orr's remaining in London, for on receipt of your words of praise I took up the matter at once with the Secretary, and the rest you know.'

As to himself and Mr. Wadsworth, the only thing to do, said Mr. Carter, was to be philosophical and try to forget the possibility of change, a sensible remark to make, but one not so easy to carry out. However, both of them worked along as usual, perhaps savouring the gaieties of the season with a little more piquancy just because of that possibility of impending doom. But as the months went by and nothing happened, they began to get quite cheerful and even to make plans for the winter.

But, alas, their optimism was misplaced. The execution was only postponed, for in August the newspapers informed Mr. Wadsworth that after his long service at the Embassy he had been superseded and that Mr. Hugh Gibson was to take his place. To treat him like this, not even to break the news by cable, but let him read it in the newspapers, was so discourteous that it could hardly be credited. Poor Mr. Wadsworth was dumbfounded, especially as there was no mention of promotion elsewhere, though later he went to Persia and from there to South America. Here was another case of the newspapers being told things far too soon, and even the Foreign Office had remonstrated officially from time to time when new developments in negotiations in which they had a part were given to the press without their first being consulted. Mr. Gibson, it fell out, did not know about his proposed transfer either. He wrote tartly that he wouldn't be along for some time. Now only Mr. Carter's fate remained undecided.

Mr. Orr, kind, gentle, and most intelligent, had interested me in the possibility of a card index for the Embassy correspondence — a fascinating new toy — and shown me how to start it. He also had a most methodical mind, and generously helped in many ways to make things easier for me. I remember his giving me a copy of 'England and the English,' written by Mr. Price Collier, an American, because he thought I ought to know what informed Americans thought about England.

There had come a new typewriter, of a make I did not know, and from the first I was prejudiced, saying it was harder to work with than the old one. So, to prove whether this was true, we made a scientific test, placing on the same key of each a miscellaneous collection of pennies, scissors, and other handy implements to see which took the most weight to register. My old typewriter won easily, so Frank walked off with the new one.

Mr. Reid returned from a brief visit to America in October, during which Mr. Carter was Chargé d'Affaires for the last time, and a few days later came the cabled announcement which we had been dreading ever since Mr. Taft came into office. Mr. Carter had been appointed Minister to Rumania! Somehow I had never thought it would really happen, for I could not conceive of the Embassy without him, dominated by his personality, his constant kindness and his humour. And to send him to the Balkan States, a comic-opera place where a trained American diplomat was absolutely wasted! Mr. Phillips was to succeed him. That was meagre comfort, though if Mr. Carter must go there was nobody we could welcome more sincerely than Mr. Phillips, who had been with Mr. Choate and knew us all, and had maintained his interest in the Embassy constantly. Mr. Phillips cabled Mr. Carter immediately, asking when he expected to leave London as he himself wanted to take a vacation before sailing. That, to his relief, gave Mr. Carter a little more leeway, as now that the actual crisis was upon him he hardly knew for a few days which way to turn. Those days were full of gloom. What would happen to me? Would Mr. Phillips bring his own secretary and leave me with only the official clerical work to do? Mr. Carter laughed. 'He won't if he's a wise man,' he said.

As I helped to pack up some of the familiar furnishings of Mr. Carter's desk, it seemed to me, as it did when Mr. Choate left, that this was again the end of an era. There was much changing of diplomats everywhere, the usual sadness of partings, the usual packing-up of homes and treks to new countries, new languages to be learned, new manners to get accustomed to, new aspects of diplomacy to get acquainted with, new difficulties about schools for children and climates for wives. Excitement, too, promotion, suspense, disappointment, all the ever-widening ripples that come from the central change of President and which the people at home know so little about. The change at London was typical of what was going on in every capital, with what was called 'promotion' to justify it. I was very sorry for Mr. Carter, but when I truthfully analyzed my emotions I knew I was sorrier for myself and for the disturbance of my own little world.

Mr. Henry White was also 'out' at Rome, owing, as the gossips said, to a slight put upon Mr. Taft many years before when he and his wife were honeymooning in England, and when, in Mr. White's absence, he was given tickets to see the State Coaches, when what he actually wanted was to enter the front door of Buckingham Palace as a guest, and meet the King. But Mr. White knew nothing about it at the time, and Mr. Hodson, who had given him the tickets, thought he was doing the right thing. Of such small incidents is history sometimes made.

The formal notice, stating that Mr. Carter, 'having been

designated by my Government Minister to the Balkan States, will relinquish his post as Secretary of this Embassy some time next month, and Mr. William Phillips, lately Third Assistant Secretary of State, will be appointed in his place,' went to the Foreign Office on the twenty-first.

The King received Mr. Carter and expressed his great regret at his leaving, and the Pilgrims gave a dinner for him, at which both the Ambassador and Sir Mortimer Durand spoke, and to which Mr. Carter made a brief reply — he was then no speaker. The Ambassador in a pleasant little speech said:

> For fifteen years... Mr. Carter has been connected with our Embassy. For nearly one third of that whole time he has acted as my chief secretary — literally as my right hand. Others have told you what they and this whole community have found him — how faithfully he served the great people whose Government sent him, and how acceptable he has made himself to the great Government that received him and to the people of this chief city of the English-speaking world. Let me limit myself to saying very simply that during the whole period of our official connection no Ambassador could ever have received from his First Secretary more loyal, zealous, intelligent, and efficient service.

So Mr. Carter went to Rumania alone to present his Letter of Credence and then returned and sailed with Mrs. Carter for America on leave. He wrote me from the *Lusitania*: 'We are sailing off and thinking of those left behind. Need I say how much my thoughts wander to you, for it is a truism that I will miss you more than anyone else in England....' Surely the most charming compliment a secretary could ever receive!

15

Mr. Phillips's wedding in England. The death of King Ed-
ward VII. Mr. Roosevelt as Special Ambassador at the funeral
and why he rode in a carriage. Miss Mildred Carter's wedding.
The Newfoundland Fisheries Arbitration at The Hague.

1910

Mr. PHILLIPS settled down at once, and seemed to feel very
much at home. He was in many ways entirely different from
Mr. Carter, more precise, more official in his manner, but very
kind and friendly. It must have been an interesting experience
for him to retread an old road after only six years' absence,
and in that time to have jumped from the bottom of the ladder to next to the top. The newspapers had a good story
about his arrival, and described the great reception given to
him, but there was not a word of truth in it. Actually he arrived late at night, and only Frank, the Despatch Agent, and
his own butler met him. The next morning he came down to
the Chancery, went over everything, caught up with the recent happenings as though he had never been away, and about
noon the Ambassador came in, casually enquired if he had
come yet and if so would he go in and see him. Reception, indeed! But though neither of us mentioned it then — it didn't
seem cricket to do so — it was Mr. Choate that he missed
most.

In between many exasperating details which kept him running up and down to Dorchester House — for the Ambassador did not come to the Chancery much — Mr. Phillips
looked for both a town and a country house to which to bring

his bride on his return from New York, where he was going in a week or two to be married to Miss Caroline Drayton. The house agents trod on one another's heels all day long offering the perfect house, and Seymour (Mr. Carter's butler and now Mr. Phillips's) spent his time going to see residences picked out as especially suitable and later returning to tell sad stories of disadvantages which the agents had overlooked. Finally, almost in despair, Mr. Phillips asked me whether I thought he could rent Mr. Carter's house which was standing empty. I could see no objection, but for some reason not quite clear then Mr. Carter refused, and so Mr. Phillips fell back on one not nearly so suitable, but in the right part of London.

His plans to be married in New York, however, were shattered by the sudden death of Mr. D. O. Mills, Mrs. Reid's father, and the Ambassador's immediate departure to join Mrs. Reid in New York. As Mr. Reid would not permit Mr. Gibson, who had arrived a few weeks before, to take charge, Mr. Phillips was obliged to cable his fiancée what must have been a very hard message, to say he couldn't come. Even his quiet dignity could not entirely hide the strain under which he was working that winter afternoon of the next day as he sat in the Ambassador's chair looking out into the dingy street and trying to be interested in routine. I was working with him, and altogether it was slow going.

When the door opened and the messenger brought in a cable, I returned to my desk in the corner. I heard him rip the envelope and there was a moment's silence in which I, too, held my breath, for I suspected who it was from. Then he jumped up from his chair and, rushing over, handed it to me, his face transfixed with relief and joy.

I read something like this: 'Sailing with my father for England. We will be married at Rogate. I will attend to everything.'

What a splendid sport! Just the right type for a diplomat's wife! And right up to the wedding day, February 2, how busy we were with the preparations and how gay he was! He seemed to dance as he walked in and out.

An English country wedding, in the village where the future Mrs. Phillips had spent many years of her girlhood and was well known, was substituted for the fashionable New York function (for which the invitations had already gone out). A special train took a few guests down from London, Commander and Mrs. Simpson, Mr. and Mrs. Orr, Mr. Gibson, the Consul-General and Mrs. Griffiths, Miss Colgate, Mr. Wadsworth, Mrs. French Vanderbilt, and myself. We had our lunch on the train, the first regular meal I had ever had while travelling — sticky buns and cups of tea handed in through the window at stations *en route* with the empty cup left under the seat being our economical habit. Mr. Gibson, who sat opposite to me at the tiny table, couldn't seem to believe that anyone as old as I had never eaten a meal on a train before. Being a Californian I assume he was used to the 'great open spaces' I was always hearing about, where one not only took meals on the train while it travelled over the deserts, but slept there, too.

Rogate Parish Church, a very tiny one, was crowded with friends and gaping villagers, and the bells jangled merrily. As it was so near to the house of Captain Warren, from which they were married, the bride and bridegroom walked to the church down the garden path, for it was a mild February day with a fair amount of sunshine. The church was beautifully decorated, and the organist came down specially from Southwark Cathedral to play the wedding march. The village was also decorated with flags across the streets. The bride was perfectly bewitching in her beautiful white satin dress with long train and cobwebby veil, a vision of fragile loveliness, and the groom was radiant. Both tall and slender they made a most handsome couple. A short reception with toasts followed, and then the train, which had been shunted on the siding to wait, carried us back to London. Next day I paid the bills, thanked the various officials for courtesies, wrote Captain Warren for boxes of wedding cake for some people who had been overlooked and might feel hurt to be forgotten, and took care of the odds and ends, while Mr. Gibson and Mr. Orr kept the diplomatic flag a-flying. But in two or three days Mr. Phillips was back, for a Chargé d'Affaires can't even have a honeymoon in peace.

'Mr. Phillips has made many new rules for our general conduct' — I wrote to one of the ex-secretaries a week or two later — I kept up a correspondence with most of them. 'He sees each of the secretaries at different hours and goes over their work with them, and inferentially doesn't want them wandering into his room at any hour as they had been in the habit of doing in Mr. Carter's time. He is also going to initial all despatches and Notes before they go to the Ambassador for signature, and to sign all the letters to Consuls, or better still have them signed by the Ambassador....'

Mr. Phillips's desire to improve relations with the Consuls was a clever move and very welcome all round, for there had been more or less friction between the two Services in London for years. The Consuls in England resented their minor status and the fact that, not being accredited to the Court, they were left out of many Court functions. Only a few months before, the New York *Sun* had attacked Mr. Reid furiously, and the Embassy was certain that the whole trouble was because the Consul-General and his wife had not been invited to the King's Garden Party at Windsor. Mr. Reid kept quiet under the attack when the Embassy felt he should have justified himself. For in that particular instance the Lord Chamberlain had especially requested that the Embassy ask for invitations for visiting Americans *only*, thus eliminating all the permanent American Colony in London.

The Consuls were always touchy about their social status, with which actually the Embassy had nothing to do. I dare say the Embassy might have been a bit more tactful, and the

Ambassador could just as well have signed the letters to them if anyone had thought of it, instead of their receiving instructions through 'young puppies at the Embassy.' But the Consular Service seemed to suffer badly from inferiority complex, and the Rogers Act, passed after the War making the two Services interchangeable, was probably at least in part inspired by disgruntled Consuls who wanted their share of the limelight. They succeeded in getting the measure through, but only time will show whether it is an improvement, for the functions of the two Services are so entirely different that a man eminently successful in one might not be equally successful when transferred to the other.

Some years afterwards I was talking over this amalgamation of the two Services with one of the American lawyers in London, who was fierce in his criticism and foretold failure for it on the ground that it was not in accordance with the psychology of nations. It was he who reminded me that one of the men most active in bringing it about was Mr. R. P. Skinner, Consul-General at London during the World War, a splendid man who did fine service and was much liked in that capacity. Indeed, the lawyer thought he would have made a most successful head of a large corporation in the United States. Mr. Skinner went to Washington to help Representative Rogers put through the Rogers Act, and a few years later was appointed Minister to Greece.

The fight for the vote which Englishwomen were making all through those years with a passion that left the men puzzled and hostile became a diplomatic one when some American women joined in the campaign — for they had no votes either. Among these was Miss Alice Paul, of whose activities I had read from time to time — I never met her — with great enthusiasm, for I, too, was a militant. Coming to London she got arrested, was brought before the magistrate charged with throwing a stone through the window of the Guildhall while a political banquet was in progress, and sentenced to a month's imprisonment. In accordance with the tactics of the suffragettes of making the most of every situation and getting as much free advertising for it and the cause as they could — for they had no money to pay for it — Miss Paul at once proclaimed her American citizenship and appealed to Washington for aid, and although the American Government could not intervene officially they instructed the Ambassador to do what he could. Mr. Reid was much annoyed — he didn't like suffragettes — and with his somewhat grudging help the British authorities thankfully released Miss Paul, wanting no American martyrs on their hands. They had enough native ones — some of whom laid down their lives for the cause before it was won. But they insisted that Miss Paul return to the United States without further ado, and she of course was obliged to go.

In his official report to the Secretary of State Mr. Reid showed his bias by stating that Miss Paul had thrown a stone through the window of the Guildhall 'which almost hit the head of the Prime Minister.' I was furious at this 'almost' for how could she know where her stone would land? And to drag in the name of the Prime Minister was, I felt, only for the purpose of making it worse! So I took my courage in hand and went to Mr. Reid and explained my views, asking him to change the despatch. But, after listening with freezing politeness, he rose to his feet, bowed low and dismissed me, with the remark that it would stand exactly as it was, that it was a true statement, and that he hoped Miss Paul would remain in the United States in future!

I had never felt more humiliated in my life, but it was up to me, as a member of the organization, to make the protest, and, after all, the snub I got was very small compared to what my militant comrades were going through. But it was hard *enough*, especially as I knew that the only person at the Embassy who had any sympathy whatever for me was the jolly, somewhat unconventional Mr. Gibson.

WILLIAM PHILLIPS
1912

Mr. Gibson made only a brief stay at the Embassy, which was perhaps just as well, for he and Mr. Reid were too unlike ever to be congenial. Mr. Gibson actually didn't seem to know the difference between a duke and a dustman! He seemed to think they were made of the same flesh and blood! So when Mr. Huntington Wilson, Third Assistant Secretary of State, asked him to be his secretary, he accepted and returned to Washington. He worked very hard for three or four years for Mr. Wilson, reported to be something of a slave-driver, and as a reward was given an 'easy' post, the Secretaryship at Brussels, to which he was appointed in the spring of 1914! A Mr. Fred Morris Dearing was to succeed him, but would not arrive at once. Mr. Gibson told us he was sorry to go, but the American papers announced that he had asked for a transfer.

The engagement of Miss Mildred Carter to Viscount Acheson was announced in London in February, and in writing me from Rumania about the details Mr. Carter told me he had given her his house in Chesham Street. So that's why he couldn't let Mr. Phillips have it! I was relieved, for his refusal with no explanation had seemed so unfriendly. She was to be married in June from Dorchester House, and I knew that meant an Embassy reunion of many old friends. Mr. Phillips was also glad that he would at last have a chance to see Mr. Carter — they had not met since their new appointments — for there were many matters in relation to the Embassy that he was most anxious to discuss with him.

The Ambassador went for a few weeks to Cannes to escape the fogs that were so bad for his asthma, but returned at the end of April because ex-President Roosevelt, on his way home from his hunting trip, was to visit him, and the prospect made Mr. Reid nervous.

While Mr. Reid had been away Mr. Dearing arrived. He seemed friendly and able, but looked shy and rather delicate, and hated draughts as much as a Frenchman. We had little time to do more than welcome him and pass along much work, for the whole Embassy was engaged in arranging for Mr. Roosevelt's entertainment. I wrote letters of polite regrets all day long to people who didn't in the least mind asking for invitations to parties which they seemed to think Mr. and Mrs. Reid would give, and I suppose the Secretaries wrote dozens more. Hundreds of letters had been forwarded to Mr. Roosevelt in Egypt, and we knew he had accepted some invitations, but as we didn't know just what these were we could make no further appointments until he sent on his list. There was a story going the rounds that among these was one from the Pilgrims, signed by Lord Roberts, who always signed himself, 'Roberts, Field Marshal,' and that the reply — in Mr. Roosevelt's own handwriting — came to 'Mr. Roberts, Field Marshal of the Pilgrims.' Surely Mr. Roosevelt knew better than that! Mr. Reid, always the most hospitable host, had also written to know if there was anything special that Mr. Roosevelt wished to do in London, and to his horror he received a reply saying that what the ex-President really wanted to see most of all was a prize-fight!

It was perhaps not to be wondered at that everybody was worried at the coming of this super-'hot potato' and was praying that there might be no 'incident' to mark his visit. The news that he was bringing his Rough Rider outfit scared everybody, for he might want to wear it! The Paris Embassy, always fussing about something, wrote to ask whether he was to be addressed 'Honourable' or 'Colonel,' and were told it must be Mr. or Honourable, but not Colonel. The Bishop of Southwark wanted him to visit the Harvard Chapel, and the City Remembrancer, in charge of the seating of the banquet at the Guildhall where the freedom of the City of London was to be conferred upon him — a very great honour — and overwhelmed with requests from Americans — sent them to the Embassy, and Mr. Dearing was given the thankless task of dividing the sheep from the goats. Poor Mr.

Dearing, so eager, so industrious, and yet so ignorant of London social conditions, had a very difficult time. But he had a gentle humour that made everybody want to help him, and great intelligence, and when his list was completed, it pleased the Ambassador very much.

One of the highlights of Mr. Roosevelt's visit was to have been the dinner given for him by the Ambassador at which the King had promised to be present. But His Majesty's health had been causing anxiety all through the spring, and, although his physicians urged him to do so, he would not relax, but allowed his engagements to pile up as usual. Queen Alexandra was making a visit to Corfu, and one of the first intimations the British public had that anything was wrong was her hurried return — she travelled night and day as soon as she heard that the King was worse — and the fact that he did not meet her at the station as usual. Her son met her instead, and broke the news that the King's life was about over. . . . His death came on May 6 and was so sudden that the people were stunned. They could not believe it. Why, wasn't it only last week that . . . Didn't he go to . . . It was just the other day . . . It can't be true!

On the actual day of his death his horse Witch of the Air won the spring two-year-old plate at Kempton Park. There had been a question as to whether in view of his condition the horse should run, but the King insisted, and as he ran to victory the King's life was ebbing away while the thousands of his subjects, all unaware, were giving him a tremendous ovation.

There was overwhelming grief everywhere, especially as people began to realize that, keeping up a brave face, he had actually worked himself to death. He had been a most popular King, neither too good nor too learned nor too high-and-mighty, with a human side that had made him beloved by all classes. Always a good friend to his people, he had mixed with them freely and fearlessly, and his tastes and theirs had been alike in many ways. He had corresponded with President Roosevelt from time to time, showed great personal friendship to the Ambassador, and always made sure that Americans were treated by the whole Court with generous cordiality. It was not at all certain that this pleasant state of things would continue with the new King, for naturally his own personal likings would enter into some extent, and as Prince of Wales he had not shown any particular enthusiasm for Americans.

As it seemed opportune that Mr. Roosevelt should be in London at this particular moment, the Ambassador enquired what other countries were doing in the way of sending Special Ambassadors to the King's funeral. Then, as no word came from Washington about the appointment of a Special Ambassador, Mr. Reid cabled that France, the other great Republic, was sending a special delegation as well as an Ambassador to the funeral, that no other special delegations were known of except royalty, but, if they thought it proper, the appointment of Mr. Roosevelt would be entirely agreeable to him, and it was believed it would be well received in England. The State Department cabled their willingness and appointed Mr. White to assist him, with the rank of Envoy Extraordinary and Minister Plenipotentiary. A notification that ex-President Roosevelt would attend as Special Ambassador was sent to the Foreign Office and also a copy of a Resolution adopted by the House of Representatives expressing their sorrow. The new King asked Captain Cloman to ride with the Headquarters Staff in the funeral procession, and the State Department instructed the Embassy to send a handsome wreath in the name of the President either through Mr. Reid or Mr. Roosevelt as seemed most appropriate.

The funeral, on May 20, was most impressive. Soon after nine o'clock the King's procession left Buckingham Palace for Westminster Hall, where King Edward's body had lain in state since the day before. The German Emperor and the Duke of Connaught rode beside the King, and behind them came a group of royal personages forming a band of reigning monarchs and princes such as probably had never before been brought together, and whose safety must have been an agonizing responsibility for the police.

Said the London *Times*:

> No King ever started on his last journey with such an escort. By the side of King George rode his cousin the German Emperor, the almost absolute ruler of the most military nation that Europe had ever known. He was followed by the Kings of the Hellenes and of Denmark, King Edward's brother-in-law; by the King of Norway, the late King's son-in-law; by the King of Spain, his nephew by marriage; by the young King of Portugal, a near kinsman . . . by the new King of the Belgians and by the King of Bulgaria. With them came the heir to the Austro-Hungarian Empire, the brother of the Russian Emperor, the heir to the regenerated Throne of Turkey, the heirs of Bavaria, Russia, and other Kingdoms, a Prince of the Imperial House of Japan, another Prince from China, and no fewer than five Princes of that House of Orleans whose names are bound up alike with the history of France and with the personal history of our own Royal Family.

Major George O. Squier, who came later to be Military Attaché, used to tell about it with much dramatic emphasis, for it was always the colourful pageantry of life that interested him.

'Seven Kings all in a row,' he would squeal. 'One-two-three-four-five-six-seven — and, my dear! — at least six Queens too. Seven Kings all riding in a row together and not a single aide anywhere. Seven live Kings, I say — Alfonso of Spain, Victor Emanuel of Italy, Albert of Belgium, What's-his-name from Sweden, Haakon of Norway, Ferdinand of Bulgaria, and of course Kaiser Bill, with his moustache so prettily curled. And not an aide, I tell you. Not one! One little bomb, my dear — and what a change in the map of Europe. Just one little bomb and the whole history of Europe might have been different. Only one . . .' The Major's voice would trail off into silence, as though he were looking long-ingly into a time when such a wholesale holocaust might have stirred up things considerably. I didn't like to tell him he had some of his names wrong, for that might have inter-rupted the flow of his thoughts. And it didn't matter. The idea was the same.

After a moment he would go on again: 'Lines and lines of officers, with stars and orders, every nation. Grandest thing you ever saw. I had on everything but the kitchen stove, but the others were even grander. Horses by the thousand — horses — horses — bands — bands — 'Dead March' in *Saul* once in a while! Carriages — more horses — regiments! And, in the middle, or rather towards the end, of all the glitter of Argentines and Austrians and Belgians and Colom-bians, French and God knows who else — along comes some State carriages, and then an ordinary carriage — an ordinary carriage, mark you — not a Royal one! — and, in it, who do you think? Why, the Honourable Theodore Roosevelt, Spe-cial Ambassador from the United States, with three other old parties. . . .'

The reason why Mr. Roosevelt rode in a carriage instead of on a horse in the London procession was obvious. It was usual for the foreign Representatives to ride, the many dif-ferent uniforms making a most brilliant spectacle. But Mr. Roosevelt was not a military man and had no regular uniform (the Rough Riders outfit did not commend itself either to the Duke of Norfolk or the Ambassador). So, after a good deal of discussion with the French Representative as to the position Republics should occupy in a ceremonial of this kind (the Duke of Norfolk seemingly oblivious that they had any pos-sible claim whatever to anything!), Mr. Roosevelt and Mr. Henry White were put into a carriage with M. Pichon, the French Foreign Minister, who was livid with rage at being put behind members of the ex-Royal Family of France, proudly riding ahead, while he was forced to content himself with such others as had no uniforms or were too aged to sit on a horse. This seemed the only practical thing to do, and both Mr. Roosevelt and the Ambassador were entirely satisfied. But Major Bentley Mott, Military Attaché at Paris and Aide-de-Camp to Mr. Roosevelt, also seemed to feel that something better could have been arranged — or perhaps thought it a good opportunity to remind the War Department that a military officer had better have been chosen! On receipt of Major Mott's report at Washington the Embassy was instructed to get a full statement from the Military Attaché as to *his* views on this seeming international insult.

In due course the State Department received a reply which was cheeky in the extreme from the delighted Captain Cloman, who had been hoping for such a chance. As a military officer he also placed the blame on the State and War Department for not having selected a military officer to be their country's representative. Captain Cloman felt that, until a diplomatic uniform suitable for such occasions could be evolved, the United States Government had better rely on their army and navy to represent them when there was riding to be done. The American silk hat and frock coat did not — in the opinion of Captain Cloman — belong on a horse. He felt that Mr. Roosevelt, 'seated on a fiery steed of unknown temper, clad in those habiliments of democracy, with coat-tails flying, in the centre of a group of mounted army officers, would have been a sight for gods and men, and certainly would not have redounded to the credit of our great American Republic. And what if his hat had blown off? Must he hold it on, or could he have a stout ribbon by which to attach it to his person?' The Captain considered, taking it by and large, that the British Government had done the only thing possible in the circumstances by hiding him from the public gaze; 'and surely if that was an insult, as some critics claim, it was also an insult to the Chinese Minister and Lord Strathcona.'

As a matter of fact — and quite outside of this occasion and the Duke of Norfolk's disregard of the existence of Republics in any social way — the British Government were probably just as glad to have a civilian appointed, for a dispute had raged for many years at London as to the precise position the representatives of the United States should take in processions. The British Government insisted on calling us the 'United States' Embassy,' whereas Mr. John Hay liked it to be called the 'American Embassy,' for that, he claimed, was the historic designation. In official processions, therefore, the representatives of the United States went along with their colleagues from Turkey and Venezuela, whereas they felt they should have been up in front with Austria and Argentina. In reply to unofficial expressions of dissatisfaction from time to time, the Foreign Office used to point out that, if on their way *to* a function they were unfortunately at the end, they were in front on the return journey. After some years, during which neither side budged an inch, the Embassy calling itself the 'American Embassy' and having their stationery so engraved, while the Foreign Office just as positively designated us the 'United States' Embassy,' the matter was taken out of our hands. The State Department began to furnish all the Embassies with letter-paper already engraved — 'Embassy of the United States of America at   ' — leaving only the name of the capital to be filled in.

King Edward's funeral procession was impressively military, to the wrath of the Liberals who said it would not have commended itself to the dead King. But the general public enjoyed it and looked upon it as an emotional spectacle and not a demonstration of military power. I am not emotional, but as I stood on the balcony of Dorchester House and watched them go slowly by, the band playing the 'Dead March' in *Saul*, and the tramp, tramp, tramping swish of the marching feet, I, too, went down into a pit of maudlin desolation, thinking of another King of England who died long ago, and, his loyal followers being unable to find a quiet burial place for him in the midst of wars, carried his body about with them for months — not a very savoury memory.

I had been invited to view the procession from Dorchester House, but, with mistaken conscientiousness, having gone to the Chancery first to see whether there was anything pressing to be done, it got so late that I feared it might be impossible to get across Piccadilly. But, well acquainted with the magic that could be wrought by a diplomatic badge or Note, I took an empty sheet of Embassy paper, put it into one of our best engraved heavily black-bordered envelopes, addressed it to the Ambassador, marked it 'urgent,' and sealed it with a large black seal of the United States. It was an imposing document, and with it in my hand I set forth. Every police-man bowed to the urgency of the communication. Being the property of a foreign Ambassador, he must of course have it at once. Whatever their doubts may have been as to the in-appropriateness of the messenger, I was triumphantly es-corted across Piccadilly by two inspectors, with thousands of people looking on, made my way back of the crowds to Park Lane, and, with the aid of another policeman, crossed Park Lane and into Dorchester House.

We read next day of the committal service at Windsor, the blue-jackets who drew the gun-carriage up the hill, with the Royal mourners and foreign representatives following on foot, and applauded the decision of the Duke of Norfolk, whose delicate task it had been to squeeze all these Personages into the little Saint George's Chapel, to have it a Garter funeral, as the best means of safeguarding the susceptibilities of all. This meant that the Knights of the Garter would take their rightful places in the front seats, Saint George's Chapel being the headquarters of this most illustrious Order of Chiv-alry of which the Monarch was always a member, leaving the others, not members of the Order, to crowd in where they could.

So Edward VII slept with his fathers and George V reigned

in his stead, though he would not be crowned King until the following year. Until then the Court would be in mourning, and there would be little entertaining. For the new Queen Mary thoroughly believed in being in mourning if one was supposed to *be* in mourning, and none of the Royal Family was allowed to go to the theatre. Ascot that year was known as Black Ascot.

French dissatisfaction against their position in the London procession continued to seethe, and they would have liked Mr. Reid to espouse their cause along with his own. It must have been a most difficult question. The Special Ambassadors of Republics could not expect to be put ahead of family, and the ticklish business of how the Ambassador of a Republic ranks with the actual head of a smaller State, who is also a relative, must have been the cause of many headaches for the Court authorities. Although Mr. Reid realized this — and probably Mr. Roosevelt did, too — he was disinclined to let any chance go by that would seem to minimize the importance of the United States, so he cabled to Washington and said he was ready to make an informal protest such as the French were said to be making, and suggested adding that the United States would hesitate to send special representatives on any future occasion unless they could be assured that, with the exception of any Monarchs that might attend, such representatives would be given the same position as the ordinary Embassy (who ranked according to the length of time the Ambassador had been at the Court). The Department replied, with some hesitation, that he could do unofficially as he chose. But Captain Cloman's laughter, his picture of Mr. Roosevelt on a horse clutching his silk hat and trying to keep on the plunging animal were so funny that I think Mr. Reid decided it was better to forget, for there is no record that he ever did anything more. It was just as well that Captain Cloman didn't know that Mr. Reid had suggested Mr. Roosevelt's appointment!

Mr. Roosevelt managed to squeeze in several interesting engagements before he left for home. He went to Oxford to deliver the Romanes Lecture, and to Cambridge. He also made his 'Govern or get out' speech at the Guildhall in which he criticized the British Government for their weak policy in Egypt, and which the London newspapers announced under the heading of 'Roosevelt Tells Us How to Govern Egypt.' But what he said was so forceful and à propos that, although there was some natural criticism on the floor of the House of Commons, it was felt that what he said was true. Several members of the British Government had been consulted beforehand, and had assured him of their appreciation, and even Sir Edward Grey had been given a hint, so it was said.

A few days later Mr. Roosevelt joined Sir Edward in a walk through the New Forest to Southampton, where, being both nature-lovers, they enjoyed the satisfying experience of getting acquainted with the birds and flowers, and renewing their friendship. After he went Mr. Roosevelt sent me an autographed copy of his 'Strenuous Life,' which naturally I was delighted to have.

Miss Mildred Carter's wedding at Saint George's Church, Hanover Square, that summer was as brilliant as it could be with the Court in Mourning. Mr. and Mrs. Carter came from Rumania, there was a large gathering of ex-diplomats and many old friends at Dorchester House, which Mr. and Mrs. Reid had lent for the wedding. My old diary describes it:

> The church was packed so full that some people did not get in at all, and the aisles were filled with late comers. Among the ushers were Mr. Ogden Reid and Mr. Grant-Smith. The music was lovely, as in addition to the choir of Saint George's, the Children of the Chapel Royal, as the choir of the Chapel is called, also sang, and looked most picturesque in their long red coats. Mr. Carter was very pale and ill, and was just prevented in time from walking up the church on the wrong side of the bride, and during the whole service seemed very broken up.

Mr. and Mrs. Carter afterwards received the guests at the head of the grand staircase, while the bride and bridegroom met their friends in the library.

I wore a purple chiffon dress, which sounds almost funereal, but wasn't, and drove back from the church with 'Bunny' Carter, who had somehow either got overlooked when the principal guests left or had waited until the end to make sure that everyone was provided for.

I had been worried as to whether I ought to wear black and finally wrote to Mr. Carter to make sure.

> On no account should you wear a black frock [he replied]. In the first place, one is dispensed from mourning on a wedding day and in the second, the wearing of black (by the order of the Court) is to be discontinued by the public after the 17th of June and restricted to those only who are about the Court. It is the worst possible luck to wear black at a wedding....

There was one bright spot about the King's death. It automatically ended the Courts and Levees until just before the Coronation of George V.

Mr. Orr's successor, Mr. Sheldon Crosby — I wondered idly if all these new men had taken examinations — arrived in time for the King's funeral and the Carter wedding. He was a broad young man, extremely friendly, but very conscious of himself and his beautiful clothes and nails, and a rather chubby person. 'Chuffy' — the nickname he had seemingly always had — was casual and did not take his work too seriously in those days when he was very young. Who could have guessed that he would blossom into a serious diplomat? He parted his blond bushy hair in the middle, was slightly Oscar Wildeish in appearance, and had long curling lashes. He soon had lots of friends, but oddly enough always seemed lonely to me. He used to twirl his moustache to show off those beautiful hands, and romance was always subtly lurking in the offing.

It seemed to be up to me to keep a maternal eye upon him, so when one day, coming quickly out of my room, I saw him on his way to the front door with a handsome bunch of flowers in his hand, turn tail and hurry back into Frank's office when he saw me, I followed.

'Lovely flowers,' I said.

'Yes,' he said, glaring at Frank, who giggled from the other side of the desk.

'Who are they for?' I asked in my best schoolmarm manner.

He made no reply, so I fixed my eye on Frank until, unable to resist the pressure, he informed me that the manicure lady had given 'Chuffy' such a marvellous manicure that he felt that nothing less than a bunch of flowers could convey his appreciation — and was just about to take them to her in person.

'Better give them to me,' I said. He handed them over most grudgingly. I turned over the card attached. It was his official card. 'And it is not wise to attach your Embassy card,' I went on solemnly.

He sighed gently. 'All right, Grandma,' he said.

After the excitements of the summer were over, Mr. Phillips parted with his appendix, and feeling the need of rest, went home on leave with Mrs. Phillips, telling me in his good-bye note from the ship to 'Please keep Mr. Dearing in order and don't be too hard on the Ambassador.' I had arranged to go for my holiday, too, but the Ambassador asked me to postpone it because, 'the other secretaries are so inexperienced!' I would have gone without a holiday forever for that! Mr. Reid could be a subtle flatterer when it suited him!

Almost at once I began dutifully writing to Mr. Phillips as I had to Mr. Carter when he was Councillor. One of the first bits of news I had to give him was that Mr. Dearing had been ordered back to Washington *en route* for Mexico, and how sorry we were to lose him — especially me, as his taste in literature and poetry and his way of sizing-up a situation and making it very broad and all-inclusive interested me — and that he had actually sailed within a few days, leaving only Mr. Crosby to keep things going. I also said we had heard by way of the diplomatic grapevine that he was moved because it was considered a waste of time to keep in London a man who understood Spanish. It reminded me of my early days when, in filling up questionnaires for the State Department, no one ever admitted that he knew Spanish.

We heard that in Mr. Dearing's place a Mr. Leland Harrison, then in the Legation at Peking, was coming. Mr. Phillips wrote that Mr. Harrison was experienced and very nice and that he knew we should like him, so that was reassuring, although I was sure that no newcomer could ever be as pleasant as Mr. Dearing. Mr. Crosby, however, on learning that Mr. Harrison had polo ponies and other evidences of wealth, and that he would probably take a house near to the Ambassadors, was quite spiteful. 'I expect His Excellency is simply counting the days until he comes,' he snarled. 'And what does he want with a house, and him a bachelor?'

The last chapter in the long Newfoundland Fisheries quarrel now being arbitrated at The Hague was actually in sight. The amount of interchange of documents and information was almost overpowering, and even after the American Counsel reached The Hague they kept sending for more.

On September 7 the long-awaited decision was reached, carefully framed, it seemed, to recognize merit in the contention of both sides. Thus was another cause of bad blood eliminated. It was the end of a long story, during which we had become very familiar with the habits and ways of the cod. It was a relief to have it over, but what possible use was all this knowledge of codfish now?

16

The Coronation of King George V. American participation, with Mr. John Hays Hammond as Special Ambassador. The Naval Review. Mr. Huntington Wilson's visit to Constantinople. Mr. Carter is appointed Ambassador to the Argentine, and is then dropped from the Service.

1911

T HE entire spring of 1911 was one chapter of toil and turmoil with our small American part of the preparations for the Coronation of King George V. By the middle of January applications had begun to pour in from America from many who wished to be 'added to the Embassy list,' the usual formula. These applications must be disposed of if the Embassy were not to be entirely swamped later on, so, to give him something definite to say, Mr. Phillips asked the Earl Marshal what space would be available to Americans in the Abbey or in the official stands. He was informed that 'invitations to foreigners would be limited to those who compose the various official delegations, with the exception of such few individuals as the King himself may desire to have invited.' Thus were the hopes of many blighted.

'Already people are applying for seats for the Coronation and for the Courts,' I wrote Mr. Choate in February, 'and it looks like being a record season. There are to be no Courts before the Court Mourning ends in May, but four will be squeezed in between then and the twenty-second when the Coronation takes place. Luckily the presentations made to the late King hold good, so the Embassy won't have to represent everybody.'

It was lucky that the Court mourning gave time for the innumerable arrangements that had to be made for the Coronation. These changed from day to day, and sometimes, when I was tired of going over our lists, sympathizing with those who wanted to get in and couldn't and still more with those who had to disappoint them, I would try to visualize the tremendous amount of work and responsibility that lay behind a Coronation; the processions of people coming from the ends of the earth, not only English of all degrees, Canadians, Australians, South Africans, Indians, British diplomatists recalled to 'kiss hands,' but no foreign sovereigns.

And yet this seeming impossibility was entirely possible to the experienced Court officials and Foreign Office, who could straighten out any tangle, and apparently, if called upon, arrange a Court pageant to include the whole world without having the slightest detail go wrong, or anyone be left out. How the officials kept their courtesy, tact, and decision in the face of conflicting opinions and demands was amazing. It didn't matter how many things went wrong, how many changes of plans there were, they were always apparently unemotional, almost casual and blandly polite. To the most preposterous enquiries they returned brief notes that settled the question, if not amicably, at least politely and implacably. They never took the slightest chance of an ambiguous sentence, nor of having a word misunderstood.

Perhaps there were mistakes behind the scenes, little things may have been overlooked. Almost every day, as the climax approached, some new detail was decided on. Our correspondence with the various Court officials was a perfect maze, and the Foreign Office, who usually expected to conduct, or at least to be advised, of all correspondence between an Embassy and other departments of the British Government, soon gave up the struggle and we corresponded direct, for even the omnipotent Foreign Secretary couldn't keep his august finger on every pulse!

As early as February the appointment of Mr. John Hays Hammond as Special Ambassador for the Coronation was announced at Washington. A week or two before, when the Embassy was asked to enquire whether Mr. Hammond's appointment would be acceptable, there was a moment of consternation, for no one had forgotten Mr. Hammond's connection with the Jameson Raid and the Boer War, and the events connected with his imprisonment in South Africa. It really seemed to the Embassy that almost anyone else would have been a more tactful choice. But the British Government accepted Mr. Hammond's appointment cordially and he at once leased 1 Stratton Street, Piccadilly, for the entire season. Therefore, when the Master of the Ceremonies, who had to find lodgings for all the Special Ambassadors and delegations, wrote to know whether Mr. Hammond had made arrangements for his stay in London or whether the British Government should take care of him, Mr. Phillips replied that the Stratton Street house had been leased and Mr. Hammond would need no accommodation provided for him.

The Court officials, therefore, assuming everything was settled, proceeded to arrange matters on that basis. It developed, however, that there was some misunderstanding about the house on the part of the State Department. Mr. Chandler Hale, Third Assistant Secretary of State, had informed Mr. Hammond that the British Government would provide him with quarters during the time he was their guest. Mr. Hammond cabled this to Mr. Phillips, saying that he would just as soon be at Stratton Street, but would do whatever the Embassy thought was proper. Mr. Phillips then cabled Mr. Hale that the British Government had not supplied a special residence, as they understood Mr. Hammond had provided for himself; that in any case Mr. Hammond's British and American staff would be the guests of the British

Government, with one exception; that if possible they would like Mr. Hammond to put up one of them, or, if he could not, to provide a staff waiting room.

Still Mr. Hale was not satisfied. He was insistent that the British Government entertain Mr. Hammond during the actual days of the festivities. Was he afraid that some precedent was about to be violated? Was the British Government trying to get out of something it owed the United States? The Stratton Street house looked out on Piccadilly along which the Royal Procession was to pass. Mr. Hammond, knowing this, had taken it for the season, and why should he move out for a few days and live somewhere else to satisfy the State Department?

To clear up the mess Mr. Phillips cabled Mr. Hammond again *via* Mr. Hale to reassure him that he was not being slighted, and that a residence would have been provided as a matter of course had it been necessary. Mr. Phillips also informed Mr. Hammond (and Mr. Hale) that Mr. Reid had made a similar arrangement at the Jubilee and at the last Coronation when he was Special Ambassador. To change the subject, Mr. Phillips asked for the names and ranks of the American members of the staff, and the State Department, thankfully grasping at the chance of dropping the matter of the house, stated that Mr. Hammond would be assisted in England by Major-General Adolphus W. Greely, U.S.A., representing the War Department, and Rear-Admiral Charles E. Vreeland, U.S.N., representing the Navy Department, and that Mr. William Earle Dodge, a private citizen, would act as Secretary of the Special Embassy.

The limited space set aside for American newspaper correspondents caused almost a riot among them. There had been forebodings of trouble all the spring, so when the Foreign Office informed the Embassy that only four seats would be allotted to United States correspondents on Coronation Day and two for the procession through London on the following day, we knew there would be dissatisfaction. The Ambassador, perhaps unwisely, himself decided that the Associated Press and Laffans Service should have two of the seats, and that the others could be arranged among the men themselves. Mr. Phillips wrote them this, and instantly the United Press protested and declined to participate, saying they were entitled to equal treatment with the Associated Press and Laffans because they served more papers. Most of the other correspondents also came to the Embassy and stated their views at considerable length, emphasizing their personal claims, but the United Press went them one better. They complained to Washington with such effect that the State Department categorically instructed the Embassy to get a ticket for the United Press representative. The Embassy, therefore, got the ticket after an acrimonious exchange with the authorities and the other newspaper men, and the entire correspondence was sent to Washington for their information. How the whole newspaper question was finally solved I don't remember, but just about that time the Society of American Correspondents in London was formed, and in notifying the Embassy of its inauguration the Secretary requested that all future communications affecting the collective interests of American correspondents in London be addressed to him. I have an impression that they probably resented Mr. Reid's interference now that he was no longer an editor.

Late in April the Foreign Office informed the Embassy that black knee-breeches, black silk stockings, and pumps would be required by the Foreign Envoys and their suites attending the Coronation Ceremonies; later another notification said that the King wished all foreign Representatives attending the Coronation to arrive on the nineteenth of June in plain clothes; and again, still later, another note stated that it had been decided that members of His Majesty's Household and British officials would not leave cards on foreign Princes and Representatives and consequently they would not be expected to leave cards on any member of His Majesty's Household or British officials. It was carefully explained that this procedure was adopted solely with a desire to relieve members of foreign suites from a formality which took up considerable time and caused much trouble.

Americans had begun to arrive early to make sure of not missing anything, and many were presented at the four Courts in May. The last Levee took place on the twenty-ninth. Mr. J. P. Morgan was presented in the Diplomatic Circle, and Mr. William Forbes Morgan, Mr. Albert Cook Myers, and Mr. Edward Bringhurst in the General Circle. Mr. Myers, as I remember, being a Quaker, refused to wear a sword, part of the regulation Levee dress, so was given permission to omit that ornamental fixture. Mr. Phillips assured him that no damage could possibly be done with it, but as it was symbolic he refused to wear it.

On May 19 the Foreign Office informed the Embassy that seats to view the Coronation Procession had been reserved on a stand in Parliament Square for members of the Corps Diplomatiques who had not received invitations to the Abbey. The same day came another note saying that seats had been reserved on a stand in Parliament Square for members of the Special Embassy to view the procession of the day *after* the Coronation. But everybody preferred to view it from Mr. Hammond's house in Piccadilly, he having cordially invited the whole Embassy to come there.

Next came fifty tickets for the State Service at Saint Paul's Cathedral, distributed somehow with much heart-burning and many critical remarks.

Decorations came next! Mr. Hammond cabled he had arranged to have his house decorated, so the Embassy cabled for a special grant for the Chancery, and the State Department appropriated one thousand dollars. Mr. Reid looked after the decoration of Dorchester House.

Now came an invitation from the Admiralty to the members

of the Corps Diplomatiques and their wives to witness the Naval Review to be held at Spithead on June 24 and asking for the names of those who wished to go. Special trains, they said, would leave Waterloo Station early in the morning for Southampton, where the guests would embark on a vessel which would convey them round the Fleet and take up a station from which the Review could be seen. Everybody accepted, but at the last moment deserted and spent the day on the U.S.S. *Delaware*, the American ship sent to take part in the Review.

Towards the end of May came a most impressive, though unofficial, document informing us that a hundred American business men were coming to London to see some of the English manufacturing establishments under the auspices of the Boston Chamber of Commerce. As they proposed to arrive actually in Coronation Week, the Embassy cabled them to postpone their visit because nothing could be done for them then. But they came, nevertheless, 'manufacturing establishments' being probably another name for the Coronation.

June came all too soon. Mr. and Mrs. Hammond and their suite arrived on June 19 — Mr. Hammond in plain clothes as instructed — and were met by the Duke of Connaught at the station. Even the smallest detail of that seemingly unimportant event had all been arranged, for two weeks earlier Major Crichton of the Lord Chamberlain's office had told the Embassy that Mrs. Hammond might, if she cared to, accompany Mr. Hammond in the Royal carriage on his arrival, but should not do so on Coronation Day, and that she would receive an invitation, with Mr. Hammond, to the State Banquet. We were also informed that Mr. Hammond's British staff would be Lord Sandhurst, Colonel B. R. James and Captain Sowerby.

On June 20, Mr. Hammond was received by the King and on the following day by Sir Edward Grey. The night before, he attended a Royal dinner at Buckingham Palace, called a 'family affair,' at which the heads of missions were present, to the number of eighty-seven, the smaller fry coming in afterwards to be introduced.

By this time the Embassy had begun to receive many gifts which Americans — strangers to him — had sent for the King, and there was the usual advance notice of the coming of various people to tender poems, flowers, addresses, and what not. One gentleman from Atlantic City led the procession with a gift of Irish point lace, while another patriot living in London wrote to the Office of Works for permission to erect the Stars and Stripes on the American group of statuary on the Albert Memorial, saying that in previous years he had had permission to decorate it with flowers. The harassed Office of Works sent the letter to the Embassy with a note saying that, while they discouraged the decoration of statues as a rule, the possibility of putting a flagstaff on a group of statuary seemed to them grotesque and could not be permitted, and, please, if the gentleman wrote to the Embassy, would they kindly let him know how the Office of Works felt about it? Luckily the gentleman never wrote!

I can never forget that Coronation morning. I reached London many hours after the twelve thousand police and sixty thousand soldiers from every part of the Empire under the command of Lord Kitchener had taken up their stands along the line of march. That had been at daybreak, about three o'clock. Now it was after nine, a sunshiny day of summer, magical, gay. As I walked along Piccadilly hundreds of people were sitting along the edge of the curb, everyone happy and excited, while hundreds and thousands more were standing behind them. Many had been there all night. It was a bit vulgar, occasionally, bless their Cockney hearts, the coster girls, and the men who put an arm round your waist as you went by and then apologized profusely: 'Beg your parding, I'm sure. Only a Haccident.' Hawkers went up and down selling balloons and occasionally sold boxes on which those at the back could stand. As soon as the deal was completed, they hurried away, for when the policeman appeared they knew he would order the box removed as a public danger. No one seemed tired, for the hours of waiting were part of the fun and there would never be a Coronation again in their time! How often I had stood among them on other occasions, or sat on the edge of the pavement until it was almost time for Whoever it Was to come along. The police were always friendly and dogs trotted up and down and lone soldiers galloped back and forth on mysterious errands and bands played. As I passed I heard a man say of George V: 'Yus, 'e's a good man, so I've always 'eard. But 'e'll never be like 'is father. Now 'e was a card if ever there was one. They say he was 'ard to please, touchy and a mite too fond of the ladies. But 'e was a real King.... *This* man? Oh, there'll be no trouble about 'im. 'E's a fine man and a good man too. Ain't it funny that we don't like the good men quite as much as we do the larky ones? But we don't.'

I wasn't one of them this time. I was a guest of the Special American Ambassador. The sun poured in as we sat at Mr. Hammond's window, and I occasionally turned my head to watch Miss Lillian Woodward, Mrs. Hammond's secretary, a very beautiful woman, who had been in London with the Clomans and was now acting as hostess in Mrs. Hammond's absence at the Abbey.

The people who had been invited to the Abbey had been told to be there at eight o'clock — 'and die of starvation before it is over' — commented Mr. Harrison bitterly. Among these were the Ambassador and Mrs. Reid, Mr. and Mrs. Phillips, the Naval and Military Attachés and their wives, Mrs. J. H. Hammond and Mr. Harrison, all in Court dress. Only Mr. Hammond would drive in the Coronation Procession.

The morning drew on as we watched the crowds, until after about three hours had crawled slowly by there came a hush in the streets. Church bells began to peal, the police waved their hands, women and children stood up from the curb, and men took off their hats, as far down the empty road the first soldiers of the procession could be seen coming along on their superb horses, prancing, glorious. Then came more and more, famous regiments with their colours, every man in perfect uniform on a perfect horse clanking by, each seeming to grow more splendid until there burst upon us the Royal glass coach with its eight cream ponies and postillions in their scarlet coats. Inside the King and Queen could be seen, both bowing graciously from side to side, acknowledging the delirious cheers and shouts, while the band close by blared 'God Save the King' as they passed slowly by. Then came other Royalties, Military Attachés of foreign Embassies in their varied uniforms, the German in cream and gold far outshining all the rest, and then more soldiers and sailors, a perfect sea of glittering swords, helmets, medals and decorations made even more striking by contrast with the soberer blue and white of the Navy. Among the carriages was the one containing Mr. Hammond, and as he passed his house he leaned far out and waved his hat to his guests.

While the great pageant went on in the Abbey and we waited for the procession to return, we had lunch, and I spent some time in a secluded nook with Mr. Carter — who was staying with the Ambassador and Mrs. Reid — talking about all the happenings. It was grand to see him and to have time to chat without interruption. He told me about Lady Acheson's baby and his pride in being a grandfather, of things in Bucharest and in Constantinople, where he had been sent on Special Mission, and of his hopes that he would be promoted soon to a capital where his years of diplomatic experience would count.

I was very sympathetic and happy to be with him, but all the time I thought of the hints I had gathered at the Embassy, that there would be no promotion for him such as he deserved.

But there was nothing I could do, not even to tell him what I suspected. I hoped it might prove to be only gossip. So I gave him all the bits of news, and hoped that when he got to Washington, where he expected to go later in the year, he might find that a change of heart had preceded him.

After the procession had passed by again on its way back to Buckingham Palace, I took the train to Portsmouth to see the Illumination of the Fleet that was to take place that evening prior to the Naval Review of the following day, when I was to join the party on the *Delaware*. Eighteen foreign warships were to be there, in addition to the most formidable gathering of the British Fleet that had ever been seen.

That evening we walked along Southsea Front, my cousin and I. It was one of those raw, rainy evenings that send a chill through the bones of people who are foolish enough to imagine the season for thin clothes has come. We stared out at sea, but there was not a single sign of life or light anywhere except an occasional tiny flare as though someone hidden behind the night had lighted a match. It began to rain hard, but, defiant of such minor discomforts, we waited patiently. On the stroke of 9.30 a gun was fired, and at the same instant a long line of golden ships on a black background came flashing into life, stretching for miles down the Solent, all with their prows pointed the same way, at the same angle, and at equal distances apart — like a line of automobiles parked with the right front wheel to the curb. A continuous stream of rockets began to go up from the ships and similar ones from the shore. Searchlights played up and down illuminating the scene for miles, and the streams of different coloured rain from the rockets fell over the ocean in fairy cascades. I had never seen anything more splendid or awe-inspiring. The sheer contrasts of light and darkness were so daring, and the long line of mysterious golden monsters coming up the horizon proclaimed most appropriately the Coronation of a Sea Emperor.

The next morning I got to the beach early, for we were to be ready to go to the *Delaware* by half-past ten. It was not, however, until 11.30 that the special train on which the rest of the Embassy travelled from London arrived. Immediately thereafter we went aboard a small dinghy and set forth upon the choppy waters of the Solent to reach the American ship some distance down the line. The water slopped right over the side of the boat occasionally, and I heard a few suppressed groans. Owing to the swell we could not even use the *Delaware's* ladder, so the two ships were put end to end, and as our little cockleshell was much lower in the water than the battleship, a ladder was suspended across and we climbed the ladder as best we could. It would have been impossible had not several of the sailors passed us from one to the other, and finally hauled us aboard with our skirts disarranged, our dignity gone, and our hair 'all to pieces.'

The Captain met us cordially and gave us the use of the officers' cabins, and after lunch — during which Mr. Blake gave an exhibition of agility in handing a cup of soup safely over several heads for a special friend of his — we were escorted over the ship. That over, we returned to the deck to hear the Captain's instructions. The principal item seemed to be that when the order to 'man ship' was given everybody not in uniform must be below and stay there until released. So we were bundled down and took up our places at the various portholes from which a good view could be had without being seen. By this time the visitors had reached all the ships, and the coming and going of small skiffs was over. Guns began to fire, and there was the excitement of impending events. Down the empty stretch of water towards us came the beflagged Royal Yacht *Victoria and Albert*, with the King standing on the bridge. Queen Mary was not in sight. She was not a good sailor and the day was very rough. As the yacht passed each ship with its yards manned and its flags flying, we could hear various renderings of the National

Anthem. As it came alongside the *Delaware*, we heard the order barked above to stand at attention, the ship's band played 'God Save the King,' the guns fired a salute, and everyone gave three cheers. The yacht passed on down the line, the music growing fainter and fainter. Then it began to grow louder as the yacht turned to come back again. After it had passed once, we had seen the whole show, so when it had gone by three times we were more than ready to go ashore. But there we had to remain, while flags waved, guns fired, and bands played again and again, until we were thoroughly tired out. The end of the Review was announced by a simultaneous salvo from the guns of every ship all together — a most alarming and ear-splitting racket — and then we were at liberty to board the dinghy bobbing up and down in the water alongside and return to London feeling that the King was now properly installed.

I had my share of attention from one of the ensigns who was my devoted attendant most of the day and on leaving tenderly tied round my arm a band with the name of the ship embroidered on it. We promised to correspond always, but, alas, I have long since forgotten his name.

Almost immediately after the Coronation came the Agadir crisis when Germany sent the *Panther* to Morocco, another warning to the English people that Germany was getting ready to challenge their naval supremacy by securing a foothold on the Mediterranean. For once, however, the British Government was awake, and the German ship was withdrawn. But those incidents did not make for peaceful relations!

By August the festivities were over. Mr. Phillips went to Switzerland and Mr. and Mrs. Hammond returned to America.

Mr. and Mrs. Choate sent me an invitation to their Golden Wedding on the sixteenth of October at Stockbridge, Massachusetts. How I wished I could go and see America! However, it was very pleasant to be remembered, and we sent them an appropriate cable wishing them continued joy and happiness.

During the late summer Mr. Carter, who had been unofficially notified that he was to be appointed Ambassador to the Argentine, and aware that Buenos Aires was considered one of the most expensive of all posts, paid a visit to South America to see whether he could afford to accept. He soon discovered that it was out of the question. But without waiting for his decision the State Department announced the appointment, and in declining it — for financial reasons alone — he was dropped. I was full of sympathy for him, for he had been in the Diplomatic Service all his life.

His friends were furious, particularly Mr. J. P. Morgan, a gentleman of decided likes and dislikes, who, living in London so much, understood better than most the worth of Mr. Carter's work. So, although the American Government did not care to retain his services, Mr. Morgan was not slow to take advantage of them. For many years he had tried to tempt Mr. Carter to leave the Service, and this was his chance! Soon Mr. Carter found himself transferred to the field of international banking, with greatly augmented income, permanence in office, and all the things the lack of which in the Foreign Service made it so unsatisfactory as a career.

I can't seem to remember just when the flesh was put on to the skeleton about Mr. Huntington Wilson's visit to the Carters in Constantinople, which was reported to have played its part in Mr. Carter's leaving the Service. But when the unofficial side of this visit came to light, it seemed to explain much.

Poor Mr. Carter! Sorry as I was I couldn't help laughing, for I could just imagine how he had suffered, with his exquisite feeling for diplomatic etiquette, his knowledge of social usage and all the rest of it, when he found that he was probably sent from Bucharest to Constantinople to be host to Mr. Huntington Wilson when that gentleman, as Assistant Secretary of State, made an official visit to the Sultan.

The Sultan, it seemed, had invited representatives of many nations — including the United States — to visit him for two days, and in turn the others had come, stayed at the Palace, been fêted, and gone. For some reason best known to himself Mr. Wilson preferred not to stay with the Sultan, but at the Embassy, and this came as a great and not altogether pleasant surprise to the Carters. It may be that they — Mrs. Wilson was with her husband — wanted to stay longer, or that they didn't like to be visiting a foreign sovereign, for they were somewhat inexperienced in the etiquette of Courts. Whatever the reason, they with their suite arrived at the Embassy — and stayed two weeks. Mr. and Mrs. Carter had to turn out of their rooms and sleep in the attic so that the Wilsons should receive the consideration due to their exalted rank, give dinners and receptions to do them honour and take them to see the sights. Everyone liked Mrs. Wilson, a charming little lady much younger than her husband, who was in a state of happy adoration of him every minute of the day, boasted of getting up in the night to commit to paper the pearls of wisdom which fell from his lips, and had the general attitude of expecting everybody else to be silent when he gave signs of speaking.

To make the Embassy more habitable, Mrs. Carter had enlivened the drawing-rooms with many photographs brought from Bucharest. Mr. Theodore Roosevelt graced the piano; Mr. John Hay, Mr. Choate, Lord Lansdowne, King Edward VII, Queen Alexandra, and many others were scattered about. It was a most interesting collection — though to Mr. Wilson's suspicious eye there was a curious omission, that of the present President, Mr. Taft. This annoyed Mr. Wilson, and Mr. Carter's explanation that none had been sent only seemed to add a sinister note. Perhaps this man, acting temporarily as American Ambassador at Constantinople, wasn't so much in touch with things in the United States as an Ambassador should be! Even the President didn't seem to know him well!

That something unfriendly was afoot was obvious to the Carters and disturbed them, for this man had power over their future. Mr. Wilson's suite were friendly but wooden-faced, Mrs. Carter rode in a hired fiacre for the entire two weeks because the Wilsons had her carriage, and Mr. Carter was worried as to what would be the outcome of his work on the Chester Concession, to arrange which he had ostensibly come from Bucharest.

At the official banquet given by the Sultan, Mr. Wilson sat on the right hand of His Majesty, with Mr. Carter on the left. Everyone knew that the Sultan was practically an idiot, his brain gone, but in spite of that Mr. Wilson intended to make the speech on which he had been faithfully working ever since his arrival at Constantinople. (Had he, too, like Mark Twain, sold it to the American press?) When the proper moment came he stood up and spoke most eloquently. It was a happy speech, full of friendly words to the Turkish Empire. Everybody listened with interest except the Sultan, who knew no English and didn't bother to have it translated as it went along. Indeed, he acted very bored. Finally it came to an end. His Majesty took his eyes from the ceiling, coughed, and, turning to an official sitting opposite at the table, rapped out a quick word.

Without a moment's hesitation this gentleman rose to his feet and made an even more felicitous address, saying that His Majesty the Sultan was much honoured by the presence at his Capital of the distinguished Mr. Wilson from the United States; that he was much moved by this demonstration of amity; that he had nothing but love and friendship for the great country across the sea which had sent him; and more in the same general strain. That finished, Mr. Carter made a brief address, for Mr. Wilson's benefit as the Sultan wouldn't know what he said anyhow, emphasizing the fact that he was a hundred per cent American with hardly an outside thought from the furthering of American interests abroad, and resumed his seat.

Curious to know what it was that the Sultan had said to the man opposite which had had such a dynamic effect, and happening to run into Sir Gerald Lowther, British Ambassador, a few days later, he enquired:

'What was it the Sultan said to the man opposite — the one who made that excellent speech?'

'Oh,' said Sir Gerald, 'all he said was, "Say something to that feller," and then, when you finished, "Now say something to the other feller." Good little speaker, that interpreter.'

Then followed other dinners, and a reception for the missionaries, everything done graciously and efficiently, for Mrs. Carter was an experienced hostess. Mr. Carter, anxious to return to Bucharest as soon as Mr. W. W. Rockhill, the new Ambassador to Turkey, should arrive to relieve him, wondered where the money was coming from to pay the bills.

But his fears about money were groundless, for upon his return to Washington Mr. Wilson sent a generous cheque to cover the expenses of his visit, and a friendly and appreciative note. But from the Carters' point of view the visit had not been an unqualified success, and they returned to Bucharest not very happy about it.

While all this was happening in Europe, President Taft had been working on his idea of an Anglo-American treaty of arbitration to dispose of all outstanding grievances, and so lay a foundation for better co-operation in the future, a possibility that was hailed with the greatest enthusiasm in England. It seemed to the Embassy that every organization interested in peace, every church, every lodge, and thousands of individuals sent letters and resolutions expressing their gratification that arbitration might now be possible as an alternative to force. Every effort was also made by the British Government to meet the views of the United States, even to modifying the Anglo-Japanese Treaty. The new Arbitration

Treaty was published in Washington in August, but, to the disappointment of millions of peace-loving enthusiasts on both sides of the Atlantic, it came to nothing, for it was vetoed by the Senate.

17

The sinking of the Titanic. *The brilliant social season of 1912.*
Mr. Phillips leaves the Embassy. Mr. Irwin Laughlin. The
death of Ambassador Reid and the ceremonies following it.

T HE Ambassador and Mrs. Reid spent part of the winter in
New York as usual, returning towards the end of February,
bringing with them another new Secretary, Mr. Stedman
Hanks, to take the place of Mr. Elliot Bacon who had resigned. We noticed a great change in the Ambassador. He
seemed frailer than ever. He and Mrs. Reid had entertained
the Duke and Duchess of Connaught in New York and it must
have been a responsibility as well as a pleasure to have a man
who was both Governor-General of Canada and a member of
the Royal Family to protect. The English papers had had
much to say about this international visit across the border,
and were extremely friendly, all except one. The articles in the
latter were so disagreeable that we could only assume that
its correspondent had been left out of something, or perhaps
the editor had been omitted sometime from some function.

Mr. Hanks was very young, the youngest man we had ever
had at the Embassy, only twenty-two in fact, a Harvard
graduate of the class of 1912, tall and thin, blond, disarmingly
friendly and unsophisticated, with no understanding of the
grave responsibilities which pertain to being part of an Ambassador's staff. But though uninformed he was not bashful;
rather like a streak of sunshine indeed, breaking upon our

dignified solemnity. Our gods were not his gods and apparently he had no great respect for ours. He thought the Embassy took itself most seriously considering how unnecessary it was in the up-to-date business world of 1912, and the shoes he wore outraged the sensitive soul of Mr. Cresson, another new Second Secretary, and a much older man.

He and Mr. Reid, however, got along famously, and to have such a young man around worshipping him must have made the Ambassador's days very pleasant. His eagerness to be useful was infectious, though occasionally misplaced, and his *faux pas* and extreme ignorance amused Mr. Reid. Mr. Cresson, and such others as must always try to educate the young, took him in hand, and he received his education with just as much zest as he did everything else, fighting every inch of the way! But everything Mr. Reid did or said was perfect in his eyes, and I used to call him the Child Samuel — with his 'Speak, Lord, for thy servant heareth' attitude.

Mr. Reid was critical and irascible when his health was poor, but underneath there must have been a large vein of sweetness which Mr. Hanks tapped. For his own good, however, Mr. Reid often got his young Secretary into trouble. There was the time that Mr. Hanks received an invitation from the French Embassy to a dinner party. He proudly showed it to everybody, but his ardour was considerably dampened when he was told the answer must go in French. As Mr. Hanks's French was not such as would pass muster from one Embassy to another, the whole staff took turns in helping him, and consequently the acceptance that reached the French Embassy was so flawless that, believing him to be a first-rate French scholar, they put him between two French ladies, neither of whom could speak a word of English! He reported next day that they all had a perfectly *lovely* time, they chatting volubly in French and he in English!

Mr. Hanks was so thoroughly scared on the day when he was to be presented at Court that Mr. Reid, in pity, took him with him into the special entrance reserved for Ambassadors. But the haughty guards with long staves who escort Ambassadors into the Throne Room had no intention of acting as escort to such as he, so one of them gave him a poke with his stave to separate him from the Ambassador, and while Mr. Reid went forward properly escorted he slunk in behind — a long way behind. It was at that Court, I think, that Mr. Reid had such a difficult time with the long silk stockings he wore with his knee breeches. They couldn't be found anywhere, and it was finally necessary to strip the stockings from one of the footmen so that His Excellency could attend the Court.

Mr. Hanks was always rushing in to tell Mr. Phillips of discoveries he had made which astonished him more than they did anybody else. When he was staying with Lord and Lady Acton, he said that he heard one of the German guests say openly that Germany intended to blow up all Europe in five years. 'Aren't you going to do something about it?' he asked Mr. Phillips, wide-eyed. Mr. Phillips asked what he would suggest. He had nothing to suggest, but kept on repeating his alarm that they might have meant it, although no one else seemed to think it was anything more than a conversational pleasantry or a bit of boasting, apparently not even Lord and Lady Acton, whose son was among the first casualties of August 1914.

It was at Ascot that Mr. Hanks put his foot in the way of Royalty. Walking across the Royal Enclosure he came upon Mrs. Reid chatting with Mrs. Symington. Trying to be useful again (no one having told him Mr. Hodson's famous 'proffered services stink!') he rushed over to a chair near-by, casually tossed the cloak that was on it to the ground and brought it triumphantly back for Mrs. Reid to sit on. But it happened to be the chair belonging to the lady who was being escorted by the King of Portugal, and His Majesty, returning just then, was most irate, and even inclined to be abusive. Mrs. Reid and Mrs. Symington melted away, and the Boston papers came out later with a story, 'Young Stedman Hanks a Friend of the King of Portugal!'

Once he told of sitting next to Mrs. Pat Campbell, the famous actress, at a dinner, and as he listened to the chatter as to the things he knew nothing about he felt that he had wasted a lot of time. College by contrast was so provincial! Now he was seeing things at first hand, and he had the aspect of a young bird with its bill open for anything that might drop in. Every morning he had something new to repeat to Mr. Reid, and the Ambassador, tired, his race nearly run, looking back on a full life in which these incidents were ordinary, enjoyed listening, and in return sandwiched in many bits of good advice. So the young man's letters began to improve, and he became a little less sure that everything as he had learned it was correct. He had long since emerged from a grub into a resplendent butterfly, with spats and buttonhole and silk hat complete, and had all the makings of a man of the world.

Mr. Reid was just the type of broad-minded, cultured leader that such a young man needed, and it interested me to hear Mr. Hanks say years afterwards that he felt there could be nothing better for any young man than for a short time to be associated with a fine leader and to sip from his cup a little of the champagne of world contacts and social amenities. To any young man who had sat at the feet of men like Oliver Wendell Holmes or Whitelaw Reid or Joseph Choate he felt the world would be forever nobler and more varied in its implications and possibilities than it could ever be for those who had never surveyed it from that elevated vantage-point, or actually participated in it. The trouble in the United States, as he saw it, was the lack of enough men with worldly experience. The experience he felt to be so necessary was not mere intellectual equipment to be got in the seclusion of college halls. What he wanted for eventual leaders was something actual, not theoretical, actual experience with, and

participation in, the world where history was being made —
a glorious adventure.

The sinking of the *Titanic* in April filled everyone with
horror. The Atlantic had become so safe that nobody thought
about it any more. But now the finest and newest ship of all,
on its maiden voyage, had struck an iceberg and sunk with
great loss of life. Fortunately none of the Embassy staff was
aboard, though the passenger list contained the name of a
relative of one of them. This gentleman, who did not sail as
arranged — Frank told me a woman had persuaded him to
linger — apparently overlooked the necessity of letting his
wife in the United States know of his change of plans, nor,
when the disaster occurred, did he inform her that he was not
on board. The same day, therefore, a frantic cable came from
her asking for news, and Frank, deeply shocked that she
should be so unnecessarily anxious, telephoned the gentleman
about the cable, assuming, of course, he would reply. Two
days went by, and then came a second cable, beseeching us to
find out something as the poor lady was prostrated with
anxiety, and on again telephoning, Frank learned that the
husband had not bothered to cable, and said casually that he
probably wouldn't. This was too much for warm-hearted
Frank. He reported the matter to the Ambassador, and Mr.
Reid, likewise incensed, instructed Frank to tell him to cable
to his wife at once! I always felt it was a pity he wasn't on
the *Titanic*. He would never have been missed!

The splendour of the pre-war Embassy may be said to have
reached its apex that summer of 1912. A great number of
American diplomats and others were presented at the Courts,
and Mrs. Reid was handsome in grey with silver brocade.

On June 6 the famous 'Hundred Years Ago' Ball, a pageant
of the Regency, took place at the Albert Hall, Mr. Phillips
representing Lord Melbourne and Mr. Hanks Beau Brummell.
As one of the English papers commented, 'One rather regrets
that these two essentially English characters were not por-

trayed by Englishmen.' All the men wore the garments of the dandies of the early years of the nineteenth century, and Mr. Phillips and Mr. Hanks looked splendid. Mr. Hallett Johnson, still another Third Secretary who had recently come, was Lord Allen. It was a great ball, in which all the notable figures took part, and the splendour of the costumes with the loveliness of setting is said never to have been surpassed in any London spectacle of the kind. It must also have been a sort of nostalgic occasion, and some of the newspapers thus envisioned it, for one of the stories began, 'It was a splendid world that we lived in a hundred years ago...'

There was also a State Garden Party at Windsor Castle and a State Ball in honour of the visit of the President of France. Mr. and Mrs. Phillips gave some quiet dinners, but Mrs. Phillips was not well enough to do much.

The end of the season brought rest for everyone except the Ambassador, who, tired though he was, went to the opening of the University College of Wales and made a stirring address on Thomas Jefferson, who was of Welsh descent. Mr. Reid asked: 'Who will name the achievement of any other man of Welsh or British blood which has more largely influenced the world for good than that empire-shaking document [the Declaration of Independence] that saved Great Britain for itself and saved America for herself?' In Mr. Reid's speeches his appeal was always to some lofty intellectual and moral ideal or some great achievement. He was not much given to the emotional school of Anglo-American oratory, but rather to explaining and impressing upon his English audience what their ancestors and their descendants had done in the wider spaces of the United States, working out the same problems of democracy and freedom with which they themselves were faced. He counted on their understanding and their pride in being a part of the same great experiment. His view was always wide, noble, rather impersonal. On one occasion he gave me a printed copy of one of his addresses on the stupendous growth of the United States, which he called 'The greatest event of modern history.' Its force and imagination and the grand sweep of the picture gave me a compelling feeling of the probable great destiny of the United States. What a pity, I thought, that England had been foolish enough to let this splendid country separate from her. If it were only part of the British Empire still, nothing would be impossible, not even world peace.

It was in October that Mr. Phillips, to my stupefaction and sorrow — I thought he at least would be more or less of a permanency — told me that he was leaving the Embassy. He wanted to go home, he said, and build a house and put his roots down deep into the soil of his homeland. He didn't want to be away from America long enough to become expatriated and lose touch with it. He said that he woke one morning as though a call that would not be disregarded commanded him to go. He didn't, however, want to leave the Diplomatic Service. When he had built his house, learned to know his neighbours better, and assumed some responsibility for his part of New England, he would be ready and eager to return to the Service and go wherever the State Department might care to send him, for in going away he would know that there was his home waiting for him to come back to. Mrs. Phillips's health did not improve and the baby daughter was not robust, so he hoped that some draughts of good New England air would benefit them both. To make sure that the Department of State realized that he was not resigning, he wrote a careful letter in which he explained the whole situation, for this taking time off, with the expectation of being reappointed later, was something unusual.

The official notification of the change came in a cable to the Ambassador from Mr. Irwin Laughlin, Councillor of Embassy at Berlin, announcing his appointment as Councillor at London, and one to Mr. Phillips asking whether he might rent his house. Mr. Phillips told me how relieved he was that such an experienced and able diplomat was to take his place, a man who had seen service in many countries, was much respected everywhere, an excellent choice, and a man he knew we should like. . . .

We were all sorry to have Mr. Phillips go — however fine his successor might turn out to be — though everyone sympathized with his wish to live for a time at least in America, and give Mrs. Phillips a chance to regain her health. We hoped that one day he might come back as Ambassador, for he had so many of the qualities which fitted him for high office, reticence, dignity, good manners, and intense interest in the cultivation of the higher ideals of peace and friendship. In England, as we knew, there would be many friends and admirers to give him a hearty welcome.

The day before he left a luncheon was given to him by the Pilgrims, presided over by Sir Gilbert Parker, at which he made a brief speech acknowledging the kindness, the hospitality and true friendship he had received during the time he had been in England. The same afternoon I went up to say good-bye to Mrs. Phillips, who had been very kind to me. Being happily married herself she seemed distressed when I told her that I had no immediate intention of marrying, and paid me a very sweet compliment by saying, 'Oh, I *hope* you will. You have so much to give!'

Almost before we realized it Mr. and Mrs. Phillips were gone. A complete stranger had come instead of whom we knew little except that he was a cousin of Mr. Grant-Smith's, was quiet, the owner of a beautiful house in Tokyo where he had lived while stationed there and still retained for sentimental reasons, and had been recently married to Miss Thérèse Iselin. I liked his trim, careful way of dressing and speaking. He wasn't much like the amusing Mr. Grant-Smith, I decided the morning after Mr. Phillips had sailed, when he came in, bade me good morning, bowed stiffly, and hung up his hat on the same hook that had been used by Mr. Phillips and before that by Mr. Carter. Did he want me to move into the other room? I enquired. Certainly not, said he, shaking his head violently — a habit of his, I discovered later. He preferred to have me right at hand, for there would be many things he would want to ask and he had heard that I knew everything! I was quite ruffled, but discovered it was only a mannerism and that his habit of speaking dryly hid a very sensitive and tender heart. I liked his clever face, his penetrating blue eyes, his gleeful chuckles when he was amused, his subtle, delightful, and sometimes calculated humour (something like Mr. Grant-Smith's on the whole), his habit of seeming to weigh respectfully everything that was said to him. I asked him once why he paid attention to people who didn't seem to know what they were talking about, and he replied that he was always willing to take advice from those who knew — even the garbage man!

The first few weeks I was busy paying bills for Mr. Phillips, helping to effect the transfer of the house to Mr. Laughlin, and many other things in connection with club responsibilities and the shipment of furniture, tapestries, etc., to Boston, and spent so much money that I was almost scared, for every letter to Mr. Phillips was a request for more.

Working with Mr. Laughlin was not easy at first, for he was so very different from Mr. Phillips. One had to know how to handle him. He understood diplomacy and diplomatic etiquette to the last comma, and on the whole, possibly because of his varied experience, was more of a cold internationalist than any other diplomat I had met. A most cultivated and interesting man who knew many languages, he could be most aggressively American when he had the slightest suspicion that any foreigner was trying to 'put one over' on him or his country. To my horror he actually seemed to feel that some of the bland statements of the Foreign Office were 'bunk.' He distrusted everything that sounded like oratory, though he could, when the occasion demanded, write letters that were nothing more. He used the most polished French and English, and I used to think resentfully (having no accents on my typewriter, for it had come from Washington without them and I hadn't had the sense to have them added) that he used French just to annoy me. But he had been in so many capitals where the social and formal correspondence was carried on in French that it had become second nature to him, and I dare say that he thought a note in English lacked the flavour of one written in the more stately French.

The one capital he had not enjoyed was Berlin, and part of his rancour was the result of a spirited quarrel he had had with the local authorities there, who insisted that he erect a perfectly unnecessary brass handrail up a staircase that went up between two walls in his house — a horror! he said, shuddering. Naturally he claimed his diplomatic privilege and no handrail was installed. But he never forgot, and when anything was said about Berlin he would say, 'Well, what can you expect of people like that?'

All this effervescence of emotion about bygone trifles was vastly entertaining to me after the placid, kindly Mr. Phillips, and the cheery, amusing Mr. Carter. However, I soon grew to like Mr. Laughlin very much and to sympathize with his slightly acid criticisms of people and things. He did not suffer fools gladly, and Frank's universal excuse for many shortcomings, 'that the man who never made a mistake never made anything,' which had always evoked a tolerant smile from everyone else, infuriated Mr. Laughlin. He had extremely high ideals of diplomatic efficiency, and I learned much from him that has ever since made me more reasoned and discriminating in my likes and dislikes and a good deal more conscious of and intolerant of stupidity.

A story that particularly amused me was that, sitting next to a gushing lady one night at dinner, who was expressing agitated horror at the report she had heard that when he had lived in Siam he had had boa constrictors in his garden, he replied, 'Not boa constrictors, my dear lady. Pythons.'

Mr. Reid was almost a dying man when Mr. Laughlin arrived. The trip to Wales had been too much for him and he never regained his strength afterwards, though he struggled right up to the last to attend to his diplomatic duties. Mr. Laughlin was most attentive and helpful, on hand all day long carrying on the Embassy work with ease and leaving the Ambassador nothing to do but sign the completed Notes and Despatches, which he did from his bed. I suppose I ought to have guessed how ill he was, but somehow the thought of his dying never crossed my mind. I had actually arranged to go to Switzerland for the winter sports, and it was not until the day before Mr. Reid's death that Mr. Laughlin hinted that it would be safer for me not to make final arrangements, as I might have to cancel them, and Mr. Hanks corroborated this and told me with tears in his eyes that the Ambassador was very bad indeed. So that's why everybody had been so depressed! I had thought the trouble was with myself, that I was tired and wanted a change, but it was something much bigger than that! I stared at Mr. Hanks and he at me and I realized then that Mr. Reid would not recover. It was a bitter moment for both of us.

The following day — a Sunday — the Ambassador passed on at noon and Frank telegraphed me — we had no telephone at home — and I started at once for the Chancery, for there would be many things to do. I was still full of emotion and fear, fear of the unknown death which drags even Ambassadors away, though I was comforted by the thought that this frail old man who had worked so hard to foster peace and good-will between his country and England had now gone to sleep for good, and not even the most urgent cable from Washington could wake him again.

Our first official duty was to inform the Foreign Office and the Secretary of State, for the death of an Ambassador is no ordinary passing, but an international event, and Mr. Reid was the first American Ambassador to die at his post in London. Mr. Laughlin cabled Washington:

> I have the sad duty of announcing to you that the Ambassador died today (December 15th) at Dorchester House at ten minutes past 12 o'clock. Pending definite instructions I have assumed control of the Embassy as Chargé d'Affaires.

Telegrams were also sent to the President, the King, Sir Edward Grey, to all of Mr. Reid's former private secretaries, and about fifty friends in America.

The following day in the House of Commons the offer of a battleship to take Mr. Reid's body back to the United States was made, and later in the day this offer was officially confirmed in a Note from the Foreign Office. The State Department told Mrs. Reid to please herself, and she accepted. On Monday afternoon also the Abbey authorities called and said the King desired a Memorial Service to be held in Westminster Abbey, and the Master of the Ceremonies confirmed this.

That same morning Mrs. Reid sent a message that she would like the whole staff to come to Dorchester House in the afternoon. We went and saw Mr. Reid for the last time, looking very peaceful, all the lines of fatigue gone from his face. The room was filled with beautiful flowers, and a large wreath from Queen Alexandra at the foot of the bed. Mrs. Reid was too weary and upset to see us.

Among the small duties which the Ambassador had been unable to carry out was the presentation to Major Squier of the Elliott Cresson medal, which had been sent from the United States with the request that he do so. It had arrived when he was weak and he spoke about it once or twice, worried that it had not been attended to. Now it was too late, so Mrs. Reid asked the Major whether he would receive it from her instead, and the next day he went to Dorchester House in full uniform and received it, and with it a gold watch no thicker than a half-crown which she had had inscribed to him from the Ambassador. He was exceedingly touched and pleased.

The cruiser *Natal* was chosen as the funeral ship and the Captain notified Mr. Laughlin that three cabins would be placed at the disposal of relatives. But Mrs. Reid decided that she and the rest of the family would sail by a fast ship the same day and so be ready at New York to receive the *Natal* on its arrival. Then followed many cables from the Navy Department as to the time the *Natal* would reach Nantucket Light so that the arrangements for meeting and escorting it into New York Harbor should be perfect, and just when everything was settled another cable came saying that the President would like to attend the funeral service and as he could not be in New York until January 4 the arrival of the *Natal* must be delayed until then.

I wrote to Mr. Phillips:

Mr. Cresson was given charge of the arrangements at the Abbey for the Memorial Service, and, assisted by Canon Westlake of the Abbey, Mr. Johnson, Mr. Fairbanks [who had finally come to be clerk of the Embassy], Mr. Synge of the Foreign Office, Sir Arthur Walsh and a girl lent by Mr. Brittain of the Pilgrims, managed to get the tickets issued. Canon Westlake, a friendly soul, helped valiantly, as he knew the places where the distinguished people should sit, and there would be many of them, for, in addition to Royal representatives and members of the British Government, the French Ambassador had decided that all the *Chefs de Mission* should be invited. This ticket distribution was made at the Chancery, so every time I crossed the hall I was called in, but as Mr. Laughlin needed me I could not be of much assistance, though I undertook to send out the cards for the Diplomatic Corps, as nobody else (except Mr. Laughlin, of course) knew just how they should be addressed. But all through the afternoon people kept coming in to ask me trivial questions until at last Mr. Laughlin, busy beyond belief, told Frank to lock the door of our room from the outside and not let a soul in on any pretext whatever! By this drastic method we got through.

The Memorial Service was entirely beautiful and fitting, the music restrained and the service not too elaborate. There were no uniforms, as the King had ruled otherwise. I can never forget the haunting music of Chopin's 'Funeral March' played very fast as a recessional, with the silver trumpets making such a swell on the crescendo that death indeed seemed swallowed up in victory.

But to me the departure of the Ambassador's body from Victoria Station on the first lap of its long journey home was the most impressive and moving part of the whole week. A group of us stood in the dismal station, trying to keep warm that chilly morning, while we waited for the procession to arrive. The platform was filled with soldiers drawn up opposite the train, which was composed of several coaches with the funeral coach, lined entirely with purple velvet, in the centre. The coffin, covered with the American flag, came along the familiar streets from Dorchester House on a gun-carriage of the Household Cavalry, escorted by men of that regiment in their scarlet cloaks, and there was an additional escort of half a battalion of Scots Guards, the band of the regiment, and the pipes and drums of the Second Battalion. As the procession marched into the station, the pipers were playing 'The land of the Leal,' and they continued while the coffin was put into the train. Then the 'Flowers of the Forest' was played. After that there was a silence, and that was broken at last by a brass band which gave one verse of 'Abide with me' with such depth and sweetness that everyone was in tears. Then followed another long silence while a few last details were attended to, and finally, as the train began to move very, very slowly out of the station the other verses of the old hymn came hauntingly and rather softly through the

frosty air, with everybody, both in the train and on the platform, standing with bowed heads. . . .

There was not a movement on the platform until the hymn
was finished, long after the train had vanished round the
corner.

But I wasn't even allowed to forget business at a time like
that, for just as he was about to step into the train with the
others Mr. Laughlin changed his mind and came hurrying
down the platform and whispered to me to prepare a despatch
to the State Department for his signature giving a full account
of the whole week. . . .

It was a representative group at the station. There was
Mr. Ogden Reid, who had arrived from America the night
before with his wife, too late to see his father alive, the
Honourable John Ward and the Earl of Granard, Mr. Laughlin,
Captain Symington, Major Squier, Mr. Cresson, Mr. Johnson,
Mr. Hanks, Captain Walsh, Mr. Petherick and Frank Gurney
of the Despatch Agency, the Consul-General, Frank Hodson,
a number of Civil War Veterans in uniform, and a goodly
number of the American residents of London. Representing
the American Society were Mr. F. C. Van Duzer and Mr. R.
Newton Crane, and Mr. J. Arthur Barratt represented the
International Law Association.

I had a few words with Mr. Ogden Reid, whom I had not
seen since he went back to America the year before to be
married to Miss Rogers and to assume charge of the New York
Tribune. There was much to say, but we couldn't say it. Mr.
Reid was wonderful. Although he was pale as death and
looked very tired, he went from one to another speaking to
all with his cordial good manners, forgetting no one, for this
was his only opportunity, as he was sailing with his mother
again that afternoon.

So ended another Embassy. The magnificent Dorchester
House, testifying to Mr. Reid's conception of the duties and
responsibilities of his high offices, was closed, and even the

stone eagle over the *porte cochère* looked forlorn. Whatever Mr. Reid's critics may have thought, whether they believed in wealth as a *sine qua non* for an Ambassadorship or whether they didn't, there is no doubt that a country is judged by its representatives and the way they live and conduct themselves. Thousands of Americans had been the recipients of Mr. Reid's hospitality, as well as thousands of English and other Europeans. Cabinet Ministers, Ambassadors of other Powers stationed in England, a cross-section of the leaders of the time, had relaxed and discussed their problems in the friendly atmosphere, and the Secretaries of the Embassy had thought of Dorchester House as a second home. Nothing could ever be quite the same again, for it was not likely that a man with the combination of Mr. Reid's distinguished qualities and the ability to carry out his mission so completely in accordance with his own ideas would again be appointed to London. Mr. Reid was a most appropriate man to be sent to England as Ambassador, for he was of the *grand seigneur* type, quiet, reserved, dignified, a type understood and much liked in England, and therefore sure to be successful. He had given himself unstintingly in every way, and during his time the American Embassy truly represented the power and prestige of the United States.

18

Mr. Woodrow Wilson becomes President of the United States.
Mr. William Jennings Bryan is appointed Secretary of State.
The Panama Canal Tolls question. Mr. Walter Hines Page
comes to London as Ambassador. Colonel and Mrs. Edward
M. House. Celebration of one hundred years of peace between
the United States and Great Britain.

1913

As one drops the torch another takes it up and carries it forward. For several days, especially while occupied with the details necessitated by the change of authorities, my thoughts were not on diplomatic business, but with Mr. Reid, seeing the coffin set in the waist of the grim battleship, listening to the screeching and moaning of the winter wind, and the lapping of the waves against the side of the ship on the boisterous Atlantic — going home for the last time. Then we read of the arrival and the grand funeral service at the Cathedral in New York (with President Taft and T. R. glaring at each other across the choir, as Mr. Phillips wrote me afterwards), and of special, rather poignant interest to us, the number of former Embassy Secretaries who had managed to get to New York to do this last honour to their old Chief, Mr. Phillips, Mr. Augustus Jay, Colonel Slocum, Captain Gibbons, Mr. Arthur Orr, Mr. DeLancey Jay, Mr. Hanks, Mr. Hoyt, and one or two others.

The sad Christmas over, during which Mr. Laughlin managed to get a few days' rest in Ireland, the New Year was ushered in with the old ominous feeling of insecurity and change, owing to the coming into office of another new President on March 4, this time a Democrat, Mr. Woodrow Wilson.

The Republicans had been in office so long that a Democratic President seemed a disaster. Aside from any change of policy that might result there was the more immediate question of what might happen at the Embassy. The Republicans had gone some distance along the road towards a 'merit' system. But the Democrats were not committed to the 'merit' policy — or at least had not yet had a chance to express their views — and everybody realized that as there must be many Democrats eager to hold office, and whom the new President would wish to honour, there would inevitably be wholesale changes.

Even the outgoing Republican Senate had seemed to feel no great responsibility for the orderly progress of foreign affairs, for it looked as though the new Administration might begin its duties on March 4 with most of the Embassies minus some of the most necessary part of their personnel, owing to the fact that the Senate had neglected to confirm any of the diplomatic appointments which had been made for several months. In February, therefore, the State Department, much concerned, had been obliged to cable Mr. Laughlin that, failing confirmation of his appointment on or before March 3, he must that day vacate his office and leave London as soon thereafter as possible, leaving 'one of the other Secretaries in charge.'

Now Mr. Cresson had been granted leave of absence to go to the United States, so 'one of the other Secretaries' could mean only Mr. Hallett Johnson, the new Third Secretary, a young man of twenty-four who had been in the Diplomatic Service but a few months. Similar instructions to vacate were also sent to the other men whose appointments had not been confirmed: Mr. Joseph Grew at Berlin, Mr. Grant-Smith at Vienna, the Minister and Secretary at Brussels, the Minister to Siam, and several others.

Aside from the personal hardship of breaking up their homes suddenly and returning to the United States, the Senate's procrastination was especially serious as most of the unconfirmed men were the experienced career diplomats on whom nearly all of the responsible work naturally fell. Indeed, the situation at London was absolutely unprecedented, for it would mean not only a complete cessation of diplomatic negotiations (for Sir Edward Grey would probably be reluctant to carry on business with such a very young man), but when a new Ambassador was appointed he would arrive to find no experienced Councillor on the ground, and this would impair the success of negotiations he might be called upon to continue.

The Panama Canal Tolls question was still undetermined, the chaos continued in Mexico, with divergent British and American views, and there were a number of lesser matters unfinished. It was particularly hard on Mr. Laughlin, who had been in London such a short time, and in those few weeks had been swamped with the sad responsibilities connected with the death of the Ambassador, and now found himself about to be deprived of his office. He also had Mr. Phillips's house in London on his hands, the lease of which did not contain a 'diplomatic clause' enabling him to break it if he were transferred.

But awkward as these personal tribulations were, they did not bother Mr. Laughlin very much. What *did* trouble him was the Embassy's being left without one experienced official — and that horrified and alarmed him. So after thinking it over he sent one of his perfectly worded cables to his State Senator, Mr. Oliver, and others to Mr. Root, Mr. Lodge, Mr. Choate, and Mr. Phillips, all of whom would understand the seriousness of the London situation. Senator Oliver indeed realized it immediately, and took the cable at once and read it to the Senate. It conveyed the picture so unmistakably that at the very last minute, actually on March 3, the Senate not only confirmed Mr. Laughlin's appointment, but all the others as well. The Embassy at London in charge of a 'diplomat of twenty-four' no doubt settled the matter.

Poor Mr. Cresson was the only one to lose out. He had nobly — but without telling anyone — cancelled his passage when he found he might be left in charge, and then, when Mr. Laughlin's appointment was confirmed, he found he might just as well have sailed in the first place. To make it worse the newspaper men seemed to imagine there was something queer and kept asking him why the Senate was not informed he was on the job. They made his life miserable looking for something disagreeable that didn't exist.

Almost as soon as Mr. Laughlin had become Chargé d'Affaires a period of difficult and exacting work began, so it was fortunate that he was well liked by Sir Edward Grey. Guatemalan finances were upset, and Mexico was entirely disrupted, with the United States supporting one rogue for President and Great Britain another.

But, disturbing as these were, they were trifling compared to the bombshell that had been exploded by President Taft the previous August in his Message to Congress giving preference to American ships using the Panama Canal, in defiance of the Hay-Pauncefote Treaty of 1901. In that treaty Great Britain had given up a former treaty which had precluded either country from building a canal in Central America, and had permitted the United States to build it in return for a guaranty of equality in the use of the Canal. Now that the Canal was approaching completion, however, Mr. Taft didn't at all like the bargain that had been made. He claimed that, as it was being constructed by the United States wholly at its own expense, upon territory ceded to it by Panama, the United States enjoyed the absolute right of ownership and control, including the right to allow its own commerce to use the Canal upon such terms as it saw fit.

Naturally the English did not agree, and there was a great

rumpus; Ambassador Reid was much worried. The matter had come up in the House of Commons in October and Sir Edward Grey told the House he had informed the Government of the United States that should there eventually be found to be a difference of opinion in the interpretation of the Treaty that could not be settled by other means, the British Government would ask that it be referred to The Hague for arbitration.

The American reply was sent to Mr. Laughlin on January 17 for presentation to Sir Edward Grey and began, 'It may be stated at the outset that this government does not agree with the interpretation placed by Sir Edward Grey upon the Hay-Pauncefote Treaty'; and proposed, in case of a continued difference of opinion, that the question be settled by — the Supreme Court of the United States! Mr. Laughlin was instructed to read the whole long document to Sir Edward Grey and then, if he wished, to hand him a copy. It must have been a happy occasion for them both!

There the matter rested until the new President could decide upon it, the Foreign Office being fully conscious of the landslide of policies and personages that would come on March 4. Probably they hoped that the new President, not being a lawyer, might see the Treaty as the simple document it was.

On March 4 Mr. Woodrow Wilson became President and Mr. William Jennings Bryan Secretary of State, and immediately thereafter the usual undignified search began for a man willing and able to make the financial sacrifice necessary to be Ambassador at London. Many Democrats who were suitable could not afford to consider it, and as all the rumours and counter-rumours were aired in the American press, people in England were all agape at this bargaining for a position which they considered far above and beyond politics. So difficult was it to find the right man that Mr. Phillips wrote me that it almost seemed as though Mr. Laughlin would be left at London as permanent Chargé d'Affaires.

Among those specially mentioned as possibilities, were Mr. Richard Olney and President Eliot of Harvard, who both declined, and later the name of Mr. Walter Hines Page was added to the list. But when the newspapers actually announced Mr. Page's appointment and added that he was sailing for England shortly, Mr. Laughlin, much incensed at having heard nothing, sent a confidential cable to the State Department asking whether it was true, and if so, to be informed of the exact date of Mr. Page's sailing. He added — in case the new people at the State Department didn't know that the appointment must be approved by the King before an Ambassador could be received — that he hesitated to take any steps until notified of the appointment and of His Majesty's *agrément*. The State Department replied that they were not yet prepared to announce the selection, that steps to obtain the *agrément* would be taken in ample time, and that the Embassy would be duly advised. A few days later Mr. Laughlin was asked to enquire whether the appointment as Ambassador of Mr. Walter Hines Page, editor and author, of New York, would be agreeable to the King, and soon afterwards Lord Morley of Blackburn, in the absence of Sir Edward Grey, replied that the appointment was entirely agreeable.

This going forward to Washington, there fell another deep silence, until on May 8 the Master of Ceremonies informed Mr. Laughlin that the King would receive Mr. Page on Friday, May 30, at eleven-thirty and that he should wear Levee dress. Mr. Laughlin cabled the Department to tell Mr. Page, enquired again the exact date of his sailing, and whether Mrs. Page would accompany him. The Department answered that Mr. Page was sailing on the fifteenth, and that Mrs. Page would come later.

Something of the Embassy's state of mind during those weeks is evident in a letter of mine to Mr. Phillips:

> Mr. Laughlin cabled his personal congratulations to Mr. Page about ten days ago and asked if there was anything he could do.

WALTER H. PAGE, AT THE TIME OF AMERICA'S ENTRY
INTO THE WAR, APRIL, 1917

He got a reply in three days saying, 'Letter follows,' but no letter has come, and Mr. Laughlin is not only embarrassed but thoroughly bored and angry to be so much in the dark — the same old story! Mr. Laughlin is praying that Mr. Page will come soon, and is wondering where he will live and whether the housing arrangements will be left to him, as well as the official ceremonial. To cheer him up I gave him a detailed account of the preparations that Mr. White and Mr. Carter had made for Mr. Reid's coming!! Meanwhile house agents and persons wishing to give dinners in Mr. Page's honour make poor Mr. Laughlin's life a burden, and a great bundle of letters have come which he warned me to be sure *not* to open in case they might need attention!! Mrs. Charlie Alexander tells us that Mr. Page is sailing on the twenty-third of May. When Mr. Laughlin heard that, he said a naughty word as he had been hoping he would not have to send in the list for Ascot and arrange the last two Courts. You remember how he hates the social end? . . .

We are also having a mass of correspondence about the agricultural commission which has just started for Rome and is coming back through Europe. A reception committee has been formed here and the Board of Agriculture is taking great interest in it. The indefatigable Mr. Lubin, the American agricultural representative at Rome (you remember him?), writes long letters every day and seems to think it is his province to keep everybody else's nose to the grindstone. Of course that only makes Mr. Laughlin reluctant to do more than he actually must. 'Why such a hurry?' he said viciously the other day. 'It will be something nice for Mr. Page to do when he gets here! . . .'

Then began the arranging for the Ambassador's arrival, now set for May 25. Mr. Page cabled acceptance of a dinner to be given by the Pilgrims on June 6 if that was convenient to the Embassy. On May 14 Mr. Laughlin talked with the Foreign Office about the official reception, complicated because the King was on a visit to Germany, and the following day Sir Edward Grey wrote that he hoped Mr. Page would make it convenient to call at the Foreign Office on May 26 or 27 at four-thirty; Mr. Laughlin chose the twenty-sixth at four. He also informed the Consul at Liverpool of Mr. Page's expected arrival there, asked the Foreign Office for the free entry of Mr. Page's motor, and made arrangements with the Coburg Hotel where the party were to stay until they found a house.

Mr. Page arrived at last, accompanied by his son Frank and by Mr. Harold Fowler, his secretary. Frank Hodson, who went with the rest of the Embassy to meet him, came back to the Chancery looking very subdued, and in reply to my eager questions said crossly, 'Nice enough people, friendly and all that. Seemed a bit quiet...' and that's all I could get of him.

The following morning, accompanied by Mr. Laughlin, the new Ambassador came down to '123,' stared round with an almost hostile eye, and met the rest of us. At first glance, with his rather dowdy appearance and big nose, I thought he was one of the ugliest men I had ever seen. But he was so cordial and indeed there was something so wistful about him that I knew I was going to like him — indeed, I did already. His attitude was unhurried, almost meditative, and, like so many other Southerners, he looked gaunt and hungry as though he had been short of food during the Civil War and had never been able to make it up. His son Frank Page was a younger, better-looking edition of his father, and Mr. Fowler, a shorter and stockier young man, had a friendly grin on his most amiable face, while a determined wavy curl stood up enquiringly on top of his head looking over at me. 'So this is the famous Chancery,' said Mr. Page at length, having taken in every defect. 'Well, I don't think much of it. I should have thought Uncle Sam could have done better than this all these years.' Mr. Laughlin gave a faint smile, but said nothing.

Some of the ceremonies were omitted because of Mrs. Page's absence, but had to be gone through when she and her daughter arrived about a month later. On May 30 the Embassy cabled that the Ambassador had presented his Letter of

Credence, and on the same day notice of his arrival was sent to his fellow Ministers and Chargés d'Affaires — he called on the Ambassadors at once. The note to the Ministers, written in French, amused Mr. Page, and in fact all the ceremonial interested him enormously. 'So that's the way it's done,' he would say with a chuckle, handing back some diplomatic document.

Mr. Page's speech at the Pilgrim Dinner was well received, but the American newspapers took their first dig at him very soon, by reporting that he did not attend the King's Birthday Dinner and reception, and when Mr. Laughlin told the reporters that they were mistaken and that Mr. Page *did* attend, they calmly said that his name was not on the official list given them and hinted there was some trouble somewhere. But if they hoped to get a rise out of the astute Mr. Laughlin, they were disappointed.

Writing to Mr. Phillips I told him of those first days, adding:

Mr. Page is a pleasant and kindly person, rather countrified, I should say, and not nearly as smartly groomed as the immaculate Mr. Laughlin. He already acts as though he was tired of meeting so many officials, but I am sure he likes every bit of it. He enjoys the social part most, and has every day filled with engagements. His son Frank is supposed to be looking for a house for them, to assist him in which he has apparently enlisted the assistance of every lady he has met, so they are always calling him up to make suggestions until now whenever the telephone rings it is assumed to be for him. Mr. Fowler, the Ambassador's secretary, is quite a competent one, and is so businesslike that I can't believe it can last. Wait until he gets to know some of the girls; then he won't set such a good example. At present he gets down here early in the morning, rushes to lunch, hurries back, and stays until six o'clock. You can realize how busy he is when I tell you that he does everything for the Ambassador that was done for Mr. Reid by at least three people, and in addition he leaves cards and makes lists of callers and that sort of routine that was formerly done by Mrs. Reid's secretaries. I was soon called in to help, too, Mr. Laughlin having told Mr. Page I knew everything, and Mr. Page unsuspiciously taking the statement at its face value! So I have been having a merry time — it still goes on — trying to instill into their resisting American heads some of the subtleties of British social custom, which they call 'bunk' and are all for disregarding entirely — just to teach those English things they ought to have learned long ago — to which you may be sure I always make suitable retort. Someone is always dashing in to ask me questions like, How do you address a Marchioness? And what *is* a Marchioness, anyhow? Is Lady V. *The* Lady or only Lady? When is a Lady The Lady and when is she only *A* Lady? What must I wear to a Royal Garden Party? — and having heard and disapproved — Why should I if I don't want to? Should the Ambassador accept this invitation, and if not why not, etc., etc., etc.

London society seems to enjoy Mr. Page. He prefers to go about alone to evening parties, and has no liking for the usual courtiers who usually attend on an Ambassador wherever he goes. Apropos of this it seems that one evening when he was going to five different dances one after the other, Mr. Cresson, a profound believer in the etiquette that the Ambassador should be suitably escorted at all times by a member of his staff, enquired solicitously who was to go with His Excellency that evening. Profoundly shocked to learn that Mr. Page proposed to go alone, he offered himself as escort. Mr. Page thanked him most politely, but was careful not to commit himself either to time or place, so, as Mr. Cresson didn't take the obvious hint, he never managed to catch up with the Ambassador, though he pursued him diligently from one place to another all the evening. Next morning when Mr. Page was informed of the agitated search that had gone on for him all over London, he said, 'Too bad, too bad,' with a twinkle in his eye. After that no other Secretary ever volunteered his service.

Mr. Page is very quiet in the Chancery. He leaves almost all of the diplomatic work to Mr. Laughlin, whom he consults about everything. He signs whatever is put before him without comment and seems quite satisfied with things as they are, except that he continues to wail about the Chancery being the worst little hole he has ever seen and he can't imagine how Mr. Choate and Mr. Reid were ever content to do business there.

Mr. Page, of course, doesn't realize that to them and their predecessors and associates it has become almost hallowed ground. He may grow to like it better as time goes on. I hope so, for no other place could ever seem the same. It is full of memories and the spirits of the diplomats who have been and gone. I tried to explain it to him one day, but he said he could not yet look upon it through such sentimental spectacles.

Mr. Page sees a great many people at the Chancery, an hotel being even less appropriate for the purpose than ' 123.' As happened when Mr. Reid first came, all the old standbys and pests have asked for interviews, and your special friend Mrs. J—— has already written several letters many pages in length. All those who were held at arm's length in Mr. Reid's time are now sending invitations, and we have continually to warn Mr. Page about getting involved.

There was to have been a Royal Garden Party next week, but it has been cancelled because the authorities are afraid of the suffragettes. The cards for the last Court were also withdrawn and new ones of a different colour substituted because of a hint that some of the suffragettes had invitations and intended some fun with them. All the places like Hampton Court, Windsor Castle, The Tower, are closed also, a great trial to American visitors who usually go to see them in their thousands. To try to make up, the Lord Chamberlain's office have given us permission to issue cards to any Americans known and vouched for as not being of the suffragette persuasion. So now I write on an average of about ten letters a day asking for privileges for one or other of the closed places for people we know all about. We don't take chances on others however estimable they may appear, for Mr. Laughlin is deadly afraid that one fine day a suffragette — either American or English — will manage to get in and he doesn't want the Embassy implicated. I plague him by telling him I shall write an application for myself and a few trusty friends, and that, as a member of the party it is no more than my duty. He says it makes his blood run cold!

Colonel and Mrs. E. M. House were also in London. Everybody liked them, though there were slight embarrassments from time to time because of Colonel House's semi-official, but undefined, status. Mr. Page had been assured by Sir Edward Grey that he, as Ambassador, would continue to be the only source through which the British Government would make their communications to the United States — whoever else the President might send — and that he could rest assured that nothing would ever be told to Colonel House that he did not know also. The House family knew people in London and their daughter had been presented at Court in Mr. Choate's time. But they didn't know the difficulties of securing invitations for Americans for Royal parties at the last moment.

Arriving at the beginning of Ascot Week, Mrs. House announced casually to Mr. Page that she would so much like to go down to the races in the Royal Enclosure. But the thirty passes allowed the Embassy that year had been gobbled up weeks before. To any ordinary applicant the Embassy would simply have regretted that it was too late, but what with a new Democratic President and the seeming importance of this Mr. House, they wanted to try to find some way to get Mrs. House in.

The Lord Chamberlain, the Master of the Ceremonies, and all the other Court officials had moved their offices to Windsor for the week and couldn't be reached. So far as they were concerned the Ascot passes were finished with and they could now watch the races in peace. An Embassy consultation evolved a brilliant idea. Major Squier was delegated to escort Mrs. and Miss House (Mr. House did not want to go) to the course and try to bluff his way into the Royal Enclosure, a most unheard-of proceeding, the method to be left entirely to his discretion. He himself had a card, and it would all depend upon whether he could get the ladies past the eagle-eyed conscientious keepers of the gate. So, all dressed up in gala silk hat and frock coat, very nervous, he took the ladies down, and, by dint of strategy of a high order — he got them in. Mrs. House would have been surprised if she had known what a bombshell her innocent request threw into the Embassy. Major Squier, however, was most boastful of his success, and when asked to tell the story once more for the fiftieth time or so he would swell out his chest and begin dramatically, 'I drew my sword...'

The celebration of the one hundred years of peace that had prevailed between the United States and England since the signing of the Treaty of Ghent on December 24, 1814, by John Quincy Adams 'politely if not hopefully,' which had begun just before Mr. Reid's death, went on all through 1913 and the early months of 1914. At the Pilgrim Dinner given in connection with this in July Mr. Page made a memorable speech in which he said:

> It is an inspiring spectacle — and history can show none other such: these two great kindred nations, one on each side of the well-ploughed sea that unites them, standing at the end of a century of peace, liberty-loving as of old, and looking forward, confident of the broadening of the bounds of freedom yet; regarding government as a living, ever-changing instrument of human progress, made by man for man's advancement and not for the mere maintenance of any political creed, yet none the less cautious in experiment and change.

This question of peace, with all its appeal to kinship, comfort, understanding, and brotherhood, was to be the principal burden of our days for many months; not so much the ideal — that could be taken for granted both in the United States and Great Britain — but a possible practical program that in case of disputes would give time for heated tempers to cool before going to war. This was Mr. Bryan's old idea, now translated into treaties which he hoped to sign with every other nation, a step in the right direction, and, at the time, seemingly easier to secure than limitation of armaments. Perhaps it was *too* simple!

The season over, and the time of vacation come, I took the momentous step of making the acquaintance of the other side of the lantern of my Anglo-American work. Several people I had known at the Embassy had invited me to visit them and see America for myself instead of only talking about it, and I was to go first to visit Mr. and Mrs. Ogden Reid and Mrs. Whitelaw Reid, and then on to various other places. Mr. Page professed to be most regretful that I was apparently going to spend all my time in what he called the 'marble halls of the multi-millionaires,' and said if I couldn't manage somehow to escape I shouldn't know in the least what the real America was like.

To offset the evil effects of too much luxury — he said — he gave me introductions to some other people, 'for, you know, Americans are a simple people on the whole — not like most of the diplomats you have known.' He urged me to see things on my own, and if I got lost to ask a policeman — just like London! He gave me letters to his business associates and to his brother, a Congressman from North Carolina living in Washington, and took a most genuine interest in all my plans. He told me I should have the privilege of tasting good coffee for the first time in my life, and that I must be sure to eat everything that was offered me — 'and you will be surprised that there are so many other things than cabbage.' How kind he was, and how human! He also wrote to his son Arthur about my visit. I did not know this until many years later, when, in compiling the Page Letters for publication, Mr. Burton Hendrick came across the letter and very kindly gave it to me. I can't help including it here.

Hooke Court, Beaminster, Dorset.
July 27th, 1913.

DEAR ARTHUR,

There has been in the Embassy for a long time a very capable little woman named Miss Emily Bax. She is English and her status is a stenographer. But she has served so long and has learned so much about the work that she is really a sort of secretary of the Embassy. Anybody else might go or might die and not be long missed; but if she were to go the Embassy would be out of gear. She's a very sensible, modest, well-bred, quiet little woman. Mrs. Reid is very fond of her and so is Mrs. Phillips.

They have invited her to spend her vacation in the United States and she will sail August 12th. I have asked the Government to increase her salary and I want her to have a good time. It has occurred to me that she would enjoy meeting you and Mollie and seeing the Press, etc. If convenient I suggest your taking her home with you for a few days (if you have room); have some of the others (Sam, if he's back) do the same thing. Pass her around and let her see how we live and work on our side the Atlantic. She's a very nice little person, indeed. Mrs. Reid will entertain her and I've told her that you'd be glad to see her. I'll send you her American address when she goes.

Affectionately,

W. H. P.

To my Silent Son.

*I discover the United States, am entertained by Embassy friends,
visit the Department of State, and return to London.*

1913

In August of 1913, therefore, another Christopher Columbus
set sail to discover a new world, with something of the same
sense of expectation and adventure as the first one, but, unlike
the first, in a cabin on 'A' deck of the SS. *St. Louis*, filled with
flowers, presents, and telegrams, and very conscious of the
fact that even the Department of State had been requested to
accord customs facilities to this 'distinguished visitor'!

It was my first long voyage, and I enjoyed every moment
of it, seeming to hear something of the same mysterious call
which had lured so many of my forbears into a seafaring life.
I, too, felt at home, at peace, as the great ship churned its way
towards the shores of America and the stars twinkled down
through the balmy velvet night.

After a week we began to sail slowly up New York Harbour, and as I stared fascinated at this new world, so peaceful
in its early Sunday morning beauty, with the first rays of the
sun dancing along the edges of all sorts of roofs and treetops
— and the bluest sky above that I had ever seen — there came
towards us very fast down the stream, on its way out to sea,
a small motor boat crowded with a band of happy men with
fishing rods and baskets. As the little boat skimmed past,
the men stood up and waved a welcome, and, waving excitedly back, I knew that I was going to like America.

As a 'distinguished visitor,' examination of my baggage was dispensed with and I was among the first to leave the boat. Mr. Ogden Reid was on the dock to meet me, and leaving the luggage to Albert, his butler, whom I had known well as the doorman at Dorchester House, Mr. Reid drove me up and down some of the principal streets to point out interesting spots, and then on out to the country to Ophir Hall, the home of Mrs. Whitelaw Reid where he and Mrs. Ogden Reid were living. He drove so fast that I was scared out of my wits, but when he turned to enquire whether it was too fast for me, I shook my head and thereafter we went faster.

After a few days Mr. and Mrs. Reid took me with them to the camp in the Adirondack Mountains to which Mrs. Whitelaw Reid had already gone. I was given a compartment to myself in a reserved sleeping-car, and before I went to bed Mr. Reid took me through the rest of the train to show me how most Americans travel at night. Walking gingerly down the narrow middle aisle I was shocked to find that nice people actually slept in two layers one above the other on each side, with only heavy green curtains to hide them from the public. I was sure I could never bring myself to do that! We stared out at the Hudson, a beautiful and majestic river, along which the train was travelling, and passed a boat going our way all lit up, with a band playing, and searchlights darting up and down picking out romantic spots. I did not see how anyone could sleep with so much light and noise, but Mr. Reid said that most people who travelled on those boats didn't want to sleep!

It was getting light when I was told to get up, and we had breakfast, the butler going off somewhere and returning with a special pot of tea for me. Fortunately it had all been taken away when the train stopped with a terrible jerk. We climbed out and found motors waiting. After a long drive through beautiful woods, we came out on the side of a large lake, where a big boat was waiting, and in it we steamed across to the other side, to a dock on which Mrs. Whitelaw Reid, smiling, was waiting to greet us. At this most marvellous camp I learned to sail a boat, banged my nose against my first screen door, was bitten by my first mosquito, at a party at a neighbouring camp danced the 'grapevine' — a fellow passenger on the *St. Louis* having kindly taught me, a Mr. Scranton of Scranton, the combination amusing me vastly — and ate strange but delicious new foods, including corn on the cob, which I firmly declined when I saw how it had to be eaten, but was finally persuaded to try.

My last morning at Camp Wild Air, when Mr. Reid took me 'over the carries,' was perhaps the best of all. We climbed into a canoe soon after half-past five (Mrs. Reid got up to make sure we had a good breakfast and to fasten my dress behind), and Mr. Reid, looking tall and handsome and energetic, paddled it across the lake to some landing-place he knew. There we got out, climbed up a narrow, steep path, me in front and he behind carrying the canoe like a helmet on his head, until another lake came into view through the trees. We slid down a steep path, got into the boat again, and paddled across the strange lake — and repeated this procedure until we had completed a circle over seven places where the canoes must be carried — and so home. As the canoe nosed along, we seemed to be alone in the world, for there was not a sound or a ripple on the water except those we made, and the trees came right down to the water's edge. It was lonely and chilly and sparkling, like champagne, until the sun rose.

A drawing-room had been reserved for me at Utica, where I changed for Chicago, but when the train came in, all the space that remained was an upper berth, so I took that with secret delight and enjoyed the climb in and out and the view of the ceiling as I lay in bed staring out at strange heads passing below. Mrs. Reid would have been surprised if she could have seen me after all the trouble she had taken to have me travel in royal state! The only thing that worried me was that my trunk had not come on the train and the official said it had probably been put on the New York train instead — as indeed it had!

With Mr. and Mrs. Orr in Chicago I went to a week-end party at Lake Geneva, during which we drove, perched up on a high waggon loaded with hay, to a large picnic at the lakeside, and ate our supper by moonlight. Lots of other people came, and chops were fried and corn was boiled (we ate it like a lot of animals, gnawing up and down the ears), and afterwards we sat round and sang songs to the music of the banjo while the headlights of the other cars, parked in a circle round us, made an enchanted elfin setting.

In Chicago I saw my first baseball game — though the gentlemen who sat one on each side of me always forgot to explain why a play was good because they were watching for the next — bought a hot brown velvet corduroy coat and skirt which took my fancy in Marshall Field's, to the stupefaction of Mrs. Orr, the temperature being somewhere in the nineties, and listened to real lions roaring in Lincoln Park as I lay snugly in bed. Mr. John McCutcheon, the famous cartoonist of the Chicago *Tribune*, who had been with Mr. Roosevelt in Egypt, gave a dinner party for me at some fashionable hotel and then took us all to see Elsie Janis dance, and the following day gave a tea for me in his apartment on the tenth floor of a new building facing Lake Michigan — a lake with a lighthouse on it! His floor was finished, but those underneath had only the girders in place, so it was like climbing up into a great bird's nest. Mr. McCutcheon also gave me several of his cartoons which I prize very highly.

From Chicago I went to Boston by way of Niagara Falls, and spent a most enjoyable day there with a perfect stranger, a nice girl who told me she and her husband had been on the train from Chicago. He had suggested she see the Falls while he went on to New York, and had told her to ask me to go with her, saying he would arrange for dinner for us at a hotel in Buffalo on our return. Of course I was delighted, and we had a happy day, crossing into Canada so that I might send cards home from still another foreign country, and in the evening we parted with much regret, she to go to New York and I to Boston.

Mr. Phillips met me at Topsfield, and as we drove out of the little country station we passed a white church with a tall slim tower just like every picture I had ever seen of a New England church. The air seemed to agree with Mrs. Phillips, for she was stronger and lovelier. Mr. Phillips took me to Harvard — where he was acting as a sort of secretary to President Eliot — to see the beautiful glass flowers, and to Boston to see the various sights, while in his library at home I saw his official commission as a member of President Theodore Roosevelt's 'Tennis Cabinet' with crossed racquets at the top.

We went to tea one afternoon with two charming ladies — the Misses Loring, who lived in a little house overlooking the sea, and had hundreds of white pigeons which they loosed and which flew round and round like a snowstorm.

All too soon I had to go, and another night brought me to Washington, where I stayed with the family of Mr. Page's brother. He and Mrs. Page were very kind to me. Mr. C. L. Cooke, who had been for a time in the Embassy and was now in the State Department, showed me all over and introduced me to Mr. Bryan — I didn't remind him that I had met him before — and I heard what the State Department thought of the Embassy, in some respects not quite so flattering as our regard for ourselves.

I thought the building very unimpressive. It was dark, with long gloomy corridors, and the doors, with slats to let in the air, were unfamiliar to me. It was so terribly hot that I didn't see how anyone could work at all. I was shown how the filing was done, how the different departments were divided up, and was of course specially interested in the one that dealt with the London routine business.

My time was now up and I must sail, but Mrs. Whitelaw Reid sent a cable to Mr. Page asking for another week, and that week I stayed with her at her house in New York which she opened for the purpose. I had a chance to see many friends, went to theatres, did some shopping — for Mrs. Reid, with her usual generosity, gave me more than enough money to pay for everything — and bought many souvenirs to take home.

One day I went to the Doubleday Page plant at Garden City and had lunch with the partners at a large round table in a big room, the only other woman being Miss Comstock, Mr. Doubleday's secretary, who was invited so that I should not be alone among so many men!! I answered most discreetly many leading questions, and heard the Ambassador referred to as the 'Doubleday-Page Ambassador' — for don't we pay his salary?

One evening I had dinner in another part of Long Island with Mr. Jay and his lady of the flowers, and another day he showed me the Stock Exchange in New York and I took pictures from the top of the Singer Building — the highest building I had ever been in in my life.

Another afternoon Mr. Dudley Field Malone, Third Assistant Secretary of State, came to call on Mrs. Reid and me, and she took the opportunity of questioning him thoroughly on Mr. Wilson's policy in regard to the Philippines which was the reverse of Ambassador Reid's. She did not approve of Mr. Wilson or the Democratic Party, and seemed to feel that the United States was well on its way to rack and ruin!

When the moment of departure could no longer be postponed, Mrs. Reid saw me off, putting me in charge of Colonel John Greenway, and as I sailed down the Bay, a lump in my throat, seeing the shore drift into the haze and a freshening breeze quicken the ship, I had a feeling I should return some day. Indeed I could now, for Mr. and Mrs. Ogden Reid had invited me to come back when the season of 1914 was over and 'take a sporting chance with Fate,' as Mrs. Reid put it — and I had agreed to think it over.

My visit to America had done something to my eyes! London seemed smaller and different. The sun shone more uncertainly and diffidently, almost as though it didn't want to be too intrusive. The gentle blue mists that lay a veil of romance over the dingy buildings seemed a sorry substitute for the clear-cut outlines of America, and, in comparison with the dramatic heights of downtown New York, London seemed insignificant.

It was good to be home again, however, with cool, moist days, my own family with its simple ways, and all the humdrum happenings to hear about. A holiday of that sort was almost too stupendous. It made such a call upon one's powers of amazement that things got out of proportion. One couldn't see the more simple aspects of America for the big happenings every minute. It was too much for me to assimilate all in a lump. I was bewildered.

Yes, it was good to be home again. I went back to work with increased interest, having now, since I had seen the State Department, a much better idea of the workings of the central diplomatic machine. Now I understood better the reason for delays, for refusals to grant seemingly ordinary requests, and I felt that I understood the Secretaries better, now that I knew something of their background. Funnily enough, they seemed more foreign, to be Americans away from home rather than visitors to England. I could also better sympathize with their criticisms of our weather, their grumbles that there was never a glass of drinking water anywhere, and that the eternal drink, when it did come, was always tea — and 'damned poison, too,' as one young man used to add passionately.

Poor things, I reflected, away from their country of brilliant sunshine, heat, ear-splitting thunderstorms, peanuts (their name for our vulgar monkey nuts), baseball games, sleeping-cars, coffee, the New York Subway, and Ice-Cream! Now I knew what they were homesick for. It was for that intangible helter-skelter, vivacity, and unexpectedness of life in America which is so amusing and such a splendid tonic when one is young. But it was the sunshine, so clean and transparent, that captivated me.

Mrs. Ogden Reid's offer to come back was strangely tempting. But how could I bear to leave the Embassy and how could I leave my family? I tried to put it out of my mind, hoping it would die, but instead it persisted, managed to intrude itself at inconvenient moments — when I was tired with the same old routine and obliged to work such long hours that there was little time for life outside. Then those wonderful days in the Adirondacks drifting along in a sailboat would come back to me, the peaceful afternoons, with glasses of iced tea and little cakes, and a tennis court waiting for someone to get up energy enough to play — such luxury and leisure as I had never known before! It didn't help for Mr. Laughlin to tell me that working in the United States was an entirely different proposition from going there as a guest, and that he didn't for a moment think I should like it.

I couldn't help feeling, however, that while I had been away things had subtly changed. There was, for instance, a Miss Margery Ford, an American, installed as stenographer to the Ambassador, who seemed to be quiet and friendly and to know her job. She would relieve me of a lot of routine, Mr. Laughlin explained. I began to think they hadn't missed me much, although all pretended they had, and said how delighted and relieved they were to see me back. Perhaps it was I who had changed. Was Fate pushing me towards New York? I protested that I preferred to remain in London. Well, then, was I content to remain at the Embassy? No, I wasn't. Did I want to leave England? No — a thousand times No! Didn't I, then, want to go back to the United States sometime? Yes, I did. And so the battle went on.

20

The repeal of the Panama Canal Tolls Act. Mr. Page's troubles over his speeches. The opening of the World War, and how it affected the Embassy.

1914

Tʜᴇ winter of 1913–14 passed rather uneventfully at the Embassy, for the United States was still little more than an onlooker at the boiling cauldron of European controversy, which, although it had seemed likely to explode in war at any moment during the last few years, had yet managed to keep on simmering harmlessly. Most American diplomats had almost come to regard this state of apparent imminent eruption as something permanent, not to be taken too seriously, and among the masses in England the repeated cry of wolf had long since begun to fall on bored or deaf ears. Lord Roberts must be getting senile to be so hysterical about the possibility of German attack.

Surrounded by this almost paralyzing atmosphere, indeed hardly conscious of it, as they endeavoured to carry out policies of the United States far removed from the grim reality around them, the Embassy was kept occupied. The happenings in Mexico continued to cause Anglo-American friction because the unsympathetic attitude of the British Minister at Mexico City towards American policies was reflected by the Foreign Office. The protection of British subjects and their concessions in times of political disturbance was part of the irritation, until after a time a hint came floating by that if the United States would not intervene to protect, not only

British but other foreign interests in Mexico, Great Britain would be forced to take some action that would be resented as an interference with the Monroe Doctrine.

However, long before the question became urgent enough to call for a showdown, the attention of the world was concentrated on Europe, and in the turmoil of its new responsibilities as a neutral in the World War the Embassy practically forgot it. So true was this that a few weeks after the war broke out a newspaper man, calling on Mr. Laughlin for news for his paper in the United States, and having exhausted every other topic enquired,

'Oh, by the way, how's Mexico?'

'Mexico! Mexico!' snapped Mr. Laughlin irritably, 'and who's he?'

In contrast to diplomatic friction there was a pleasant little interlude in the early spring when the New York and Chicago Baseball Teams arrived in England, and on the very day of their arrival the King enquired whether they intended to play a game, because if so he would like to attend. The King's wish was passed on to the teams and a game immediately arranged. A list of the personnel of the teams was sent in advance by Mr. McGraw to the Embassy for the King's use, and the match was played at the Chelsea football ground before a large crowd. Mr. Page and Mr. Laughlin sat, one on each side of His Majesty, in the centre of the front row of the grandstand, and judging by the laughter, all had a good time. The King asked many questions, with both the others answering and pointing out specially fine bits of play. Once or twice they were only saved from black eyes by the netting.

Many English people were sitting near me in the row directly behind the King, and as none of them knew anything about baseball, and I had seen one game in Chicago, I undertook to explain it, and might have gone on had I not encountered a chilly look from Mr. Laughlin, which silenced me. The English audience did its best to follow, but were only really excited when a catch was made, for they knew about that from cricket. So towards the end, trying to liven things up, some of the outfielders began to indulge in private stunts, and these were such a great success that when the game finished, the whole crowd was full of cheer and good-fellowship. As we came down the stairs after shouting ourselves hoarse when the King left, I heard one man say that he thought there might be something to baseball, after all!

In March, 1914, just a year after President Wilson assumed office, came the longed-for repeal of the Panama Canal Tolls Act. The President went before the Senate and asked for 'the repeal of that provision of the Panama Canal Act of 1912 which exempts vessels engaged in the coastwise trade of the United States from payment of tolls, and to urge upon you the justice, the wisdom and the larger policy of such a repeal with the utmost earnestness of which I am capable.…'

'We consented to the treaty,' he said, meaning the Hay-Pauncefote Treaty, 'its language we accepted if we did not originate it, and we are too big, too powerful, too self-respecting a nation to interpret with a too strained and re-fined reading the words of our own promises just because we have power enough to give us leave to read them as we please. The large thing to do is the only thing we can afford to do, a voluntary withdrawal from a position everywhere questioned and misunderstood.'

That must have been a blow for Mr. Taft!

So the Act was repealed, and there was tremendous relief and satisfaction in England, for if this was an indication of Democratic policy and of Mr. Wilson's way of conducting international business, it was felt that Anglo-American relations were in good hands. There was a brand of fair thinking and good-will that had been scarce in many of the negotiations of recent years, and Mr. Wilson's feeling for the sanctity of treaties was welcomed and praised on every hand.

I rather wondered what the President had meant by 'we did not originate the language,' for a package of notes that we had found at the Embassy and forwarded to Washington the year before had been filled with suggestions and counter-suggestions about every point and almost every word. These showed that even if, as President Wilson claimed, the United States did not 'originate it,' Mr. Choate, Mr. Hay, and Mr. White had evidently made as many suggestions as the British Government. Or, if Mr. Wilson meant 'we did not originate the treaty,' then who did? For wasn't it the United States who wished to get the Clayton-Bulwer Treaty out of the way so that they could build the Canal?

Poor Mr. Page was having the usual troubles trying to please both his British audiences and the diverse elements in the United States. He couldn't seem to believe that there were, as there always had been, unfriendly and suspicious people in the United States ready to pounce on anything said by the Ambassador to England that might be construed as 'truckling to the British.' Mr. Choate, who had been especially subjected to that form of criticism, could have warned Mr. Page about it. But Mr. Page was lacking in that brand of protective colouring; he was unused to having his every word weighed to find if it could be used to his disadvantage; he was, in short, so unversed in the discretion which his diplomatic office imposed upon him that he was always liable to get into hot water. He had been warned many times, and the remark made by a reporter at a Navy League Dinner had been repeated again and again for his edification. This individual — called a 'sneaking whelp' by Mr. Page — had listened to what he said at the dinner, and, as he got up to go, yawned and said, 'Well, there's nothing in it for me — nothing for which his recall can be demanded.'

So on March 12, when a cable was received from Mr. Bryan informing the Ambassador that a 'Resolution has been adopted by the Senate containing a request that you furnish it without delay with a copy of your speech at the annual dinner of the Associated Chamber of Commerce in London in which you are reported by the newspapers to have made the statement that the simple meaning of the Monroe Doctrine is that the United States prefers that no more land shall be gained in the new world by European governments and that you declared amid laughter that the pleasure of building the Canal had been greatly enhanced by the knowledge that the British would derive most benefit from its use' — Mr. Page was perfectly furious and aghast. A further cable, however, reassured him that the request was made simply in compliance with the Senate Resolution and did not imply criticism by the President.

All Mr. Page had said was: 'I will not say that we constructed the Panama Canal even for you. For I am speaking with great frankness and not with diplomatic indirection. We built it for reasons of our own. But I will say that it adds to the pleasure of building that great work that you will profit by it. You will profit most, for you have the greatest carrying trade. . . .'

Mr. Page was having continued difficulties with his finances, too, discovering that it cost far more to be an Ambassador than he had expected. He had begun to feel that he could not afford to remain in London, and yet he did not want to embarrass the State Department. The Embassy, full of sympathy, yet feeling he was oversensitive, hoped he was airing his troubles long and loud in Washington.

But when it was hinted that Mr. Bryan — Mr. Page's *bête noire* — was about to descend on Europe and deliver speeches in behalf of his peace treaties, Mr. Page felt that the limit had been reached. He was not the only one perturbed, for it was a serious breach of international etiquette for any official — especially a Secretary of State — to make speeches in a foreign country, except only after a formal invitation to do so had been given and accepted, and the speech delivered under the supervision of the inviting Government with appropriate ceremony. However, in the end Mr. Bryan didn't come — perhaps he didn't receive enough encouragement — and Mr. Page didn't resign.

Mr. Cresson was transferred to Central America along towards spring, and in his place, to be Second Secretary, came a Mr. Edward Bell, a regular cyclone, with flashing black eyes, uncertain temper, brilliant intuitive mind, and a flood of invective that reminded me of the best efforts of a bargee. At first glance he looked like the quietest sort of conventional gentleman, perfect in every detail, and his attitude towards Mr. Laughlin and the Ambassador was most respectful. But let any little thing happen to disturb him, and off went the lid! Frank Hodson would fly from him, and everybody else gave him a wide berth. But, apart from boiling up like a bottle of soda water whenever he was crossed, he was one of the most charming as well as amusing men who was ever at the Embassy, so dynamic, so unexpected, so thrillingly interesting! He soon guessed that I liked him and wasn't in the least afraid of him, and we became very good friends. There were many times when I would sit and laugh while he harangued about some trifle that wasn't even worth a thought. In the end he would sometimes laugh, too, a bit apologetically. Like Mr. Grant-Smith, he seemed to feel that sinister forces were at work to undermine the United States, and kept a wary eye on what he called — glaring at me — 'that Foreign Office of yours.'

It wasn't until the World War came that Mr. Bell's greatest usefulness began, and then he was a tower of strength, for he took over and was entirely responsible for one of the most difficult of all jobs in wartime — spies and secret-service activities and the checking-up of many people who were prancing round the world on mysterious errands, mostly unlawful! He used to say that what he had learned had so disillusioned him that after this he would not trust his own mother under oath!

There was nothing of the friendly helping hand about him. He believed in leaving people to their fate if they hadn't enough sense to find their own way out of difficulties. I remember, in those early war days, a telegram coming from an unknown Austrian lady addressed to her husband whose whereabouts was entirely unknown, in which she said, 'Answer at once or I shall kill myself and the children.' Mr. Chandler Hale was in charge of the Austrian division of the Embassy, and Mr. Bell telephoned the telegram to him.

'Oh, how dreadful!' said the sympathetic Mr. Hale. 'But what shall I do? How can I find the man? Who would know?'

'That's your job,' said Mr. Bell blandly; 'but you'd better get moving and do something.'

'Yes, but what?' almost wept Mr. Hale.

'I wouldn't presume to interfere with your department,' and Mr. Bell unfeelingly rang off.

'How could you?' I reproved him as he slammed down the telephone.

'Oh, I just want to see what sort of brain-wave His Nibs will have. I'll call him in a few minutes and see what we can do.' And of course he did, for he knew the ropes much better than Mr. Hale.

During May the King and Queen of Denmark paid a State visit to their British relatives and there were two Court Balls. Among those who attended the second were Mr. and Mrs. Cornelius Vanderbilt. As I remember, Mrs. Vanderbilt and her children went on to Switzerland immediately afterwards, and when the war broke out, Mr. Vanderbilt set forth to rescue them with four different passports issued by the Embassy (absolutely against all rules) to cover various contingencies — one for himself and Mrs. Vanderbilt, one for her and her children and nurses, one without the nurses, and the last for Mr. Vanderbilt alone. With all these precautions they had no difficulty in getting back to London. I wonder whether he ever turned in those extra passports!

There were two further Courts in June, at the first of which Mr. and Mrs. Ralph Page, Mrs. Edward Bell (wife of the Second Secretary, recently married), and Miss Esther Cleveland were presented in the Diplomatic Circle, and on June 28 came a notification that the Court would be in mourning for a week for His Imperial and Royal Highness the late Archduke Franz Ferdinand of Austria Este, K.G., C.V.O., to go out of mourning on July 5. Little did we realize that the assassination at Sarajevo of this rather obscure man and his sad little morganatic wife (so proudly riding beside him in state that day for the first time in her life) was the match that was to light the conflagration that would sweep away the world we knew. That the moment was so imminent we did not dream.

Colonel House had just finished an unofficial trip to the various European capitals and reported that he found no comfort anywhere. He was worried at the obvious signs of coming war, especially in Germany which he described as a charged dynamo. But, whatever the Government may have known, the people of England were unaware of any particular tension. Irish affairs were bordering on civil war and the suffragettes were talking of blowing up the House of Commons. Hundreds of thousands of Americans were in various parts of Europe, and the assassination of the Archduke meant nothing to them. Who could have foreseen that the international line-up of treaties and *ententes* to promote peace would, when the match was struck, be found to be nothing more than an obligation on each nation to protect itself by aligning itself with one side or the other? The *Entente Cordiale* obligated England to go to the assistance of France in case Germany attacked her (it did not obligate her to send an army), and the guaranty of Belgian neutrality given by many nations, including both Germany and England, must be upheld. If France was attacked or Belgium invaded, there was no honourable way out for England.

By the beginning of July we were all tired out, and tempers were worn ragged. The Ambassador and Secretaries had just returned from attending a Naval Review where they had seen more than two hundred British battleships lined up in the Solent — a witness to England's naval preparedness, though the gathering seemed to have no special significance — and Mr. Page had taken a house in the country where he hoped to get some rest. The Secretaries had also made plans to get away from the turmoil of London, and my thoughts were dallying idly with my future, for I had written Mrs. Ogden Reid that I would accept her offer and return to the United States in September.

Instead of the rest which everybody had been looking forward to, ominous mutterings filled the air. I began to index small items under 'Austria and Servia.' Servia had appealed to Russia for aid against Austria, who had sent her an ultimatum demanding certain satisfactions for the murder of the Archduke. Russia told her to accept Austria's demands with the exception or two, which she suggested be brought before the Hague Tribunal. But this did not satisfy Austria. Her Ambassador at Belgrade declared that nothing but complete acceptance would satisfy his Government, and left Servia for home, which, in diplomatic usage, was tantamount to a declaration of war. All this came pouring in in telegrams, notes, memoranda of most of the countries. Europe was excited and afraid.

Enquiries began to come as to what we should do 'if war comes,' and we began to hurry off communications and enquiries to the American Embassies on the Continent, vaguely fearing that something might happen to prevent their safe delivery. The Ambassador instructed the Secretaries to tell all American visitors, very quietly and without arousing their alarm, that they had better make plans to go home at once.

Everybody carried out the orders, but did it so tactfully that I doubt whether one single American cancelled his proposed trip to the Continent or shortened by even one day his stay in England until the newspaper stories became so alarming that they told their own story.

On July 31 a gathering of the Pilgrims was to be the last big Anglo-American function of peace — the Waterloo Ball of the World War! Lord Roberts, who was to have been in the chair, was 'unavoidably prevented by urgent affairs from attending,' and there were no other British officials or diplomats present — a hint to anyone of discernment — so Viscount Bryce, former Ambassador at Washington, presided. 'We are friends happily with all the world,' he said, although he must have known why Lord Roberts was not present, and that even while he was speaking Austria was bombarding Belgrade, Belgium had ordered mobilization in self-defence, Germany had recalled her High Sea Fleet, and the British Navy — which had not been dispersed since the review — had cancelled all leave and was preparing as a precaution to steam northward to take up its place opposite to the German coast. On that day, too, Germany had asked England if she intended to remain neutral in a Continental war and Sir Edward Grey had enquired in return whether Germany intended to respect the neutrality of Belgium according to treaty.

Was Lord Bryce at this critical moment making a personal appeal for understanding with the other half of the Anglo-American world when he said:

> Just as the Thames, which rolls below the windows of this hotel, is composed of millions of drops of water, so the friendship of the two countries rests upon the individual friendships of thousands and thousands — I might almost say millions — of persons who know and esteem one another, and who are desirous that their countries should be friends even as they are friends themselves. . . . We have with the United States a special kind of friendship which is more than a friendship; it is a kind of mutual comprehension. It is what Goldwin Smith boldly

called, in days long ago, when ties had not grown so close as they are now, a 'League of the Heart.'

It almost seemed so. A league of the heart! That was what was needed, not only between England and America but between all nations, for only by that road could peace ever come to the world.

By August 2 the German troops had entered Luxembourg and Sir Edward Grey was trying to make up his mind whether England could remain neutral, for he was no sabre-rattler and realized only too well the terrible responsibility of taking his country into a great war, especially as the Cabinet was very divided on the question. But the ordinary people had no misgivings. They knew they must fight if Belgium were invaded, not only because of the treaty, but because it would never do to have German armies so close to the English coast.

In my train going home, everyone, a bit depressed, was talking of what might happen, and later in the evening my mother and I went for a stroll with Bobby Burns, a handsome Scottie given to me by Mr. and Mrs. Laughlin, and I told her all I knew about the situation. Tooting Common looked especially lovely that night, with people in their summer clothes, the band playing, and many boats on the lake. The sunset was liquid gold, a pure water-colour of delicate pastels, and as the night came down it was so quietly peaceful and beautiful that the thought of war seemed absolutely nonsensical. But that night I had a feeling of absolute despair. Was all we loved to go? The charm of the civilization that we had built up — was it nearing its end? And what about the future? It *couldn't* be that war was actually on us! And yet, as I glanced up I fancied I saw a searchlight...

Next morning, everybody else being busy with an Embassy overrun with visitors, I began to look up the legal position of strangers in a country at war, and found that friendly aliens would be all right so long as they didn't interfere and did exactly as they were told, for apparently foreigners living in

England are considered to have a 'temporary allegiance' to it, and the visitors, I was sure, would have no other thought than to get away. It was Bank Holiday, so everyone was out, wandering aimlessly up and down the streets.

I was most interested to hear that, during the week-end, sensing the coming emergency, a group of American summer visitors, Mr. Fred I. Kent of the Bankers' Trust Company, Mr. Oscar Straus, formerly American Ambassador at Constantinople, Mr. Herbert Hetzler, and Mr. William C. Breed had got together and organized themselves and several others into a committee. They had been given as headquarters — without any charge whatever — the dining-room floor on the Thames Embankment side of the Savoy Hotel, and were all ready to help their fellow citizens who had already begun to flock from the Continent in thousands. In telling me about it when he came in, Mr. Laughlin thought it positively amazing what the group had been able to accomplish in a few hours.

Later in the morning, the committee arrived in person to tell the Ambassador what had been done and ask his approval and co-operation. Mr. Page told them they had lifted a great burden off his mind, that he would head the committee (along with the Consul-General), and would turn over to them the care of all Americans who came to the Embassy for advice or relief. As everyone was clamouring for passports, and these could only be issued by an authorized officer of the Diplomatic Service in London, Mr. Gerry Greene, another new Third Secretary, was told off to the Savoy a day or two afterwards and a passport office installed there. Thus came into existence the famous American Relief Committee, which functioned until all Americans had returned home safely. To it was added almost immediately the permanent Committee of Resident Americans in London — which took over the whole work when the travelling Americans had gone home — and valuable assistance was also rendered by the Consulate-General. Of the great work done for their fellow Americans in providing money and credit, lodgings, passages, sympathy, morale, and friendship, I knew only what came to me at second hand, for my energies were taken up entirely with the overwhelmingly interesting, immediate, and varied diplomatic business.

As a matter of historic interest the list of the American Relief Committee,[1] with the various sub-committees, is included in an appendix.

If war *did* come I expected that the Embassy would exercise 'good offices' towards the various countries — that is, if the United States was to remain neutral, as I presumed she would, for she was not immediately concerned now, though if England were beaten, she might find herself next in line.

After everyone had gone that Bank Holiday evening, I tried to analyze my feelings. I knew there was general distrust of Lord Haldane, who was very friendly to Germany; uncertainty about the Labour Party and what they intended to do; a mixture of feeling about France mostly negative, and the same about Belgium. We had, of course, always half-expected the war. Lord Roberts had talked himself hoarse up and down the country until everybody was thoroughly annoyed with all the 'preparedness' talk, except that we agreed on one point, that the Navy must be kept up, whatever the cost. It was our absolute belief in the Navy that accounted, perhaps, for our seeming carelessness. We were sure that it was the best in the world, and I almost think we were sorry for the Germans. Was the Kaiser so sure of victory that he would go to the length of defying England by invading Belgium? And if he did would the British Labour Party and the other pacifists decide that that was crime enough to justify England's declaring war?

Sir Edward Grey, in perhaps the greatest speech of his career, had said in the House of Commons that afternoon, 'If in a crisis like this we run away from our obligations of honour

[1] See Appendix B.

and interest with regard to the Belgian treaty, I doubt, whatever material force we might have in the end, whether it would be of very much value in face of the respect we should have lost.'

It could not help but be war. As I realized this, I put my head down on the hard cold typewriter in sudden fear mingled with a curious thrill of excitement. One thing was certain. I shouldn't be able to go to New York. My place was here.

A footstep outside roused me. It was our postman from the office opposite, a friend of many years standing, come to say good-bye. He was leaving for Belgium that night, not to fight, he assured us, for war had not been declared, but to make arrangements for the delivery of mail. We never saw him again.

21

August 4, 1914, at the London Embassy. Stranded Americans and their efforts to get passage to America. England declares war on Germany.

1914

I<small>T WAS</small> the morning of August 4, 1914....

The train that brought me into London was punctual. The only sign of anything untoward was a sentry standing on guard at Clapham Junction, one of the largest railway stations just outside London. This sentry was the object of much interest on the part of the passengers, because of the novelty of seeing a soldier in such a spot. He looked rather forlorn and there was apparently nothing at all for him to do.

Arrived at Victoria Station, I hurried out with the rest, and took my way rapidly down to '123,' where the porter, appropriately and patriotically named George England, admitted me somewhat morosely.

I saw at once the reason for George England's gloom. It was not the quiet, dignified scene of diplomacy *in absentia* that greeted my eyes this morning. Instead, the vestibule and reception rooms were filled with men and women, with anxious faces, talking and gesticulating — and one woman in tears. The two Messengers, with Mr. Edward Bell, Mr. Greene, and Mr. Fowler, all early risers during the past week, were trying to cope with the many demands made upon them and to stem the tide of almost panic that seemed to be imminent. The harassed people had learned that all steamship

(257)

passages were cancelled 'for the present,' and they were frightened and short of money, as the ordinary August Bank Holiday had been extended by the Bank of England for an additional two days to get its finances adjusted. Currency was therefore very scarce, and even the American banks felt the desirability of conserving it.

So here the Americans were, stranded in a foreign land with a war almost in sight and no way to get home. This was more than they had bargained for, coming as they did for relaxation and culture, and they rushed to the Embassy in the hope that it might be able to bring pressure to bear on the steamship companies to release the ships. The majority of them were good-tempered and patient, but the inevitable few were outspoken in their criticisms of those who permitted such barbaric things as war to happen. Most of them wanted passports. There were many who came in merely for comfort. They wanted assurances that this catastrophe which seemed to be rushing towards them was a nightmare. This group fussed and fumed, and their sorrows seemed so fatuous and empty in the face of the real tragedies that none of us were as sympathetic as we might have been, I fear. We knew that they were in no particular danger, that they would not suffer from lack of food or lodging, but were actually in the proud position of having front seats without any participation in the war itself.

Pushing my way through the crowds, I found my desk covered with official documents. The incoming and outgoing correspondence of the last few days had shattered any fond illusions that anyone at the Embassy might have had that the struggle could be localized except by a miracle, and we all realized that the end of this day would probably find England drawn into the great European conflict which had been in the making for years, but which had been definitely brought up on to the horizon by the assassination of the Archduke.

Conscious as I was, that morning, of impending tragedy, I

had the routine of the day to keep me from thinking. Opening my desk, I set to work. A request from the Foreign Office to restrict our use of the cable to messages absolutely necessary; an enquiry about one of the ships in a German harbour; a notification that a certain Consul's appointment was satisfactory; a cable from Washington asking us to secure the arrest of a man wanted by the State of Pennsylvania for forgery, and his return to the United States; one or two replies from the Foreign Office to questions asked on behalf of certain Government departments of the United States; a reply from Washington to the enquiry as to whether anything was being done by the United States to promote peace on the Continent; and several telegrams from prominent people in America asking us to look after their various friends and relatives supposed to be in London.

By the time these were all indexed, Mr. Laughlin arrived, much worried at things in general and harassed by the crowds of people, many of whom recognized him, through which he had to pass on his way in. Almost on his heels came Ambassador Page, who also with some difficulty forced his way in and into his own room. There Mr. Laughlin joined him, with the day's correspondence in his hand, but, apparently without stopping to read it, Mr. Page came out again after a few minutes, went into the reception room, and began to make a speech to the assembled visitors. His cheery manner at once had a profound effect on their drooping spirits, and his common-sense attitude stabilized the atmosphere. He said that if war did come there was nothing for them to be afraid of, that their interests would be safeguarded in every way, and that he would do whatever he could to get them home as soon as possible. He asked those who had not come for anything special to leave, so that the work of the Embassy could be attended to without delay, and told them about the Committee at the Savoy Hotel.

Later in the morning, Mr. Page repeated his cheerful words

to a new crowd, many of whom had had difficulty in reaching England from the Continent, but, although some of them left, there remained a stolid group who seemed to feel safe under their own flag in their own Embassy. They sat in every corner, on the tables, and even on the narrow stone staircase that led to the second floor — to the annoyance of naval and military officers who went up and down to consult with the Attachés upstairs. Each time a Secretary went through the hall he was surrounded and questioned, and even I was called upon from time to time when one of my own sex developed hysterical tendencies.

A telephone call from the German Embassy brought Mr. Laughlin hastily back from the clutches of a despondent gentleman who said he simply *must* sail. 'Yes, this is Laughlin. Yes, we have promised already to look after things. But are you certain you will go? The German Government has until midnight to answer the British ultimatum.' But the members of the German Embassy seemed sure that no answer would be forthcoming and wished to assure themselves that their people and their property would be taken care of by their American colleagues until the war was over. They informed Mr. Laughlin that Germans of military age were leaving as fast as they could, and that most of their officials and archives would go with the Ambassador as soon as the war was an actual fact.... They said also that there would still be many Germans left, especially women and children who might need protection, and would the Embassy take care of them....

Troubles with these 'adopted responsibilities' developed immediately. During the morning an hysterical Austrian lady appeared, sent by the Austrian Ambassador. It appeared that her husband, a German, had left his hotel, she had not seen him since, and she feared he might have been arrested to prevent his leaving England. It developed that this gentleman was an agent of the Krupp Company of Germany and had waited just a little too long before making his get-away.

The British Government had the gentleman safe and sound and were not disposed to release him, though the lady promised in his behalf to leave his files behind. It reminded us of a visit which a group of Krupp agents had made to England only a few months before to see some of the military establishments. It seemed foolhardy, this showing off of new military inventions to a foreign competitor, but, with guile that Americans will understand, the program was arranged with a full appreciation of certain little German weaknesses. The party always managed to arrive at their destination at mealtime, and before any tour of inspection could be made an exhaustive banquet had to be partaken of, with much wine and speech-making, after which the delegates, dazed with too much food and oratory, were permitted to make their observations, in the complete confidence that they would understand very little of the very little that was shown them.

The morning also brought in many other prominent American business men, who, realizing that a crisis was upon them and that they couldn't get home for the present, came to offer their services in something other than relief measures. They were splendid sports, and rallied round the Ambassador with touching docility and good humour. Two or three American diplomats also, *en route* for their posts, and who had planned a day or two's recreation in London, made hasty arrangements to continue their journey. Among these was Mr. Thomas Nelson Page, Ambassador to Italy, who left hoping to get as far as Paris by train, after which he expected to have to cross the Alps to Rome by motor. We saw him go with misgivings, for there was no certainty that on some lonely Alpine highway he would not be requested to get out of his car, and find himself watching the back of it fade from sight in the hands of a group of soldiers. He had only his diplomatic rank to protect him. Mr. Sheldon Crosby, appointed to Madrid from Siam, was due to reach London any day, and Mr. Page had determined to commandeer his services to help with the passport business.

The afternoon wore away, with Americans still flocking into the Embassy. Outside, the crowds streamed by, newspaper boys calling extras pushing their way hither and thither, busses filled with anxious-eyed people lumbered by, and little groups of reserves marched along, very conscious of their uniforms and their impending glory.

A sound of martial music brought us rushing to the front window for a moment's respite. Swaggering along, in full marching equipment, was one of the most famous Irish regiments, with cheering crowds marching along beside the soldiers. The excitement was tremendous. We did not know where they were going, and neither, it turned out, did they. They had imagined, it appeared, that they were on their way to the war and were to be the first regiment sent across. But it turned out that they were only being transferred from one barracks to another. When they discovered the truth, their wrath boiled over with characteristic Irish thoroughness, and another regiment had to be called out to pacify these impatient would-be heroes.

The Ambassador returned, looking stern and anxious, about four o'clock from a brief call at the Foreign Office, and shut himself into his room to write a cable to Washington. It was very quiet and peaceful in this room, with its heavy carpet and the pictures of his predecessors staring down at him from the walls. He was tired and ill at ease, and very conscious of his responsibilities for these thousands of Americans whom he couldn't protect, cut off from home by an ocean three thousand miles wide. He remembered with a shudder that it was the belief of the experts that Germany's first naval move against England would be to send her ships into the Atlantic Ocean, and that this attempt could be expected immediately after war was declared. In their opinion a naval battle might well be fought during the coming night which in a few hours would decide the fate of the British and German navies. Sir Edward Grey had told Mr. Page officially that war would actually be declared at midnight if no answer was forthcoming from Germany. Mr. Page must now report this and his anxieties to the Secretary of State, and ask for the assistance and money that he would need to do the stupendous task which was just beginning. He felt conscious of failure, the failure of the diplomacy he stood for, to ward off this terrible thing that was impending, and he knew that he must try to convey in his cable some indication of the disorganization, terror, and chaos that surrounded him.

He sat there in his chair quite still a long time, this foreigner looking on at a tragedy that was not his, but with which he was so closely linked. He understood what unwelcome guests his fellow countrymen must be in a country faced with war to the death. Finally he began to write, and page after page of his beautiful, even handwriting was placed face downward in perfect order as he finished it — as orderly as the thoughts that he strove to clothe in appropriate and burning words. His rather tragic face (something like Abraham Lincoln's, I thought) reflected his sombre thoughts, and the feeling of the reflective mood was intensified by the sacrificial spirals of smoke rising unheeded from a cigar smouldering by his side. His secretary, Mr. Fowler, came and went noiselessly, glancing at him affectionately, and letting in a buzz of eager conversation every time he opened and closed the door. But Mr. Page heard nothing. He was completely absorbed, and the room itself was the only oasis of quiet in the whole turbulent Embassy.

Twilight and evening came late, as they do in England in August. The staff worked on unceasingly at the official business which had been so delayed all day, callers grew fewer and fewer, and the Ambassador finally left for the night after a hearty 'Thank you' to his busy helpers. By this time it was beginning to be realized by the general public that no answer was coming from Germany. The streets grew almost impassable with people intent on being in front of the Houses of Parliament or Buckingham Palace when the great moment arrived.

Poor things, how could they know, mere human atoms in the clutches of a violent emotion, what was in store for their country and their loved ones? They were filled with a clanging, rather cheap, false gaiety, whistling perhaps to keep up their courage. Girls and boys with linked arms marched merrily, the boys almost unconsciously trying to pull away as the inherited instincts aroused by the thoughts of war made them long to be gone, while the girls almost as unconsciously tried to restrain them. Older men and women with anxious faces passed along, with more understanding. They were not carried away by this glamorous aspect of war. They had seen other wars. Their loved ones had come back to them before, wounded and wasted. Some had never come back. But these thoughtful ones were in the minority. Every bus was loaded with sight-seers. There was some horse-play, some air of holiday because something unusual was astir, some boasting about 'poor old Fritz and what 'e 'as comin' to 'im, pore old chap,' and a good deal of drinking. It would be a quick war, over in a very few months, and there was nothing much to worry about.

I went out for a hasty supper about ten o'clock. Every restaurant was full, bands playing bravely, to the same assortment of gay and serious people. A steady stream of others went by, flocking towards Buckingham Palace, and the light on top of Big Ben announced that Parliament was still sitting, and that, probably at that very moment, while they were waiting for the final answer, a debate was going forward that might change English history forever. The scene in the streets showed that mixture of sublime and ridiculous which makes life for the interested observer so everlastingly thrilling.

The Embassy looked untidy and almost tawdry as I came in

about ten-thirty, with papers scattered everywhere, a feeling of dead air, and a silk hat perched rakishly on the head of the sculptured Miss Liberty, giving her a ribald and unladylike appearance. The hum of typewriters clicking upstairs in the headquarters of the Naval and Military Attachés proclaimed them still at work, and in the Messengers' office cables were being prepared in cipher. My desk was piled with new things to be done, and Mr. Laughlin sat at his absorbed in a despatch in which he was attempting to convey some sense of the general events to a far-off Government. He did not even glance up. He had a power of concentration that I envied, for all that day I had been almost carried away with the drama of my position in the midst of history in the making, seeing it from the point of view of another country which was not concerned in it for the time being except as a spectator. I was apprehensive, discouraged, and swamped in a sort of sloppy patriotism, absurd and destructive. I could not command my complete attention in the way Mr. Laughlin did, for my ears were tuned to the noises outside and my spirits were sinking as the hours drew on to midnight.

Eleven o'clock, then twelve — zero hour, with no news. The streets blazed with light, most of the population seemed to be out-of-doors this beautiful summer night, and an air of expectancy prevailed. The telephone rang a few times, and I jumped nervously, but it was only newspaper men asking for news, or anxious wives enquiring for erring diplomatic husbands. The pile of work grew less. We were all tired, and it was a final relief when the Ambassador's secretary let himself in just after midnight, although the news he brought was bad. He had just come from outside Buckingham Palace, where he had heard the news of war. He had seen the King and Queen respond to the overwhelming demonstrations of faith and patriotism and had joined in singing 'God Save the King.' In the face of the inevitable, we decided that our slight efforts could now make little difference, and that, as this was probably but the beginning of many terrible days, we had better conserve our strength for the future.

As I opened the front door to let myself out, a Foreign Office special messenger handed me a Note, marked 'Immediate,' addressed to the Ambassador. With it in my hand I walked back and handed it to Mr. Laughlin, standing by while he read it. It was the official declaration:

> The Secretary of State for Foreign Affairs presents his compliments to the American Ambassador, and begs to inform His Excellency that a state of war exists between His Majesty's Government and that of Germany.

The war had begun.

22

The United States' 'good offices' as a neutral during the World War.
1914–1916

THE day-by-day diary that I kept during the first months of
the World War, which there is no room to include here, was
left in the safe in the London Embassy until 1919, because, as
a British subject, it seemed to me more discreet, when I sailed
for New York at the end of 1914, to leave it behind. Ever
since then I have been waiting for some book to appear in
which the work of salvage to the nations at war, carried on by
the American Foreign Service during the years of America's
neutrality, was at least acknowledged. But as there has been
no book I shall try to sum up something of what I knew.
What these men — specially those in the London Embassy
— did for thousands of victims, aside from the official service
to their countries known as 'good offices,' has been far too
little known and has never received proper recognition.

August 4 found England with thousands of foreigners of
the fighting countries within her borders, and thousands of
her own people in foreign countries, all the men trying to get
home to fight. I do not remember exactly how freely Germany let Englishmen of military age leave, but England permitted Germans of military age to leave until the tenth of
August. I presume French and Italians and Austrians got
back to their countries somehow, but that again I don't remember.

The men gone, there remained the women and children to

be looked after, and these were left to the protection of the American Foreign Service. There were large numbers of foreign governesses, ladies' maids, office people, and older men and women who had somehow to be got home, if they preferred to go, or looked after if they remained where they were. Their money gave out, their freedom of intercourse was stopped, their clubs were closed, their mail was intercepted and censored, their remittances were stopped, and their very food might have been uncertain had it not been for arrangements made by the American Foreign Service with the various Governments to handle reciprocal relief funds.

The return of these persons to their homes was a tourist business in itself. The groups were collected, the passage of ships carrying them across the perilous mine-strewn North Sea rendered safe, and when the other side was reached they were passed on to other Americans — or sometimes to their own Consuls — who saw that they reached their homes. Returning groups of women and children to Germany and Austria was part of the regular routine of those early months, as was the bringing back of the corresponding British women and children.

The American Foreign Service was also the official channel for communication between the various warring Governments. If the British Government wished to find out anything from the German or Austrian Government they enquired of the American Ambassador and he had somehow to find a way to reach Berlin or Vienna — with the mails closed — and get an answer. A good part of my war diary was taken up with the trials and difficulties of communication, and as every question handled was of serious immediacy and importance there was no room for delay. The ordinary routine of peace — to send everything through the Department of State — would not do at all. It took far too long, and caused an amount of explanation that handicapped the emergency nature of the work.

A system of couriers enabled us to take care of it best and

was arranged between the American Embassies direct, but, as civilian matters in time of war are always sacrificed to the exigencies of the war itself, there was never any certainty of the couriers arriving anywhere at any particular time, for everybody was in a nervous tension of fear and hatred. All that could be done was to plan as best we could, and then wait for some sort of reply. Sometimes it came, sometimes it didn't. Sometimes we were impatient, and had a feeling that unfriendly hands were holding up communications. Sometimes we were surprised and delighted at unexpected co-operation. Naturally there were several brushes with the Department of State about the courier system, for they felt everything should go through them so that they would know what was going on, but a compromise was reached in the end by which they permitted the Embassies to act direct in the majority of cases.

The censorship brought much grief, as many people tried to get letters through to their relatives in foreign countries by way of the Embassy despatch pouches which were of course exempt from the clutches of the censor. It was hard to refuse this very human request, but as representing a neutral country the Embassy had to be continually on its guard. Some of the Consuls were not so careful, but they soon found that letters sent by them were opened by the censor!

There were minor skirmishes between the various American Embassies, all trying to expedite their part of the great job. The Minister in Switzerland wanted the London Embassy to reserve places for Americans on the special train for British subjects leaving Geneva, instead of getting a train of his own; the Ambassador at Berlin, Mr. James W. Gerard, telegraphed direct to mayors of English cities informing them of refugees about to be returned, instead of acting through Mr. Page, causing some fuss with the Foreign Office, and the Minister at The Hague told us not to send him along any more work for the present because he was snowed under.

The London Embassy also tried to find out the whereabouts of Englishmen who had been wounded and about whom their families could get no news. That was one of the most heartbreaking phases of those early weeks. It took time to get the proper exchanges of information started, so before that many English people came to ask us to try to get news about sons who had been reported wounded or missing. Some were believed to be in French hospitals which had been captured by the Germans, some taken back to Germany, and there was no way of finding out where and how they were. They could send no word themselves and there was no one to find out anything except American officials, and they could do little beyond forwarding the enquiries to the American official nearest to the scene and ask for a reply. I know that the enquiries made by the London Embassy, and its interest in the sorrows of many individuals, and their sympathetic assistance in securing information, brought relief and comfort to many, and will never be forgotten by grateful English fathers and mothers, wives, and sisters.

Then began the regular work with the prisoners of war. Bureaus of Information were set up in course of time by the various countries, in accordance with the Hague Convention. But before that there were misunderstandings and much bitterness, each Government afraid their prisoners were being badly treated. Much ill-advised publicity was given to reports made by prejudiced and uninformed persons, and the American Foreign Service was called upon by each Government to visit the camps where their citizens were and report on the care which was being given them. In addition to this many other American officials, under the direction of the Embassy, visited camps both in England and on the Continent, until the increase in the number of prisoners and the complexity of the situation called for a separate organization.

Through the American Embassies also passed back and forth lists of wounded and prisoners and dead and hospital ships and enquiries of every sort for thousands of men. One of the things I can never forget was that first list of British casualties that came from Germany. It had been delayed for a long time, and the Foreign Office, who had long since sent on the corresponding German list, kept begging us to make enquiries, afraid that the Germans might be holding it up on purpose.

It was late in the afternoon that, hurrying downstairs, I saw a bulky package lying on a chair in the hall. Opening it, for everything was attended to immediately, I spread it out, and there before me was the first British casualty list we had been waiting for so long, accompanied by many souvenirs of the dead soldiers, pay-books (on the back page of which most men wrote their wills), watches, photographs — all the pathetic aftermath of lives laid down in war. It was too much for me, so I sat gloomily on the bottom of the stairs, thinking of the cold battlefields, the misery, dirt, and final death, and of the women and children who had lost husbands and fathers. But that was no way to be neutral, so I hurried upstairs, and under cover of a third-person note sent on the list to the Foreign Office at once.

It is awe-inspiring now to remember the speed with which the war overtook us, blotting out the past instantly, and then the speed with which we adjusted ourselves to the new conditions and new needs. The transition was practically instantaneous. Overnight, diplomacy entirely changed for the time being, and either ceased to function or translated itself — as in the case of such neutral countries as Spain and the United States — into vast machines of mercy. Strange calls were made upon the intelligence and humanity of diplomats. Some of them gave their lives as certainly as the soldiers did — literally working themselves to death — and their work was always on the side of helpfulness and salvage. They took the débris of a disorganized world, filled with horror and terror unspeakable, and toiled to bring a little order out of the general chaos. Like the monasteries of an older day the Embassies and Consulates of the United States became sanctuaries, and many thousands of people caught in the maelstrom have America's diplomats to thank for a happy ending to their afflictions.

That the great humanitarian service rendered by the American Foreign Service is almost unknown is due to the fact that the Foreign Service is on the whole rather an anonymous service. Very little is known of its members (except the few spectacular men appointed for particular purposes from time to time, for whom the stage has been set to enable them to bring off a *coup* which has perhaps been worked on by the regular staff for years) with the exception of travellers and those interested in commercial and international relations as a profession; though there is, of course, a general understanding that there are American officials in all foreign countries 'protecting American interests' there.

The State Department does not advertise its accomplishments, nor does the Foreign Service. But, as I am neither a member of the Foreign Service nor a member of the State Department, I see no reason for such concealment, for, after all, isn't that the real work of the diplomat? He is not a destroyer, but a conserver, working constructively and continuously towards a more harmonious world. He is the official interpreter of one country to another. He lives in foreign lands, speaks foreign languages, is the friend of foreigners, so that his country's interests and ideals may be understood and safeguarded. The American diplomat is America personified to the millions of foreigners who will never actually see the soil of the United States; and while he is at his post guarding the outer portals, his fellow countrymen at home may rest secure in the knowledge that some of their best citizens are 'over there' watching over their interests and representing them in the councils of the nations.

And when the war was over and a shabby peace brought an

end to the fighting and bloodshed, did these diplomatic 'Good Samaritans' get their reward? I suppose they did if inward satisfaction is meant, for they got little else. Soldiers and sailors were rewarded with public acclaim, bands, medals, and promotions, and most of the men who stayed safely at home, and played a spectacular part in the limelight without danger to life and limb, got their reward too. But what did the diplomats get who carried on the dangerous work far away under all sorts of adverse circumstances, the men who laboured — and still labour anonymously year after year — to protect American interests abroad?

The British Government alone, I believe, offered some testimonial pieces of silver plate to some of the American officials who acted for them in their *enemy* countries, though, curiously enough, the Embassy at London, which had done far more than any of the others, did not share in this recognition of service. Ambassadors, of course, were offered the decorations customarily given even in times of peace on the termination of their missions, but there was no general word of appreciation and thanks when the day of peace came round. I have always wished that the Governments who were assisted so generously by the American Foreign Service had publicly thanked them. Even if Congress had not permitted their acceptance, they should have been honoured at least by an *offer* of the distinctions appropriate to their status that had been showered upon American naval and military officers of all grades.

But alas, the gesture was never made, and it is too late now. Much has happened since to make those momentous and tragic days shadowy and unreal, and there is, especially among those who had no part in them, or profited by them, a desire to blot them out, or at least to minimize them. But they should not be allowed to be forgotten. For if, as Mr. L. P. Jacks says in one of his books, each country should live and work so as to make good history for future generations to rejoice in, surely the years of her neutrality, when her Foreign

Service carried high the banner of brotherhood and helpfulness to all the world, is a chapter of American history, of which not only ours, but the generations yet to be, should be proud.

Envoi

I<small>T</small> <small>IS</small> twenty-four years now since, in December, 1914, I left the London Embassy and came back to New York to be secretary to Mr. and Mrs. Ogden Reid. By that time the Embassy had changed completely, with an influx of new people of every grade. Not only were several additional Secretaries and Attachés sent from Washington as soon as the Department of State realized the extreme emergency that existed beyond the seas, but the clerical staff grew by leaps and bounds until there was little left of the friendly pre-war 'Embassy family.' As much of my work was concerned with the diplomatic exchanges and American criticisms of British interference with American cargoes, which seemed unfair in the tremendous drama that was going on, I was not particularly sorry to leave just then, for I did not feel very neutral. In fact, the so-called 'rights' of neutrals interested me not at all, and my sympathies were all with Ambassador Page when he said he did not want a lot of legal arguments to present to the British Government.

With a mixture of emotions, and after many unsolicited and unnecessary words of good advice to my successor and friend Minnie Lovell — to take care of Mr. Laughlin and see that he didn't further stretch the fifteen or sixteen hours a day of intensive work which he had been putting in ever since the war began — I set my face towards the United States with high hopes, fortified by the fact that I had been given six months' leave of absence so that I could return to the Embassy in case I preferred to do so.

I stayed three most interesting years in New York with Mr. and Mrs. Reid, alternately enjoying the different work and the new experiences that it made possible. But, in spite of all their kindness and generosity — and they certainly did everything in their power to make that 'sporting chance with Fate' bring forth fruit abundantly, I was constantly depressed because of my subconscious realization that I had left my country when it was in trouble and was little better than a deserter.

Sailing to England for the Christmas of 1916, along with a number of British from the remoter parts of the Empire going home to fight, hearing for the first time at the ship's concert the poignant 'Keep the home fires burning,' and staring with something of horror at the tears on every side, I wondered whether I ought not to remain in England. But when calling at the Embassy, it was so entirely different that I had no possible wish to go back there, and my family thought it not only foolish but ungrateful to Mr. and Mrs. Reid if I did not return to New York.

I sailed back in February on one of the first ships to leave port after the Germans had declared their unrestricted submarine warfare on neutral as well as enemy ships, wondering if our particular ship would be sacrificed. It was the American Line, and the passengers were about fifty per cent British and fifty per cent American, with two captains, the American captain, and an English captain travelling as a passenger, whose own vessel had been torpedoed. The English amused themselves making plans to capture the ship and take it back to Liverpool as a prize. The American captain was to be made to walk the plank, and we were instructed, when a discreet knock on the cabin door in the dead of night should proclaim the fateful moment, to proceed aft armed with our fish knives and forks!

This fooling made what otherwise might have been a gloomy voyage a very cheerful one, especially as the American captain was of great assistance in suggesting improvements in the plan. The worst moment of the trip for me was coming into the brightly illuminated New York Harbour after the gloomy nights of England, where the visits of bombing planes necessitated the protection of the friendly darkness. At that moment I hated America for flaunting her safety and her seeming unconcern with the tragedies of Europe!

All through the spring I moped, and in the summer such a wave of homesickness swept me that I went to Washington to the British Embassy to get a passport to go home. But they wouldn't give it to me — women, they intimated, were at a discount; so, as soon as possible after America had joined the Allies — to my mind a gloriously triumphant outcome of Anglo-American diplomacy — I volunteered for service and went to France with the Y.M.C.A. with something of the relief with which a martyr — long under sentence of death — must go finally to the stake. The war over, I had a small part in the Peace Conference and then returned to New York vindicated and at peace with myself.

Since then life has been full of its usual ups and downs, its pleasures, its successes and its disappointments. I have received the greatest affection and kindness from hundreds of American friends, have travelled from one end of the country to the other, enjoying the varied beauties of each district and overwhelmed with the drama and the variety of it all. I have assisted in a small way with many projects that should ultimately make for a better world, and, perhaps inevitably, an outcome of my specialized initiation into its ideas and ideals, have become an American citizen — with Mr. Ogden Reid as my sponsor — a step which was not difficult for me to take, a legal transfer only, involving no violence to my soul nor to my past.

Most of the Secretaries who were with me at the Embassy

have remained my good friends. A few of them have since died, some have become important in other fields, and some are still in the Service. All the Ambassadors of my time have gone to join the great Court above, where I hope they have the honoured places near the Throne which they deserve. And the comings and goings of those who are still serving their country abroad, and the gradual growth and improvement of the Foreign Service, have been of the greatest interest to me.

In my visits to England I have been to the Embassy many times, and last summer, through the kindness of Mr. Phillips, was permitted once more to go through the archives to revive memories of pre-war events, hoping in that way to illuminate them with at least a reflection of the old fires. I read through some of the despatches concerned with the various diplomatic exchanges that seemed so vital then, pored over the old cards — resurrected from some basement for the purpose — and looked again at many notes from Court officials with their gilt edges and precise handwriting. But it didn't seem real any more. Too much has happened since, to me and to the world. The glamour of those years, the enthusiasm with which we pursued the broad and easy road that seemed to be leading us straight to a too-easy world peace, have been quenched in the disaster of the World War and the destruction, for the time, of all our hopes.

Even the Embassy Chancery at 4 Grosvenor Gardens, which we had moved into in September 1914 to give space for the constantly expanding wartime Embassy, which I had left humming, had become quiet and dignified again — though the ghosts of those who have since passed to other spheres still seemed to flutter in and out of the rooms and up and down the staircase before me.

So, as I stepped out through the front door, — I rubbed my eyes — was that Ambassador Page ahead? — into the busy London street of 1937, I realized that, precious as they had been to me, those years must now translate themselves into their rightful place in the background, to be no more than a fragrant memory of youthful endeavour in the days that are no more.

THE END

Appendix A

List of American Presentations at Court
1903—1914

TO KING EDWARD VII

Levee, February 23, 1903

DIPLOMATIC CIRCLE

Mr. CRAIG W. WADSWORTH   BY MR. CHOATE
   Third Secretary of Embassy
Hon. DAVID R. FRANCIS
   President, St. Louis Exposition
Hon. JOHN BARRETT
   Commissioner, St. Louis Exposition

Levee, March 9, 1903

GENERAL CIRCLE

Mr. HENRY CLAY EVANS   BY MR. CHOATE
   American Consul-General at London
Mr. SMITH E. LANE
Mr. SIDNEY APPLETON

Court, March 13, 1903

DIPLOMATIC CIRCLE

Hon. THOMAS W. CRIDLER   BY MRS. CHOATE
   Commissioner, St. Louis Exposition
Mrs. CRIDLER

GENERAL CIRCLE

Mrs. HENRY CLAY EVANS
   Wife of the Consul-General
Miss CLAY EVANS
Mrs. GEORGE H. B. HILL

Court, March 20, 1903

DIPLOMATIC CIRCLE

Mrs. ISAAC BELL   BY MRS. CHOATE
   Wife of former Minister to The Hague
Miss BELL

GENERAL CIRCLE

Mrs. SIDNEY APPLETON
Miss ROWENA STEPHENS

Court, May 8, 1903

DIPLOMATIC CIRCLE

Mr. WILLIAM PHILLIPS   BY MR. CHOATE
  Secretary to the Ambassador

GENERAL CIRCLE

Mrs. FREDERICK PECKHAM   BY MRS. CHOATE
Mrs. ARTHUR GLASGOW
Miss NINA GILLETT

Levee, May 18, 1903

GENERAL CIRCLE

Mr. ARTHUR GLASGOW   BY MR. CHOATE
Mr. FREDERICK W. PECKHAM

Court, May 28, 1903

GENERAL CIRCLE

Miss SOHIER   BY MRS. HENRY WHITE
Miss ALICE SOHIER
Miss MARY BIGELOW
Miss HELEN POST

Levee, June 12, 1903

DIPLOMATIC CIRCLE

Captain C. H. STOCKTON   BY MR. HENRY WHITE
  Naval Attaché
Bishop WILLIAM LAWRENCE
Mr. HUGH H. HANNA ⎫
Mr. JEREMIAH JENKS ⎬ Monetary Commission
Mr. CHARLES A. CONANT ⎭
Professor SIMON NEWCOMB
Mr. J. PIERPONT MORGAN

Court, June 24, 1903

DIPLOMATIC CIRCLE

Mr. JOSEPH H. CHOATE, JR.   BY MR. and MRS. CHOATE
Mrs. JOSEPH H. CHOATE, JR.
Mr. CHARLES F. McKIM
Miss FLORENCE HAYWARD
Miss ALICE STICKNEY
Mrs. STOCKTON

GENERAL CIRCLE

Mrs. WILMERDING   BY MRS. CHOATE
Miss WILMERDING
Mrs. W. I. WHITE
Miss PEARL WHITE
Mrs. ROBERT CHAPIN

(282)

Levee, February 29, 1904

DIPLOMATIC CIRCLE

Major JOHN H. BEACOM   BY MR. CHOATE
  Military Attaché

GENERAL CIRCLE

Mr. CHARLES AINSWORTH SPOFFORD
Mr. WADE CHANCE

Levee, March 14, 1904

GENERAL CIRCLE

Mr. WALTER NEEF   BY MR. CHOATE
Mr. LOUIS C. HAY

Court, April 22, 1904

GENERAL CIRCLE

Mrs. H. C. KNAPP   BY MADAME PANSA, Italian Ambassadress
Mrs. CHARLES A. SPOFFORD   MR. HENRY WHITE, Chargé d'Affaires
Miss FAITH MOORE
Miss MARGUERITE OSBORNE

Court, May 13, 1904

DIPLOMATIC CIRCLE

Miss ANNA PHILLIPS   BY MADAME PANSA (Mrs. Choate being ill)
Miss MARTHA PHILLIPS
Mrs. LARZ ANDERSON

GENERAL CIRCLE

Mrs. ROSS WINANS   BY MADAME PANSA
Miss WINANS
Mrs. F. W. WHITRIDGE
Miss WHITRIDGE

Court, May 20, 1904

DIPLOMATIC CIRCLE

Miss STOCKTON   BY THE DUCHESS OF MANDAS
  Daughter of Naval Attaché   Spanish Ambassadress
Miss BEATRICE MORGAN   (Mrs. Choate being ill)

GENERAL CIRCLE

Mrs. LEON GRAVES   BY THE DUCHESS OF MANDAS
Miss ENO
Mrs. GEORGE VANDERBILT
Mrs. GEORGE LAW
Mrs. WILLIAM BARCLAY PARSONS
Miss PARSONS

(*283*)

Levee, May 30, 1904

Mr. W. BARCLAY PARSONS   BY THE DUKE OF MANDAS
Mr. CHARLES VERNON HOPKINS   Spanish Ambassador
Mr. GEORGE VANDERBILT
Mr. FRANCIS BATCHELLER
Mr. APTHORPE FULLER

Levee, June 7, 1904

DIPLOMATIC CIRCLE

Mr. NELSON O'SHAUGHNESSY   BY MR. CHOATE
    Secretary, American Legation, Copenhagen

Court, June 22, 1904

DIPLOMATIC CIRCLE

Mrs. HENRY MORGAN   BY MR. and MRS. CHOATE
Mrs. O'SHAUGHNESSY
Miss ANNE MORGAN
Mr. JOHN WANAMAKER

GENERAL CIRCLE

Mrs. CHARLES WOOD   BY MRS. CHOATE
Miss GRACE ALLEN
Miss MONA HOUSE
Miss EMILY TREVOR
Mrs. FRANCIS BATCHELLER

1905

Court, February 17, 1905

DIPLOMATIC CIRCLE

Rear-Admiral CHADWICK, U.S.N.   BY MR. CHOATE
Mrs. CHADWICK   BY MRS. CHOATE

GENERAL CIRCLE

Mrs. SHAW   BY MRS. CHOATE
Mrs. AUDENREID
Miss RUMSEY
Miss SPOFFORD

Court, February 24, 1905

GENERAL CIRCLE

Mrs. HOWARD LEVIS   BY MRS. CHOATE
Miss M. H. DODGE
Miss SCHREINER
Mrs. VAN ZANDT
Miss VAN ZANDT

Levee, May 19, 1905

DIPLOMATIC CIRCLE

Mr. LEWIS EINSTEIN   BY MR. CHOATE
   Third Secretary of Embassy

GENERAL CIRCLE

Mr. LEGGETT

Levee, May 26, 1905

DIPLOMATIC CIRCLE

Mr. FREDERICK MORGAN   BY MR. J. RIDGELY CARTER
   Assistant Diplomatic Agent, Cairo   Chargé d'Affaires of the Embassy

GENERAL CIRCLE

Mr. RICHARD MORTIMER   BY MR. CARTER
Mr. LORING ANDREWS
Mr. CHAUNCEY J. BLAIR

Court, May 29, 1905

GENERAL CIRCLE

Mrs. JOHN JACOB ASTOR   BY MRS. J. RIDGELY CARTER
Miss HALLIE E. RIVES
Miss BLANCHE SHOEMAKER
Mrs. RICHARD MORTIMER
Miss MORTIMER

Court, June 2, 1905

DIPLOMATIC CIRCLE

General WOODFORD   BY MR. CARTER
Mrs. WOODFORD   BY MRS. CARTER
Mrs. OGDEN MILLS
Miss MILLS
Miss GLADYS MILLS

GENERAL CIRCLE

Mrs. CHAUNCEY BLAIR
Miss BLAIR
Mrs. LEBRETON
Miss LEBRETON
Mrs. WALLACE
Miss WALLACE
Miss MOORE

1906

    The Honourable Whitelaw Reid appeared for the first time in his official capacity at the Levee held by His Majesty King Edward VII on the 20th of February 1906. Captain J. H. Gibbons (Naval Attaché) and Mr. DeLancey Jay (Secretary to the Ambassador) also appeared for the first

(285)

time at this Levee, though previously presented to the King in private audience in January 1906 (by Mr. Carter) and June 1905 (by the Ambassador) respectively.

Levee, Buckingham Palace, February 20, 1906
GENERAL CIRCLE
Mr. WILLIAM E. CARTER   BY MR. WHITELAW REID

Levee, February 26, 1906
GENERAL CIRCLE
Mr. ALAN SANDS   BY MR. REID

Levee, May 22, 1906
DIPLOMATIC CIRCLE
Mr. U. GRANT-SMITH   BY MR. REID
Third Secretary of Embassy
GENERAL CIRCLE
Mr. ARCHER HARMON   BY MR. REID

Court, May 25, 1906
DIPLOMATIC CIRCLE
Miss JEAN REID   BY MRS. WHITELAW REID
Miss MILDRED CARTER
Mrs. JOHN H. GIBBONS
GENERAL CIRCLE
Mrs. WILLIAM E. CARTER   BY MRS. REID
Mrs. BAXTER
Miss BAXTER
Miss EVELYN BIGELOW
Miss HARMON
Mrs. MACMILLAN
Mrs. A. MERCER PELL

Court, June 1, 1906
DIPLOMATIC CIRCLE
Mr. DAVID J. HILL   BY MR. REID
Ambassador to The Hague
Mrs. HILL   BY MRS. REID
Mrs. DONALD CAMERON
Miss MARTHA CAMERON

GENERAL CIRCLE
Mrs. THEODORE SHONTS   BY MRS. REID
Miss SHONTS
Miss THEODORA SHONTS

(286)

Miss McCandless
Miss Steele
Mrs. Moore

Court, June 28, 1906
DIPLOMATIC CIRCLE
Mr. Nicholas Longworth   BY MR. REID
Mrs. Longworth   BY MRS. REID
Mr. Frederick W. Whitridge   BY MR. REID
Mr. J. G. A. Leishman   BY MR. REID
Mrs. Whitridge   BY MRS. REID
Miss Whitridge
Mrs. Leishman
GENERAL CIRCLE
Mrs. Frederick Benedict   BY MRS. REID
Mrs. John Drexel
Miss Mathilde Townsend
Miss Hallie Bremond

Court, July 13, 1906
DIPLOMATIC CIRCLE
Mr. Oscar Straus   BY MR. REID
Mrs. Straus   BY MRS. REID
Mr. Henry White   BY MR. REID
    Ambassador to Italy
GENERAL CIRCLE
Mrs. William Clark   BY MRS. REID
Miss Clark
Mrs. Mina Steel
Miss Steel
Miss Muriel Robbins
Miss Edith Levis

1907
Levee, February 14, 1907
DIPLOMATIC CIRCLE
Captain Sydney A. Cloman   BY MR. REID
    Military Attaché
Mr. Lydig Hoyt
    Secretary to the Ambassador
GENERAL CIRCLE
Mr. Robert J. Wynn   BY MR. REID
    Consul-General at London
Mr. Cyril Andrews
Mr. Chalmers Roberts

Levee, February 19, 1907

DIPLOMATIC CIRCLE

Mr. GEORGE VON L. MEYER   BY MR. REID
   Ambassador to Russia

GENERAL CIRCLE

Mr. MILLARD HUNSIKER   BY MR. REID
Mr. C. W. KOHLSAAT

Court, February 22, 1907

DIPLOMATIC CIRCLE

Mrs. SYDNEY CLOMAN   BY MADAME MUSURUS, Turkish Ambassadress

GENERAL CIRCLE

Mrs. CYRIL ANDREWS   BY MADAME MUSURUS
Miss VAN ALEN

Court, March 1, 1907

GENERAL CIRCLE

Mrs. R. J. WYNNE   BY MADAME MUSURUS
Miss EDITH CLARK
Mrs. ROBERT EMMET
Miss MARGARET HARRIS
Mrs. MOE
Mrs. MARSHALL

Levee, June 3, 1907

DIPLOMATIC CIRCLE

H.E. Honourable JOSEPH H. CHOATE   BY MR. REID
   Ambassador and Delegate to the Second Hague Conference

GENERAL CIRCLE

Mr. EUGENE PARSONS   BY MR. REID

Court, June 6, 1907

GENERAL CIRCLE

Mrs. FRANK WIBORG   BY MRS. REID
Miss WIBORG
Miss MARY WIBORG
Mrs. MELVILLE POST
Mrs. EUGENE PARSONS
Miss DREXEL

Levee, June 25, 1907

GENERAL CIRCLE

Brigadier-General HENRY COOK   BY MR. REID
   Retired

(*288*)

Court, July 5, 1907

GENERAL CIRCLE

Mrs. JOHN E. REYBURN   BY COUNTESS BENCKENDORFF
Mrs. CRAWFORD HILL   Russian Ambassadress
Mrs. HATCH WILLARD
Miss HATCH
Miss HARRIET ALEXANDER

1908

Court, July 20, 1908

GENERAL CIRCLE

Miss WYNNE   BY MADAME VILLA URRUTIA
Miss DAGMAR VAN ZANDT   Spanish Ambassadress
Miss MARION SCRANTON

Court, February 28, 1908

GENERAL CIRCLE

Mrs. FREDERICK SHERMAN   BY COUNTESS BENCKENDORFF
Miss FREDERICA SHERMAN   Russian Ambassadress
Mrs. MILLER GRAHAM
Miss JANET PECK

Levee, May 11, 1908

DIPLOMATIC CIRCLE

Mr. SHELDON WHITEHOUSE   BY MR. REID
    Secretary to the Ambassador

Court, May 15, 1908

DIPLOMATIC CIRCLE

Miss JENNY CROCKER   BY MRS. REID

GENERAL CIRCLE

Mrs. W. P. THOMPSON   BY MRS. REID
Mrs. McC. RAMSEY
Mrs. COLE SCOTT
Mrs. HENRY BACON

Court, May 22, 1908

GENERAL CIRCLE

Mrs. FRANK MITCHELL   BY MRS. REID
Mrs. HERBERT SHIPMAN
Miss MARION LITCHFIELD
Miss MARY DUKE
Miss MOIRA VAIL JONES
Mrs. LANDFIELD

Levee, June 1, 1908

GENERAL CIRCLE

Mr. EDGAR A. CAROLAN   BY MR. REID
Mr. JEROME B. LANDFIELD
Mr. FRANK W. JONES
Mr. FRANK P. MITCHELL

Levee, July 6, 1908

GENERAL CIRCLE

Mr. CLARENCE MOORE   BY MR. REID

1909

Levee, February 23, 1909

DIPLOMATIC CIRCLE

Mr. ARTHUR ORR   BY MR. REID
    Third Secretary of Embassy

GENERAL CIRCLE

Mr. WILLIAM ROCKEFELLER   BY MR. REID
Mr. JAMES STILLMAN
Mr. L. H. McCORMICK
Lieut. Commander CHESTER WELLS, U.S.N.

Court, February 26, 1909

DIPLOMATIC CIRCLE

Mrs. ARTHUR ORR   BY MADAME VILLA URRUTIA
                                  Spanish Ambassadress

GENERAL CIRCLE

Mrs. N. B. KNOX   BY MADAME VILLA URRUTIA
Mrs. CHESTER WELLS
Mrs. L. H. McCORMICK
Miss IRENE CATLIN
Mrs. WILLIAM ROCKEFELLER

Court, March 3, 1909

DIPLOMATIC CIRCLE

Mr. IRVING DUDLEY   BY MR. REID
    Ambassador to Brazil
Mrs. DUDLEY   BY MRS. REID

GENERAL CIRCLE

Mrs. WADE CHANCE   BY MRS. REID
Mrs. CLINTON CUSHING
Miss GARMANY
Mrs. and Miss BUTTERFIELD

(290)

Levee, May 24, 1909

GENERAL CIRCLE

Mr. WALTER FARWELL — BY MR. REID
Mr. CHARLES CARROLL

Court, June 11, 1909

DIPLOMATIC CIRCLE

Mr. ROBERT WOODS BLISS — BY MR. REID
  Secretary of Legation, Brussels
Mrs. BLISS — BY MRS. REID

GENERAL CIRCLE

Mrs. JOSEPH STICKNEY — BY MRS. REID
Mrs. WALTER FARWELL
Miss JULIA CALHOUN
Miss ANITA STEWART
Miss RUTH ADAMS
Miss YVONNE TOWNSEND

Levee, June 22, 1909

DIPLOMATIC CIRCLE

Commander EDWARD SIMPSON, U.S.N., — BY MR. REID
  Naval Attaché
Major BENTLEY MOTT
  Military Attaché, Paris

GENERAL CIRCLE

Mr. THOMAS NELSON PAGE — BY MR. REID
Mr. W. G. SEWALL
Mr. MITCHELL HARRISON

Court, June 24, 1909

DIPLOMATIC CIRCLE

Mrs. EDWARD SIMPSON — BY MRS. REID

GENERAL CIRCLE

Mrs. THOMAS NELSON PAGE — BY MRS. REID
Mrs. REEVE MERRITT
Miss EUDORA CLOVER
Miss ANGELICA BROWN
Miss OLGA WIBORG
Mrs. FRANCIS ADAMS CLARK

1910

Court, February 25, 1910

DIPLOMATIC CIRCLE

Mr. WILLIAM PHILLIPS — BY MR. REID
  Councillor of Embassy

(291)

Mr. Hugh S. Gibson
  Second Secretary of Embassy
Mrs. William Phillips   by Countess Benckendorff
                                          Russian Ambassadress

GENERAL CIRCLE

Mrs. John L. Griffiths   by Countess Benckendorff
Mrs. R. N. Fairbanks
Mrs. Arthur K. Buxton
Miss Jennie Tredwell
Miss Moulinier

Levee, March 1, 1910

GENERAL CIRCLE

Mr. John L. Griffiths   by Mr. Reid
  Consul-General at London
Mr. Robert N. Fairbanks

Court, March 4, 1910

DIPLOMATIC CIRCLE

Mr. Charles W. Fairbanks   by Mr. Reid
Mrs. C. W. Fairbanks   by Countess Benckendorff

GENERAL CIRCLE

Mrs. Webster Fox   by Countess Benckendorff
Miss Cecilia B. Fox
Miss Margaret Winslow
Mrs. William J. Goudy
Miss Helen Goudy

TO KING GEORGE V
1911

Levee, February 21, 1911

DIPLOMATIC CIRCLE

Mr. Leland Harrison   by Mr. William Phillips
  Second Secretary of Embassy
Mr. Sheldon L. Crosby
  Third Secretary of Embassy

Levee, February 28, 1911

GENERAL CIRCLE

Mr. John C. Calhoun   by Mr. Phillips

Court, May 9, 1911

DIPLOMATIC CIRCLE

Mr. Elliot C. Bacon   by Mr. Reid
  Secretary to the Ambassador
Mrs. S. L'H. Slocum   by Mrs. Reid

Mrs. WILLIAM CROCKER   BY MRS. REID
Miss ETHEL CROCKER
Miss AGRA BENNETT
Miss MAZIE DELAFIELD
Miss ELEANOR WEBB

Court, May 10, 1911

DIPLOMATIC CIRCLE

Mrs. ROBERT BACON   BY MRS. REID
Miss MARTHA BACON

GENERAL CIRCLE

Mrs. OSCAR IASIGI   BY MRS. REID
Miss NORA IASIGI
Miss MARGARET DRAPER
Miss JANETTA ALEXANDER

Court, May 24, 1911

DIPLOMATIC CIRCLE

Miss MABEL CHOATE   BY MRS. REID
Miss LUCY BUCKLER

GENERAL CIRCLE

Mrs. C. W. BREGA   BY MRS. REID
Miss ENDERS
Mrs. WILLIAM BOURN
Mrs. JAMES H. BULL
Mrs. MARGERY BULL

Court, May 25, 1911

DIPLOMATIC CIRCLE

Mrs. POST WHEELER   BY MRS. REID

GENERAL CIRCLE

Mrs. JOHN NICHOLAS BROWN   BY MRS. REID
Mrs. JAMES HARAHAN
Miss JULIA CHAPIN
Miss BLANCHE BARRON

Levee, May 29, 1911

DIPLOMATIC CIRCLE

Mr. J. P. MORGAN   BY MR. REID

GENERAL CIRCLE

Mr. WILLIAM FORBES MORGAN   BY MR. REID
Mr. ALBERT COOK MYERS
Mr. EDWARD BRINGHURST

Levee, June 9, 1911
No presentations and no one attended from the Embassy
Major Slocum (Military Attaché) was received in special audience
February 3, 1911

1912

Levee, March 4, 1912
DIPLOMATIC CIRCLE
Mr. Post Wheeler   BY THE FRENCH AMBASSADOR
Secretary at St. Petersburg
GENERAL CIRCLE
Mr. R. Newton Crane   BY THE FRENCH AMBASSADOR
U.S. Despatch Agent, London

Court, March 8, 1912
DIPLOMATIC CIRCLE
Mr. William Penn Cresson   BY THE FRENCH AMBASSADOR
Second Secretary of Embassy
Mrs. John C. Phillips   BY COUNTESS BENCKENDORFF
Mrs. Harry H. Hough

GENERAL CIRCLE
Mrs. James Amory Moore   BY COUNTESS BENCKENDORFF
Miss Allene Crane
Miss Estelle Wilson King

Levee, March, 11, 1912
GENERAL CIRCLE
Mr. Edward C. Dameron   BY THE FRENCH AMBASSADOR
Mr. Robert Grant

Court, March 14, 1912
GENERAL CIRCLE
Mrs. Robert Grant   BY COUNTESS BENCKENDORFF
Mrs. James B. Duke
Miss Bradhurst
Miss Margaret Perin

Court, March 15, 1912
GENERAL CIRCLE
Mrs. George Aitken Clark   BY MRS. REID
Miss Greta Hostetter
Miss Catherine Dameron
Miss Frances Dameron

Court, May 14, 1912

DIPLOMATIC CIRCLE

Mr. STEDMAN HANKS, Secretary to the Ambassador   BY MR. REID
Mrs. E. DUDLEY KENNA   BY MRS. REID

GENERAL CIRCLE

Mrs. CHARLES E. HELLIER   BY MRS. REID
Miss MARY LOUISE HELLIER
Mrs. ELMER E. BLACK
Miss ISABEL McLAUGHLIN

Levee, May 30, 1912

GENERAL CIRCLE

Mr. IRA NELSON MORRIS   BY THE RUSSIAN AMBASSADOR

Levee, June 13, 1912

DIPLOMATIC CIRCLE

Mr. EAMES MacVEAGH   BY MR. REID

GENERAL CIRCLE

Mrs. GEORGE AITKEN CLARK   BY MR. REID
Mr. EDWARD DUDLEY KENNA

Court, June 24, 1912

DIPLOMATIC CIRCLE

Mrs. FRANKLIN MacVEAGH   BY MRS. REID

GENERAL CIRCLE

Mrs. IRA NELSON MORRIS   BY MRS. REID
Mrs. BARTON FRENCH
Miss GLADYS McMILLAN
Miss ROSE DEXTER
Mrs. EDWARD T. STOTESBURY

1913

Levee, February 4, 1913

DIPLOMATIC CIRCLE

Mr. IRWIN LAUGHLIN   BY SIR EDWARD GREY
    Chargé d'Affaires of the Embassy
Commander POWERS SYMINGTON, Naval Attaché, and
Lieutenant-Colonel G. O. SQUIER, Military Attaché
    attended for first time, having been presented
    privately on arrival   BY MR. LAUGHLIN
Mr. HALLETT JOHNSON   BY MR. LAUGHLIN
    Third Secretary of Embassy

GENERAL CIRCLE

Mr. ROBERT A. GARDINER   BY MR. LAUGHLIN
Mr. F. S. PEARSON

(*295*)

Court, February 7, 1913

GENERAL CIRCLE

Mrs. ROBERT A. GARDINER   BY MADAME IMPERIALI
Mrs. A. H. ADAMS
Miss GERTRUDE EDWARDS
Miss POLLY JACOB

Levee, February 13, 1913

GENERAL CIRCLE

Mr. WALTER HORTON SCHOELKOPF   BY MR. LAUGHLIN

Court, February 21, 1913

DIPLOMATIC CIRCLE

Mrs. IRWIN LAUGHLIN   BY COUNTESS BENCKENDORFF
Mrs. NATHAN K. AVERILL   BY MRS. LAUGHLIN
    Wife of Military Attaché at St. Petersburg

GENERAL CIRCLE

Mrs. F. S. PEARSON   BY MRS. LAUGHLIN
Miss NATALIE PEARSON
Mrs. WYNN SEWELL
Miss HARRIET SPROUL
Miss LEBRUN PARSONS
Mrs. WALTER HORTON SCHOELKOPF

Court, May 7, 1913

DIPLOMATIC CIRCLE

Mr. ADRIAN ISELIN   BY MR. LAUGHLIN
Miss LOUISE ISELIN   BY MRS. LAUGHLIN
Mrs. CHARLES E. GREENOUGH

GENERAL CIRCLE

Miss HELEN MARIE STUART   BY MRS. LAUGHLIN
Mrs. ROBERT WILCOX (ELLA WHEELER WILCOX)

Levee, June 2, 1913

His Excellency the Honorable Walter Hines Page appeared for the
first time at this Levee

DIPLOMATIC CIRCLE

Mr. HAROLD FOWLER   BY MR. PAGE
    Secretary to the Ambassador

Court, June 9, 1913

GENERAL CIRCLE

Miss BERTHA DEAN   BY COUNTESS BENCKENDORFF

(296)

Court, June 10, 1913

Mr. FRANK PAGE   BY MR. PAGE
   Son of the Ambassador
Miss JOAN WHITRIDGE   BY COUNTESS BENCKENDORFF

GENERAL CIRCLE

Miss MARY ALEXANDER   BY COUNTESS BENCKENDORFF
Miss JULIA ROBBINS
Miss ELEANORE SWERINGEN

1914

Court, February 13, 1914

DIPLOMATIC CIRCLE

Mr. ARTHUR W. PAGE   BY MR. PAGE
   Son of the Ambassador
Mr. EDWARD BELL
   Second Secretary of Embassy
Mrs. ARTHUR W. PAGE   BY MRS. PAGE
Miss KATHARINE PAGE
Mrs. BELL
   Mother of the Second Secretary

GENERAL CIRCLE

Miss KATE FOWLER   BY MRS. PAGE
Miss SYLVIA DE GRASSE FOX
Miss ELIZABETH WELLS
Miss HARRIET McCOOK

Levee, February 17, 1914

GENERAL CIRCLE

Mr. CLIFFORD CARVER   BY MR. PAGE

Court, March 6, 1914

DIPLOMATIC CIRCLE

Mr. JOSEPH E. WILLARD   BY MR. PAGE
   Ambassador to Spain
Mrs. WILLARD   BY MRS. PAGE
Miss BELLE WILLARD

GENERAL CIRCLE

Mrs. MORTON DEXTER   BY MRS. PAGE
Miss MARY DEXTER
Mrs. CLARENCE MOORE
Miss FRANCES MOORE

Court, March 13, 1914

DIPLOMATIC CIRCLE

Mrs. JOHN S. PARKE   BY MRS. PAGE
Miss GENEVIEVE PARKE
Miss PAULINE PARKE

GENERAL CIRCLE

Mrs. FLETCHER RYER   BY MRS. PAGE
Miss DORIS RYER
Miss MARY NATIONS
Miss FRANCES LEGGETT

Court, June 4, 1914

DIPLOMATIC CIRCLE

Mr. RALPH PAGE   BY MR. PAGE
  Son of the Ambassador
Mrs. PAGE   BY MRS. PAGE
Mrs. EDWARD BELL
  Wife of the Second Secretary
Miss ESTHER CLEVELAND

GENERAL CIRCLE

Miss MARGUERITA PENNINGTON   BY MRS. PAGE
Miss DOROTHY DOUBLEDAY
Miss MARY SANGER

Court, June 5, 1914

GENERAL CIRCLE

Mrs. EDWARD M. HOUSE   BY MRS. PAGE
Mrs. HUGH O. WALLACE
Miss OLGA KELLY
Miss EVELYN MARSHALL

Appendix B

The American Citizens' Committee in London [1]

White Room, Hotel Savoy, Thames Embankment Entrance
(This American Citizens' Committee in London — the great Committee of relief and general assistance which operated during the first months of the World War, was made up of two committees which came into existence independently of each other as the World War loomed:

      (*a*) Committee of American Residents in London
      (*b*) Committee of American Visitors to London

These joined and functioned until the first rush of visiting Americans had gone home. Then the Committee of American Residents of London took over the whole work and continued until September 25, 1915, when it disbanded.)

Honorary Presidents: Ambassador WALTER H. PAGE and Consul-General R. P. SKINNER

                Chairman: THEODORE HETZLER
                Secretary: W. NORTH DUANE
                Treasurer: WILLIAM C. BREED

GENERAL COMMITTEE
THEODORE HETZLER, *Chairman*

JAMES G. CANNON	OSCAR BALDWIN	NICHOLAS F. BRADY
FRED I. KENT	R. GILMAN BROWN	ARTHUR WILLIAMS
OSCAR S. STRAUS	R. NOYES FAIRBANKS	W. T. POTTS
JAMES BYRNE	W. E. W. HULL	ROBERT W. DEFOREST
WALTER FISHER	R. D. MCCARTER	B. A. WORTHINGTON
JOSEPH P. DAY	H. A. TITCOMB	LEO ARNSTEIN
CLARENCE GRAFF	T. D. HOFFMAN	E. P. GASTON
FRANCIS M. WELD	GEORGE D. SMITH	A. CHESTER BEATTY
CLARENCE L. FABRI	LAWRENCE A. ARMOUR	WILSON CROSS
CHARLES L. LLOYD	THOMAS J. SHANLEY	W. F. FISHER
LUDWIG NISSEN	JAMES C. HARVEY	AUSTIN F. HOY
CHANDLER P. ANDERSON	S. STANWOOD MENKEN	JAMES MACDONALD
HARRY E. BRITTAIN	WILLIAM C. BREED	A. K. JEFFRIES

[1] This list is taken from lists lent by Mr. William Breed and Mr. Clarence Graff. These have been corrected and supplemented from copies of the *American Bulletin*, published each day for about three months by the American Citizens' Committee for the information of Americans and distributed free.

FINANCE COMMITTEE

FRED I. KENT, *Chairman*   THEODORE HETZLER   JAMES G. CANNON

TRANSPORTATION COMMITTEE

JOSEPH P. DAY, *Chairman*

FRANCIS M. WELD, Savoy Hotel
GEORGE D. SMITH, Berkeley Hotel
HARRY E. BRITTAIN
I. C. BOEY, Philadelphia
J. C. FERGUSON
JOHN GARRIGUES
J. MAYER, JR., New York
Reverend C. B. BULLOCK, Cold Springs

DIPLOMATIC COMMITTEE

OSCAR S. STRAUS, former Ambassador to Turkey, Hyde Park Hotel
WALTER L. FISHER, formerly Secretary of the Interior
JAMES BYRNE, attorney of New York

HOTEL COMMITTEE AND RELIEF COMMITTEE

WILLIAM C. BREED, *Chairman*, New York, Carlton Hotel
THOMAS J. SHANLEY, New York, Waldorf Hotel
JAMES C. HARVEY, St. Louis, Savoy Hotel
ARTHUR WILLIAMS, New York, Savoy Hotel
Professor AUGUSTUS TROWBRIDGE
Honorable FRANKLIN S. BILLINGS

CABLES

S. STANWOOD MENKEN, Ritz Hotel

WOMEN'S RELIEF COMMITTEE

Mesdames H. C. HOOVER, J. W. JENKINS, A. T. STEWART, G. FOX, L. A.
SELWYN, L. WOODRUFF, EDGAR RICKARD, P. HUTCHINS,
R. DICKSON, DEANE MITCHELL, W. T. GAUNT; Miss POLK

MEN'S RELIEF COMMITTEE

H. C. HOOVER, *Chairman*, WILLIAM C. BREED, A. H. KUEHN, F. C. VAN
DUZER, CLARENCE GRAFF, EDGAR RICKARD, R. ANNAN, W. WEIR,
R. NOYES FAIRBANKS, R. C. LATHROP, J. P. HUTCHINS

REGISTRATION COMMITTEE

L. H. SOMERS, *Chairman*, Rainbow Lake, New York
HENRY A. NAVE, M.D., *Assistant Chairman*, Kansas City, Kansas, Imperial
Hotel, London
WALLACE B. JOHNSON, Utica, New York, Waldorf Hotel, London

C. B. Francisco, M.D., Kansas City, Missouri, 3 Upper Bedford Place, London

Frederick Snare, Jr., 323 Broadway, New York (Snare & Triest), Morley's Hotel

Charles V. Maas, 87 Nassau Street, New York, Waldorf Hotel

Irving E. Mausback, 460 Riverside Drive, New York, Cranston's Kenilworth Hotel

Nelson Curtis, Jr., Jamaica Plain, Boston, Carlton Hotel

Alfred R. Teichman, Postmaster, Counsellor at Law, 260 Norman Avenue

George D. Smith, 48 Wall Street, New York, Berkeley Hotel, London

Dorothea B. Corcoran, 5221 Sheridan Road, Chicago, Hotel Windsor

C. C. Nesselrode

Joseph C. Ferguson

BAGGAGE COMMITTEE

Edward P. Gaston, *Chairman*, Salisbury Square, London

S. H. James, *Assistant Chairman*, London

BULLETIN COMMITTEE

F. J. Kingsbury, New Haven   C. L. Lloyd, London

POST OFFICE COMMITTEE

Dudley P. Lewis, *Chairman*, New York

Miss Ida G. Scott, London

Mrs. Annan, London

Miss Ruth Cooper, Northampton, Massachusetts

Miss Katherine D. Allison, Northampton, Massachusetts

Miss Mary E. Orem, Philadelphia

Mrs. E. B. Leax, London

COMMITTEE FOR EXCHANGE OF STEAMSHIP TICKETS

E. B. Wyman, *Chairman*, Shilott, New York

Mrs. Wyman, Shilott, New York

Mrs. Huntress, Boston

REFERENCE INDEX COMMITTEE

L. H. Somers, *Chairman*, Rainbow Lake, New York

Mrs. C. L. Bryant, Danbury, Connecticut

Oliver Perry, New York

Carl Foster, Regina Hotel, Woburn, Massachusetts

C. S. Miller, 51 Torrington Square, Sacramento, California

Edna Simmons, 51 Torrington Square, Sacramento, California

Elinor Simmons, 51 Torrington Square, Sacramento, California

Jean Song, Los Angeles, California

FLORENCE W. DISBROW, Newark, New Jersey
Mrs. SLOMAN, Detroit
R. L. BENSON, New York

ASSISTANTS TO SECRETARY

W. W. KENT, JR., New York   L. H. SOMERS, Rainbow Lake, New York
DAVID MARGESSON, London

ENQUIRY COMMITTEE

DR. HENRY R. MULLER, New York   DR. J. MOORE, Virginia

AUDITING COMMITTEE

THEODORE HETZLER   W. NORTH DUANE   WARREN KENT

COMMITTEE ON AMERICANS STRANDED ON CONTINENT

LEO ARNSTEIN, *Chairman*
F. W. ROE, University of Wisconsin
RANSOM H. THOMAS, JR., Morristown, New Jersey

EDITORIAL STAFF

LEO ARNSTEIN   ERNEST H. ABBOTT   S. STANWOOD MENKEN
SAMPSON H. SCHWARZ   EDWIN H. DENHAM   J. E. DENNOTT

COMMITTEE OF AMERICAN RESIDENTS OF LONDON

(This Committee came into being August 4, 1914, and ended its work September 25, 1915.)
The American Ambassador, WALTER H. PAGE, *Honorary Chairman*
The American Consul-General, ROBERT P. SKINNER, *Honorary Vice Chairman*
HERBERT C. HOOVER, *Chairman*
CLARENCE GRAFF, *Treasurer*
FREDERICK C. VAN DUZER, *Honorary Secretary*
F. HESSENBERG, *Secretary*

EXECUTIVE COMMITTEE

WALTER BLACKMAN	B. G. LATHROP
POMEROY BURTON	BERTRAM LORD
ROBERT COLLINS	A. F. MARTIN
CLARENCE GRAFF	GEORGE A. MOWER
F. HESSENBERG	FRANCIS E. POWELL
HERBERT C. HOOVER	ROBERT E. PORTER
MILLARD HUNSIKER	EDGAR RICKARD
J. P. HUTCHINS	H. GORDON SELFRIDGE
A. F. KUEHN	F. C. VAN DUZER
JOSEPH W. GRIFF	JOHN BEAVER WHITE

WOMEN'S DIVISION

Mrs. WALTER H. PAGE, wife of the Ambassador
Mrs. ROBERT P. SKINNER, wife of the Consul-General
Mrs. HERBERT C. HOOVER, wife of the Chairman
Mrs. A. T. STEWART, Vice-Chairman
Mrs. J. W. JENKINS, Honorary Secretary
Mrs. EDDY AGIUS, Secretary

EXECUTIVE COMMITTEE

Mrs. EDDY AGIUS	Mrs. J. W. JENKINS
Miss ETHEL BAGG	Mrs. B. G. LATHROP
Mrs. J. W. DICKSON	Miss DAISY POLK
Mrs. H. C. HOOVER	Mrs. EDGAR RICKARD
Mrs. J. P. HUTCHINS	Mrs. H. GORDON SELFRIDGE

Mrs. A. T. STEWART

Index

Choate letters, 34; Alaska boundary, 56; poems of, 81; and Bryan, 89; visit to London, 111; sees King, 112; death, 112; memorial service at St. Paul's, 113; Senate blocked Hay, 116; presentation troubles, 145; preferred 'American' Embassy, 178

Hellenes, King of, 175

Hempstock, Walter, 65

Herbert, Sir Michael, 55, 57, 59, 60, 61

Hetzler, Herbert, 254-55

Hill, Mr. and Mrs. D. J., 122

Hill, George H. B., 48

Hodson, Charles, office, 20-21; diplomacy of, 26; tells E. Bax some American history, 32; Carter truant, 36; newspaper receptions, 81-83; meets Ambassador Reid, 107; death, and what newspapers said, 126; famous saying, 205

Hodson, Edward, 126

Hodson, Frank, describes Embassy, 12-19; office and work, 20; and Mr. Choate, 33; succeeds his father as Messenger, 126; assists a Consul, 128; helps an old lady, 133; met Mr. Phillips, 165; sinking of Titanic, 207; and Edward Bell, 248

Holmes, Oliver Wendell, 206

House, Colonel and Mrs. E. M., 229, 230, 250

Hoyt, Lydig, 219

Hozier, James, M.P., 6

Jacks, L. P., 273

James, Mr. and Mrs. Arthur, 63

James, Colonel B. R., 191

James, Henry, 86, 116

James, Mr. and Mrs. Willie, 63

Janis, Elsie, 237

Jay, DeLancey K., arrives with Ambassador Reid, 108; morning or evening suit, 109-11; diplomatic uniform for Mr. Nansen, 114-15; attends Levee, 118; and Mr. Bryan, 124-25; resigns, 126-27; flowers for lady, 152-53; recuperating in Paris from war wound, 160; at Reid memorial service, 219; E. Bax dines with Mr. and Mrs., 239

Jay, Peter Augustus, 125, 219

Jefferson, President Thomas, 48, 208

Jetté (Alaska Boundary), 57

Johnson, Hallett, 208, 215, 217, 220-22

Kean, Senator, 27

Kennedy, Ambassador Joseph, 74

Kent, Fred I., 254-55

Kitchener, Lord, 192

Knollys, Lord, 26

Knox, Philander, 154

Krupp Company, 260-61

Labouchere, Henry, 6

La Farge, John, 97, 102

Lambert, Mr., 81

Lansdowne, the Marquess of, and Henry White, 23; Mr. Choate's call on, 33; dinner to Admiral Cotton, 55; personality of, 61-62; Mr. Choate informs L. Carter in charge of Embassy, 102; waived Ambassador Reid's call at Foreign Office, 109; is succeeded by Sir E. Grey, 117

Laughlin, Irwin, queer Americans, 132; appointed Councillor, 209-10; arrival, 210-13; illness and death of Ambassador Reid, 213-18; assumes charge of Embassy, 214; varied diplomatic matters handled, 219; delay confirmation appointment, 220-22; Panama Canal tolls troubles, 222-23; Mexican question, 221; acceptability of Ambassador Page, 224; arrangements for Page and arrival, 224-28; diplomatic work left to, 228; and suffragettes, 229; Who is Mexico? 244; baseball game, 244; and Edward Bell, 248; praises organization for war relief, 254; important duties on Aug. 4, 1914, 259-60, 265-66; Minnie Lovell to work with, 275

Lincoln, Abraham, 263

Lodge, Henry Cabot, champion of the Irish, 41, 42; Alaska Boundary Tribunal, 55-66; Newfoundland Fisheries, 116; Republican negligence in confirming diplomatic appointments, 221

London, Lord Mayor of, 59, 60

Longworth, Mr. and Mrs. Nicholas, 122, 123

(308)

Phillips, Mrs. William. *See* William Phillips, Drayton, Caroline

Phipps, Mr. and Mrs., 63

Pichon, M., 176

Pilgrim Society, 59; inauguration of, 67–68; dinner to Mark Twain, 133; dinner to J. R. Carter, 164; lunch to William Phillips, 210; Reid memorial service, 215; dinner to Ambassador Page, 225–27; one hundred years of peace dinner speech, 231; 'Waterloo Ball' of World War, 252

Porter, General Horace, 135

Portugal, King of, 175, 205–06

Reid, Miss Jean, 108, 121, 139–42. (*See* Ward, Lady)

Reid, Ogden, 142, 181, 217, 277

Reid, Mr. and Mrs. Ogden, 232, 235, 240, 241, 251, 275, 276

Reid, Whitelaw (*see also* Mrs. Whitelaw Reid), Court rehearsals, 51; appointed Ambassador, 97; house for, 98; preparations, 101–07; arrival, 108–10; leases Wrest Park, 115–16; first Levee, 118; Bryan's visit, 123; Independence Day reception, 129; dinner to Mark Twain, 132; dedicates Harvard Memorial Chapel, 136; Miss Reid's wedding, 139; cancelled presentation, 145–146; at Mrs. Ronalds's, 149; to remain in London, 155; promoted international friendships, 158; King visit, 159; Orr to remain in London, 161; speech at Carter dinner, 164; death of D. O. Mills, sails for New York, 166; 'Sun' attack, 168; Roosevelt for Special Ambassador at King's funeral, 174; newspaper men at Coronation of George V, 189; attends Coronation, 193; entertains Duke and Duchess of Connaught, 203; Stedman Hanks, 204–07; speech on Jefferson, 208–09; death of, preparations for return to U.S., condolences, etc., 213–18; comparison with Page Embassy, 227; Philippine policy, 239

Reid, Mrs. Whitelaw (*see also* Ambassador Reid), Henry James on, 116; Queen received, 109; presentations at first Court, 121; reception at Dorchester House, 147–48; personality of, 155–60; at Ascot, 205; dress for Court, 207; Emily Bax visits her in U.S., 232–37, 239

Rhodes scholarships, 28–30

Roberts, Earl, 59, 172, 243, 252, 255. (*See also* Pilgrim Society)

Rockhill, W. W., 201

Rodd, Sir Rennell, 114

Rogers, Miss Helen, 109, 217. (*See* Reid, Mrs. Ogden)

Rogers, Representative, 169

Ronalds, Mrs., 149

Roosevelt, President Theodore, Choate, correspondence with, 34; ambitions, 41; arbitrates between Russia and Japan, 79; elected President, 95; best of every bargain, 116; Sir Mortimer Durand, 127; ex-President starts for Africa, 154; Ambassador to entertain on way home, 171–73; Special Ambassador at funeral of Edward VII, 174–81; at Reid memorial service, 219; Phillips member of 'Tennis Cabinet,' 238

Root, Hon. Elihu, 35, 55, 57, 116, 221

Rosebery, Earl of, 90

Rothschild, Alfred, 149

Russia, Czar of, 135

Salisbury, Lord, 55

Sandhurst, Lord, 191

Sargent, John S., 9, 84–85, 86, 142

Scranton, William (of Scranton), 236

Selborne, Lord, 54

Seymour, 166

Shonts, the Misses, 53

Simmons, B. J., 96

Simpson, Commander and Mrs. Edward, 167

Skinner, R. P., 169, 254

Slocum, Colonel S. L'H., 219

Southwark, Bishop of, 172

Sowerby, Captain, 191

Spain, Alfonso, King of, 101, 111, 175

Spears, Kaufmann, 81

Spooner, Senator, 83

Squier, Major G. O., 175, 214–15, 217, 250–51

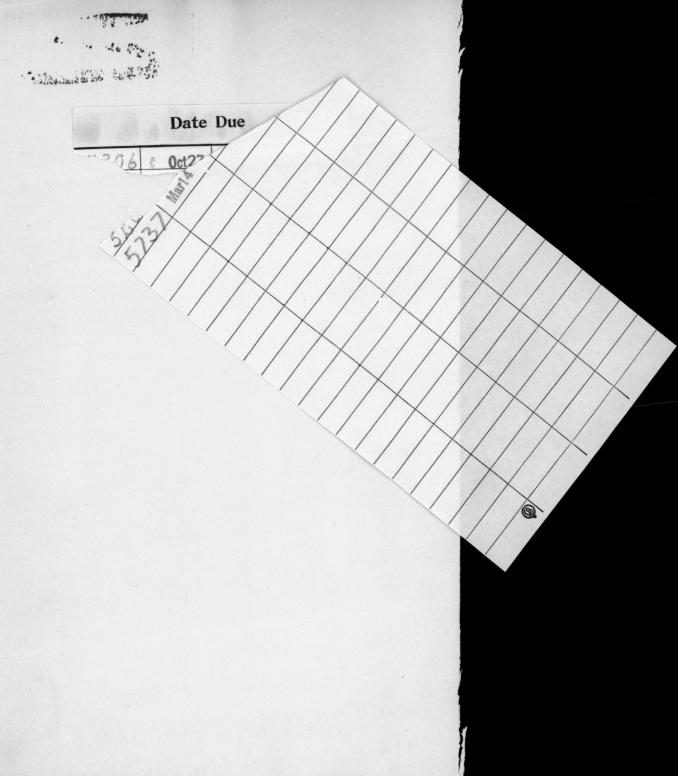